William Cook

Practical poultry breeder & feeder

How to make poultry pay

William Cook

Practical poultry breeder & feeder
How to make poultry pay

ISBN/EAN: 9783337146887

Printed in Europe, USA, Canada, Australia, Japan

Cover: Foto ©Lupo / pixelio.de

More available books at **www.hansebooks.com**

TENTH EDITION,

Enlarged and Fully Revised to date.

PRACTICAL

POULTRY BREEDER

AND

FEEDER:

OR,

HOW TO MAKE POULTRY PAY.

BY

WILLIAM COOK.

Author of "The Book on Ducks, and how to make them pay;" "The Horse: its keep and management;" "Pheasants, Turkeys, and Geese: their management for pleasure and profit;" "Fowls for the Times: the history and development of the Orpington Fowl;" Editor and Proprietor of "The Poultry Journal;" Conductor of Poultry Department "Farm, Field and Fireside;" Poultry Lecturer in London and to many provincial County Councils; &c.

PUBLISHED BY THE AUTHOR AT
QUEEN'S HEAD YARD, 105, BOROUGH, LONDON, S.E.,
AND
ORPINGTON HOUSE, ST. MARY CRAY, KENT.

ENTERED AT STATIONERS' HALL.

BROMLEY, KENT:
E. CLARKE & SON,
PRINTING WORKS, 53, HIGH STREET,
AND AT ST. MARY CRAY.

CONTENTS.

	PAGES.
GENERAL REMARKS ...	1—11

Poultry-keeping — Moral, sanitary, and financial benefits, combined with improved health—Personal attention for good results—Comparative advantages of town and country poultry-keepers—Poultry will pay —[Poultry-keeping past and present — The Author's work.

HOUSES AND RUNS ...	13—28

Houses — Hogshead houses — Lean-to houses — Perches and nests — Movable houses for fields — Confined runs—Covered runs—Open spaces used to their best advantage—The treatment of confined runs—Difficulties with regard to runs: how to surmount them—How to keep fighting cocks apart—Cheap and interchangeable runs.

MOSS PEAT	29—34

Moss Peat a permanent benefit to fowls and owners —Lime and dust, danger and dirt— Moss Peat a deodoriser—German *versus* English moss peat.

CONTENTS.

	PAGES
FEEDING	35—52

Past mismanagement and its results—Soft food and how to mix it—Meat for fowls—Eggs without shell and how to avoid them—Feeding with troughs—Stimulants for sluggish fowls—Grit, maize, and egg shells, hemp seed and boiled grain—Fish diet and fishy eggs bring "fishy" financial results—Herbs and green food for fowls.

WHICH ARE THE BEST FOWLS TO KEEP ... ... 53—61

Strain, not breed, the index of excellence—Good crosses for profit—Sitting varieties and non-sitting varieties—Where to keep one or the other for the best results.

HOW TO BREED AND WHAT TO BREED FROM ... ... 63—89

Good birds kept shews truest economy—Fertile eggs: how to ensure—Artificial incubation—Incubators: their defects and disappointing results—Foster mothers—Sitting and hatching.

PURE OR DISTINCT VARIETIES ... ... 91—154

Plymouth Rocks—Minorcas—White Leghorns—Buff Leghorns—Black Leghorns—Creve Cœurs—Dorkings—Speckled Dorkings—Hamburghs—Scotch Greys—Game—Indian Game—Old English Game—Cochins—Houdans—Wyandottes—Golden Wyandottes—Buff Wyandottes—White Wyandottes—Langshans—Brahmas—Redcaps—Andalusians—Orpingtons—Rose Comb Orpingtons—White Orpingtons—Buff Orpingtons—Diamond Jubilee Orpingtons—Anconas.

CONTENTS.

	PAGES
BANTAMS	155—157

Bantams not useless—Juvenile interest awakened and results in after life—Favourite varieties—Mistakes and pleasures—Hints as to management.

CROSS-BRED FOWLS ... ... 159—183

Cross-bred Fowls: what they really are—The utility and great value of the system, and the advantages accruing therefrom—Crossing and re-crossing Houdan-Orpington—Houdan-Minorca—Houdan-Leghorn—Houdan-Indian Game—Minorca-Langshan—Leghorn-Plymouth Rock—Dorking-Brahma—Indian Game-Plymouth Rock—Indian Game-Dorking—Indian Game-Buff Orpington—Buff Orpington-Dorking—Orpington-Dorking—White Orgington-Light Brahma—Orpington-Brahma—Leghorn-Orpington.

DISEASES ... ... 185—228

Poultry subject to many diseases—Ignorance of many people respecting this fact and the result of same—"A stitch in time saves nine"—Warm comfortable houses the best preventive of disease—Roup—Liver Disease—Leg Weakness—Gapes—Cramp—Egg Eating—Egg Bound—Crop Bound—Soft Eggs—Comb Disease—Feather Eating—Consumption—Diarrhœa and Dysentery—Dropsy in the Abdomen—Inflammation of the Lungs—Vermin—Bumble Feet in Fowls—Enteritis.

THE TREATMENT OF BROODY HENS ... ... 229—230

Broody hens in the way—Some modes of curing—The only humane and effective plan for bringing the birds on to lay quickly—The broody coop.

CONTENTS.

PAGES

PREPARING BIRDS FOR THE SHOW PEN ... ... 231—235

Novices, careless and disappointed — Untrained birds: their beauties not perceptible, and consequently overlooked by judges—Washing the birds — The care of cockerels after returning from showing.

POULTRY FARMING AND KEEPING ... ... 237—246

Questions often asked with regard to Poultry Farming—Ignorance—Failure—Distrust— Popular suspicions concerning Poultry Farming—The commencement: How to begin and how not to begin—Theory one thing and practice another in Poultry Farming.

FATTENING FOWLS ... ... 247—251

Disappointment in young birds for table overcome by fattening—Fattening coops and food—Skim milk and fat for fattening fowls—Cramming by hand and by machine—Hints for helping fattening fowls—Killing.

SURREY AND SUSSEX FOWLS ... ... 253—260

Surrey Fowls: their excellence and consequent leading position as market fowls—The Author in Surrey and Sussex—The Surrey system of Feeding—Surrey Fowls, past and present—Sharp Grit for Surrey Fowls — How Surrey people keep their chickens dry.

TO PRESERVE EGGS ... ... 261—262

The quicklime system — Buttered eggs — Eggs preserved in sawdust.

LIST OF ILLUSTRATIONS.

	PAGE.
Andalusian Cock	134
,, Hen	134
Ancona Cock	152
,, Hen	152
Black Minorca Cock	100
,, ,, Hen	100
Brown Leghorn Cock	102
Buff Leghorn Cock	106
,, ,, Hen	106
Black Red Game Cock	118
Buff Cochin Cock	120
Chicken Coop	79
Creve Cœur Cock	108
,, ,, Hen	108
Coloured Dorking Hen	112
Dark Brahma Cock	130
Diamond Jubilee Orpington Cock	150
,, ,, Hen	150

LIST OF ILLUSTRATIONS.

	PAGE
Front of Hogshead House	16
Farmer's House on Wheels	25
Feeding Troughs	41
Golden Wyandotte Cock	126
,, ,, Hen	126
Hogshead House	14
Heads of Good and Bad Layers	64
Houdan Cock	122
,, Houdan Hen	122
Indian Game Cock	118
,, ,, Hen	118
Lean-to House (showing wire netting above and below ground for keeping out rats, &c.)	17
Langshan Cock	128
,, Hen	128
Light Brahma Cock	130
,, ,, Hen	130
Plymouth Rock Cock	94
,, ,, Hen	94
Partridge Cochin Cock	120
Red Cap Cock	132
Rose-Comb Orpington Cock	140
Rose-Comb Buff Orpington Cock	148
,, ,, ,, Hen	148
Rose-Comb Black Bantams	156
Rose-Comb White Bantams	156
Small Run	27
Silver-Grey Dorking Cock	110
,, ,, Hen	110
Silver-Spangled Hamburgh Cock	114
Scotch Grey Cock	116
Silver Wyandotte Cock	124
,, ,, Hen	124
Single Comb Orpington Cock	136
,, ,, Pullet	136

LIST OF ILLUSTRATIONS.

	PAGE
Single Comb Buff Orpington Cock	144
,, ,, Hen	144
White Minorca Pullet	102
White Leghorn Cock	104
,, ,, Pullet	104
White Wyandotte Cock	126
White Orpington Cock	142
,, ,, Hen	142

INDEX.

	PAGE
Author's experiences among poultry keepers	5
Ashes and dust for runs	24
Andalusians, their plumage and laying qualities	133
Anconas	153
Author's experiences among Surrey Fatteners	253
Burying corn to give exercise	25
Boarding up runs to prevent cocks fighting each other	25
Broody hens: how to deal with	228
Broody coops: how to make and use	230
Biscuit meal for fowls	39
Boiled corn: when and how to give it	48
Birds for profit: how to breed	53
Broken eggs in nest: how to act in case of	74
Bone meal for young chickens	84
Buff Leghorns	107
Brahmas: light and dark	129
Bantams: Black Rose-comb and White Rose-comb	153
Bantams for children	153
Broken eggs in oviduct: how to relieve fowls in cases of	213
Bumble feet: how to avoid and cure	227
Buff Orpington-Dorking cross	178

INDEX.

	PAGE
Children's training and amusement: poultry keeping in regard to...	2
Continental poultry supplies: advantages of home production	9
Crosses, good profitable: egg producers and table birds ...	55
Cabbage and green food: how to keep up supply of latter	51
Chickens at hatching time, how to deal with and take care of ...	77
Chicken coops: how to make and use ...	79
Cramp: its causes, and results in case of ...	82, 203
Chickens reared under glass: their weakly condition	70, 82
Chicken rearing summarised ..	87
Creve Cœurs: their good qualities	108
Cochins: Buff, White, Partridge, Black, and Cuckoo ...	120
Cross-bred fowls: their use and advantages	160
Cramming and Crammers	254
Camphor for fowls	203
Colds: how to prevent	193
Crop bound: how to relieve the fowl ...	209
Comb disease: its causes and cure	215
Consumption: its causes and remedy	220
Dandelions for poultry	50
Dorkings: coloured, silver-grey, cuckoo, buff-speckled, and white	109
Dorking-Brahma cross	172
Diseases: how to deal with in early stages	186
Diarrhœa and Dysentery: how to act in cases of	220
Dropsy in abdomen: how to relieve	223
Evils of misleading poultry literature, and baneful effects of its influence	6
Exercise for sitting hens: care of nest during same	75
Egg-eating: how to prevent ...	205
Egg-bound: how to act in case of fowl being	207

INDEX.

	PAGE
Enteritis	228
Fowl-houses—cheap and inexpensive: how to make, fit, and place them	13
,, Hogshead: how to adapt	14
,, Lean-to: with plan for preventing ingress of rats	17
,, Movable on wheels: their uses and management...	25
Feeding: erroneous opinions with regard to	41
,, why this should be carefully attended to	41
,, when and how to give the food	42
Flint grit for poultry	43
Fish for Poultry: which birds should have it, and which should not	49
Fertile eggs: how to ensure	65
Fresh blood: its absolute importance	57, 66
Foster mothers	70
Fatteners' diet	254
Fattened poultry: prices of	249
Fattening fowls: how to tend and feed	255
Feather eaters: how to deal with and cure	218, 221
Grain for poultry: the best kinds of	47
Groats for young chickens	84
Gardens: how to utilize for rearing young chickens	85
Game: varieties and leading points	117
Golden Wyandottes: their advantages and points	125
Gapes	201
Hatching hens: how to feed and tend them	75
Hamburghs: silver-pencilled, golden-pencilled, silver-spangled, golden-spangled, and black	113
Houdans: their points and peculiarities	122
Houdan-Orpington cross	163
Houdan-Leghorn cross	166
Houdan-Minorca cross	164

INDEX.

	PAGE
Houdan-Indian Game cross	168
Heated houses : dangers attending use of	186
Indian Game : their value for crossing and table purposes	119
Incubators : failures and successes	67
Indian Game-Plymouth Rock cross	174
Indian-Game Dorking...	176
Indian Game-Buff Orpington cross	177
Inflammation of lungs : how to deal with	224
Killing	250
Liver disease : direful results of ; symptoms, causes, and cure	44, 195
Lime : its uses and its dangers	86
Leghorns : black, buff, pile, and duckwing	104
Langshans	128
Leghorn-Plymouth Rock cross...	171
Leghorn-Orpington cross	183
Leg-weakness	200
Moss peat for poultry	29
,, substitutes for	33
Meat for poultry	48
Maize for fowls : its use and abuse	45
Moisture for eggs during period of incubation	74
Management of small broods : economical amalgamation of same	76
Minorcas	100
Minorca-Langhan cross	169
Nests : how to make and place them	71
Newly hatched chickens : how to feed and care for ...	83
No-water system : author's experiences of same ...	87
Orpingtons : their origin	10
Oyster shells for laying hens	39

INDEX.

	PAGE
Orpingtons: single-combed black, rose-combed black, white, Rose-comb Buff, Single-comb Buff, and Diamond Jubilee, their spread, popularity and advantages	134
Orpingtons—Buff: origin and good points	144
,, ,, standard of	148
Orpingtons for crossing	145
Orpington-Dorking cross	178
Orpington-Brahma cross	182
Poultry keeping as an industry: past abuses, present encouragement	1
Poor man's pleasures: poultry keeping in regard to	2
Poultry keeping *will* pay!	7
Poultry keeping past and present: restrained, encouraged	8
Perches for runs: their great usefulness	23
Proportions of nutriment in various grains: table of	40
Plymouth Rocks: their advantages and peculiarities	93
Poultry farming: does it pay?	237
Practical poultry keeping *versus* ignorance	238
Poultrymen: qualifications of	241
Poultry keeping: profits of	244
Preserved eggs: various systems for keeping	261
Runs for poultry	22
Runs: covered	22
Runs: how best to arrange	23
Redcaps or "mooney" fowls	132
Roup: how to deal with	187
Strain: its importance in regard to selection of birds	53
Soft food: and how to mix it	36
Scraps: how to utilize to the best advantage	37, 38
Sharp grit for poultry in confinement: the absolute necessity of	43
Shingle *versus* grit	44
Shell-less eggs: how to avoid	39

INDEX.

	PAGE
Sulphur for poultry : its value, and risks attending its use	49
Stinging nettles for fowls	50
Sitting hens	73
Sitting hen : when and how to put on nest	72
Setting : how to manage same, and how many eggs to give the hen	74
Scotch Greys : their popularity and characteristics	115
Surrey fowls : their production and prestige	253
Surrey fowls : how tended when young	255
Show pen : how to prepare birds for	231
Scrofulous matter : how to remove from throat	190
Soft eggs : how to avoid	211
Soft egg in passage : how to remove	213
Tropical climates : non-sitting varieties for	60
Troughs for feeding poultry	41
Testing eggs at eighth day : how to detect unfertile ones	76
Unfertile eggs : how to use to best advantage	77
Ventilation in fowl-houses : how best to secure	19
Vegetables and green food for poultry	37
Vermin : evidences of their presence and how to destroy	225
Wyandottes : their points and failings	124
White Orpington-Light Brahma cross	181
Washing for show pen	234
Young chickens and vermin	86

PREFACE.

My original intention in writing the first edition of this book was to show the people of England that climate and soil were not really the causes of the great success the French met with in poultry-keeping, but that the real secret of their success lay in the practical knowledge the people generally possessed concerning the methods which were most likely to lead to the greatest number of eggs and the largest and finest table birds being produced, and the energy of those who take up this most valuable and profitable pursuit to help their small incomes, and to give them luxuries that apart from the profit so gained would have been well-nigh impossible.

In sending forth previous editions I have thanked all those who had not only read the book, but who had brought into practical use the many hints it contained, and who also had not been slow to confess honestly that the birds who for so long had been maligned and deemed unprofitable servants to mankind, were not so much to blame as those who by wrong treatment, carelessness, and indifference to the welfare of their birds, of course, rendered their lives miserable, and the good results that should have been gained as impossible of achievement as anything this course of conduct produces in things men have to do with.

Looking back to that time and scanning the circumstances of the intermediate months, the same gratitude in an increased degree naturally fills one's mind. The eighth, now in its turn the ninth, edition is all but sold out, and the books are now circulated in all parts of the world, and I can only hope that the good work of instructing my fellow men in practical and profitable poultry-keeping will go on apace, so that the interest now so manifestly awakened in all parts, and shewn in the more than ever repeated applications by the County Councils for my lectures will be fed and increased, while sound information shall, as the result of these chapters, strengthen its influence and add to its practical and utilitarian importance.

In all parts of the world the Book has found admirers and grateful readers, and some who were sceptical have been forced by sheer facts to acknowledge that those birds I at first likened to machines for converting waste and worthless matter into good and profitable delicacies, are really what they were represented, and that the "Poultry Breeder and Feeder" has indeed fulfilled its mission in a marked degree in showing people "How to make Poultry Pay." Looking back now over the years which have passed since I first sent this book forth to the public, in spite of many difficulties, I remember how it had been tossed about on the sea of controversy and conflicting opinions, the only result being that it has become better known and more widely appreciated, and its contents, like all truth, have stood the test. Poultry-keeping is one of England's best hopes for the future, calculated as it is to help in increasing the pleasure and profit alike of both rich and poor, combining intellectual amusement and profitable recreation for all those who care to trouble enough about their birds to treat them as they should. The development of the industry in England would form an interesting study, and statesmen and others are beginning to wake up to the fact of its importance, while our go-a-head cousins over the water who have, if anything, made better use of the "Poultry Breeder and Feeder" than the English, are beginning to send over their eggs and poultry, as they have sent their cattle, to the shores where so many find a market for their produce. During my journeys up and down the country I see interesting signs of progress everywhere, and the fact that I am, more than ever before, lecturing day after day in town and country districts for the County Councils, shows that poultry-keeping is more rapidly than ever assuming its proper position in our midst.

Trusting that intelligent poultry-keepers have found in the additional matter something more of help and encouragement, I send forth the tenth edition thoroughly revised and rewritten, as I have sent the former ones, with the good intention I originally had, seeing no reason to alter the name or title in any way, feeling assured—as I have more reason to do every day—that the system it advocates and lays down is indeed that which will help people to make poultry pay. Over 34,000 are now in circulation. This fact speaks for itself.

WILLIAM COOK.

ORPINGTON HOUSE,
   ST. MARY CRAY, KENT.
      April, 1898.

GENERAL REMARKS.

Poultry-keeping—Moral, sanitary, and financial benefits, combined with improved health—Personal attention for good results—Comparative advantages of town and country poultry-keepers—Poultry will pay—Poultry-keeping past and present—The Author's work.

OULTRY-KEEPING is still rapidly on the increase, and, as a consequence, we constantly hear of new breeds, new appliances, new methods, and indeed almost everything seems new, as the development of this important industry awakens in the minds of many ingenuity and powers which have lain dormant, and we feel more and more assured of the future good results which must be gained by spreading broadcast throughout our land those feathered pets which are—because they yield a handsome profit—essentially the poor man's pets, who cannot afford, as the rich do, to indulge in keeping large animals or a number of birds that are all expense and yield little or no return. Poultry-keeping as an industry offers many advantages which must appeal significantly to all those who

study the influences at work in the elevation of the poor of countries or districts. Unlike many hobbies it has an elevating effect upon those who are enthusiasts in carrying forward its interests. For children the good results that come from an early acquaintance with poultry-keeping are an important consideration. Young minds are active if they are healthy, and young hands are the willing servants of these minds, and if this activity can only be governed and trained and turned from mischief into useful efforts to excel in amusements which are instructive, a great deal is gained in directing aright those influences which make or mar young lives. Kindness to animals, regularity in attending to the wants of the birds, a certain business enthusiasm, which in these days of keen competition men who are to succeed must have, in addition to much practical knowledge, such as that gained in carpentering, to build the houses and runs, painting, whitewashing, and in many other ways might be cited as useful details, all helping to train young minds to regular and industrious habits at the time when they are most easily influenced, keeping them at home and preventing them spending their spare time at the street corners, in the public houses, or in other doubtful places of amusement.

Then the question of economy, and even sanitary benefits may be cited as by no means unimportant considerations, and in these particulars poultry-keeping may be said to achieve one of its greatest successes. There is always a great quantity of waste food, scraps, kitchen refuse, &c., which, if not disposed of somehow, finds its way into the ash bins—causing unpleasant smells, dangerous to health, and detrimental to comfort. Poultry would thrive on much of this refuse, and mixed with a little meal and hard corn, these scraps, &c., might be used as food for the birds, who in return for it would give fresh eggs and at last make a savoury dish for the table. It might be useful to hint here that in towns it would be a good plan if poultry-keepers could collect refuse from hotels, &c., as they could get a good part of their fowls' food in this way, and the birds would thrive better and produce more eggs on such food as this than any other; certainly this is better for them than any patent foods.

Thus it will be seen how valuable poultry are, and when in addition to this it is remembered that millions of English money find their way into other countries because English poultry and eggs are not produced, how important does it appear that English cottagers and others should avail themselves of the splendid opportunity that lies within their grasp. Poultry-keeping recommends itself as an industry for the poor, because the birds being so small the risk of losing stock by death or accident is not so great, and losses are not so far-reaching in their results as in many forms of live stock farming. For instance, where pigs, sheep, cows, or horses are kept, the loss of one of these animals forms a serious item, but the loss of even one or two fowls can speedily be got over, and so a poor man need not hesitate to embark upon this enterprise through fear of great losses. On the other hand, the author has found from experience, having kept all kinds of cattle and live stock, none have yielded so good a return as poultry, so that the best investment for both rich and poor is poultry keeping, and the fact of his having had some hundreds of acres devoted to this pursuit shows that he does not speak without experience.

Then to keep a few fowls only a very small space is needed, and almost every cottager has enough room to spare for this, while for larger animals his back garden would be useless, and why should it be that English cottagers have to be content with French eggs, which are oftentimes uneatable, while they may, if they choose, produce fresh eggs and enjoy the luxury of a roast fowl sometimes for dinner? In times of sickness, eggs are simply invaluable, and as this frequently comes when eggs are dearest, the persons sick, if they are poor, often cannot afford to buy them at all, and have to go without, when, if a few fowls had been kept, they might have been forthcoming. The pleasure to be gained by people of all classes, mixed oftentimes with immense benefit to their health and prospects, renders poultry-keeping an important factor in the joy of every-day life. The author has known many instances where cottagers with a small piece of ground have paid their rent and derived a great deal of pleasure by keeping poultry, while some very delicate ladies he has known have greatly improved their health by getting out into the air to attend to their birds. Poultry-keeping is a pursuit the love for which increases as a person goes on. At first it seems a little irksome to some, but the author has known many who have persevered, and success has brought enthusiasm and increased their interest until they have found in their birds one of their chief delights, independent of the profit gained. How eagerly the children expect the little chicks when the hen is sitting; how carefully she is lifted off her nest morning after morning, and then how great the delight when the little balls of fluff appear and become the pride of their young owners. And how good it is thus to interest children; nothing gives parents such delight as seeing their children pleased and interested with animals, or, indeed, any good thing. The love for animals will often check a brutal tendency in children and make them kind to these pets, when otherwise the bad influences of a brutal nature might have been left to lead them into excesses which often end seriously.

Poultry always pay for good and personal attention. The author travels about 30,000 miles a year up and down England, visiting the poultry yards of both rich and poor, lecturing, driving from farm to farm and district to district, and seeing in the course of these journeys all sorts of poultry, all sorts of poultry-keepers, and all sorts of poultry accommodation. When he is requested to pay a gentleman a professional visit, as he often is, he frequently calls on many others in the same district, and so when he says poultry-keeping pays for personal attention, he speaks from a vast experience of localities and breeds best suited to districts, as well as the conditions under which it is most suitable for poultry to be kept. He is often called in to lay out pens and yards, and in some cases where poultry-keeping has been unsuccessful he is able to detect the flaws in the system, remedy the evils, and start the person on the road to successful and lucrative experiences. He finds, among the people he calls upon, cottagers who make a handsome profit out of their fowls, and who give them personal attention and carefully provide for all their needs. On the other hand, he finds oftentimes rich men whose poultry kept and tended by others scarcely pays at all, so that working men will see that the opportunities are really very much on their side in this matter. There are books which oftentimes lead cottagers astray by saying so many fowls only should be kept on so much ground, and speak of expensive appliances, heated houses, &c., and lay down rules of a most extravagant kind; but cottagers should not be alarmed by these, but go on treating their fowls intelligently, giving them a good warm food and hard corn diet, as advised in the pages of this book, and they will help their fowls to lead the most useful of lives and give their owners much pleasure and not a little profit.

Poultry-keepers are apt, like all other people, to form comparisons. It is suggested by many persons residing in towns that country poultry-keepers have so many more advantages for successful poultry-keeping, as their birds can roam over commons and fields, and oftentimes pick up half their living. This may be so in some cases, but when we consider that in the country the pig-pail and other sources absorb a good deal of the scrap refuse, all of which goes to the fowls in towns; how much less a country producer gets for his eggs—often not more than half as much—the limited sphere he has to get customers, and then the disadvantages of selling oftentimes through a market, it will be seen that the town producer, even if it costs him a little more for the keep of his birds, most certainly has the best of it, over and above the opportunities of getting scraps,&c., from the hotels, of which I have spoken. Eggs always realise a better price in towns or good districts near a town, and to have the birds on the spot is an immense advantage, and if all things are fairly considered the town poultry-keeper will find that he has by far the greatest advantages. Six fowls penned in a back-yard in a town often lay more eggs than ten in the country, where they have several acres to roam over during the winter months, as where they have grit and corn, &c., supplied, they are fed regularly, while the chances are they do not pick up while running over the ground as much as is supposed.

One of the facts an increased interest in poultry-keeping has evolved is that poultry *will* pay. In a few instances the author has known poultry to clear from 15/- to £1 per bird where only a few have been kept, say 6 or 13 hens; and where 25 or 46 have been running, they have brought in from £9 to £20 clear profit. Of course this is where the birds have been treated properly, and the eggs, &c., have sold well in a good town or district. This profit is welcome to all, in whatever position they are placed, and it adds pleasure to pleasure when a hobby is a source of income. It was one of the habits of the late Prince Consort to make all his experiments in farming, &c., pay, and if this were the only good lesson this excellent man left behind him he would have done good work. But to the poor, how much more welcome is a little additional money to their limited incomes, and if to the joy of their children over the chickens and the nutritious eggs and savoury fowls, they are able to remember a little profit made, surely they will feel grateful for the feathered pets that have done so much to make their lives happier.

Poultry-keeping is to-day a very different thing from the poultry-keeping of years gone by. In those days of conservative old breeders, who would neither impart anything they possessed in the way of knowledge, nor sell eggs or birds, and who guarded most jealously any approach to the spread of the industry, poultry-keeping for the poor man was practically out of the question. The best he could hope for was to get a few mongrels from some farmer or other enterprising person who could supply them, and these were the birds which led so many disappointed cottagers and others to say "poultry will not pay." How altered are the circumstances of poultry-keepers now. In these days of shows and periodicals devoted to the fancy, of improved appliances and methods, when the poorest reads the experiences of the rich, and on the poultry-keeping platform the rich and poor meet together; when master vies with man to produce birds of excellent quality, and the man often beats; in these days of fair prospects, it is not surprising when we find that where one person kept poultry ten years ago, twenty keep them now, and that all over the country men and women are going in more and more for good birds and good results. The author entertains the hope that in the course of some twenty or thirty years the English people will be found producing poultry and eggs sufficient to supply all the needs of England, and so be occupying a much better position than now.

A great many good eggs are sent out from England now to Africa, America, India, France, Belgium, Holland, and

Germany and Russia, and a good number to Australia and New Zealand, and these are sold at from 4/- to a guinea per dozen, so of course good birds are produced from them.

The English breeders not only keep good birds, but are continually improving them, and these are becoming more plentiful all over the country, but the only grave defect is found in the fact that exhibitors at our shows are apt to sacrifice the laying qualities to fine feathers and good points; thus oftentimes a good breed is spoiled, because, in the eagerness to produce fine plumage, &c., the more important qualities from a commercial point of view are lost sight of. The author has been working for years to counteract this evil, and produce birds that combine exhibition points with good laying qualities, and in this he has been signally successful, almost beyond his most sanguine expectations, so that he has gone far beyond giving advice, but has proved his theories by producing the breeds and spreading them broadcast throughout the world. The laying qualities are all important in our English fowls, because eggs are such an article of consumption in this country. The cottagers and small farmers in France, Sweden, Denmark, and Russia, produce most of the foreign eggs sent to this country. These people make poultry pay well enough. The eggs have to pass through the hands of four or five middle-men, each of these making a profit for himself; how much more then should the English poultry-keeper be able to realise a good price for his eggs and get a good living. These people have pretty much the same climate as our own, and indeed in Ireland, whence we get many of our eggs also, the climate is even damper. The foreign eggs are generally smaller than those produced at home, so the home producer has many advantages over his foreign competitor for the poultry and egg trade of England.

Amid all the changes that have been wrought in the poultry-keeping world, the author has been a foremost figure. He has travelled all over the country and has been continually in touch with poultry-keepers of all classes; and in many parts, as well as at his London office and Poultry Yards and Farms, he has met boys and girls and men and women who have brought him their pets to relieve of their pain or give them advice concerning them, some coming from 20 miles round. In addition to this, he has continually answered letters which have been sent him from all parts of the world, with stamped addressed envelope enclosed for advice, which he gives gratis, he having sometimes as many as from 100 to 160 letters in a day. Thus he has striven to disseminate good sound advice, shewing that as corn was tolerably cheap and conditions favourable, how people might make their poultry pay. The Orpington fowls (so named after the village in which he lived at the time of the introduction of the first of the breeds) form some of the results of his experiments in producing a good table bird, with excellent laying qualities, combined with a good and handsome appearance, and to those already so well known he has added breeds of ducks and other fowls which have been proved to meet certain needs and necessities which exist. These are fast spreading over the world, and have taken prominent positions as some of the leading varieties of fowls. During recent years he has also made public what he for some time kept secret, viz., how he detected the good layers among a flock of birds. He gives in the book some heads of fowls, which he has had engraved from photographs taken by Mr. E. Davey Lavender, Gold Medalist, of Bromley, Kent, of live specimens of the good and bad layers of various breeds. The success of this branch of intelligent poultry management has been marked, and he has received letters telling him where, even children—some as young as ten years old—have taken his book and gone to the run and picked out the best layers quite easily. Poultry-keepers generally have also accepted this, which is proved so conclusively to be the practical outcome of intelligent observation.

Utility has been the watchword of the author, and his success in producing good profitable birds has been great, as the new breeds he has introduced to the poultry world will shew, and now he has only the desire that the truth concerning poultry-keeping may be told, believed, and proved by the many thousands of those whose lot is made up largely of want and worry, bringing them better days and brighter prospects. The illustrations in this book are drawn from life and engraved, the best birds in the author's yards being used as subjects for them.

HOUSES AND RUNS.

Houses—Hogshead houses—Lean-to houses—Perches and nests—Movable houses for fields—Confined runs—Covered runs—Open spaces used to their best advantage—The treatment of confined runs—Difficulties with regard to runs: how to surmount them—How to keep fighting cocks apart—Cheap and interchangeable runs.

POULTRY-KEEPING has its details and among them a great consideration especially to poor people is the cost of the house.

Some poor people sit down and take into consideration the cost of these things and wonder if they can afford the £2 or £3 necessary for the purchase of really suitable houses, and because they feel they dare not make the outlay they give up the idea of keeping fowls at all.

This, however, should not deter any from taking up poultry-keeping, as something cheaper might be provided just to start with, although where one can afford it it is not a bad investment to have good substantial houses and runs at the outset.

If only a few fowls are kept, say four or six, they may be housed quite effectually and comfortably in a large box or hogshead. Either of these may be bought for a few

Then, if a box is used, of course the same general principles may be observed, only the roof must be made to slant so that the water runs off.

FRONT OF HOGSHEAD HOUSE.

If only egg or smaller boxes can be obtained the house must be built, and it is well to put it up, if possible, against a fence or in a corner.

Of course the wood will be found very thin, but if there are no cracks, a nice, neat, tight, little house may be made of them, and even if there are a few cracks the birds will keep all the healthier, as fresh air is most beneficial. A house five feet square will do nicely for from 8 to 12 birds, and I have kept fowls in such houses as these and had them in full lay all through the winter.

Where poultry-keepers can afford larger and more substantial houses they may be made with feather-edge boards for the sides, &c., and the roof may be thatched, or made with ordinary half-inch boards covered with German felt. The German felt is far superior to the ordinary felt as it shillings at any grocer's shop and very neat and comfortable plain houses may be put up at very little cost, if used as follows.

Where a hogshead is used it should be laid upon the ground on its side and blocked both sides securely, so that it does not roll.

A few inches of earth or road-scrapings put at the bottom of the barrel and beaten down will make a nice level floor.

To make a window a small square opening should be cut in the back end close to the top. A piece of glass should be put in, and so a window about six inches by eight can be made. This might be fixed in a frame so that it may be opened to form a ventilator when the weather is not cold. Continuous ventilation should also be secured by boring a few holes in the front and back of the

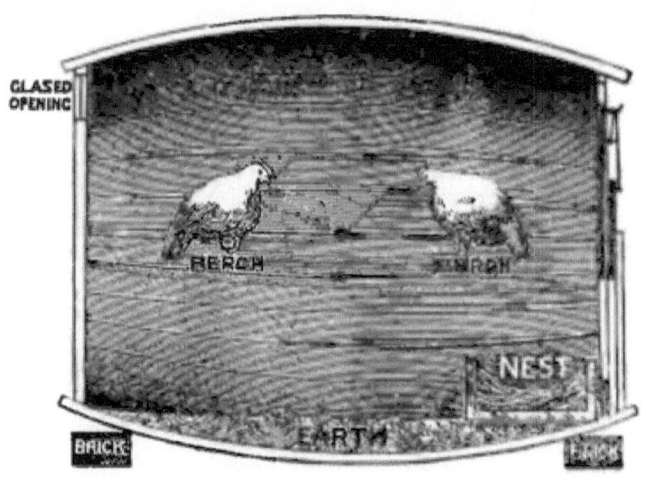

HOGSHEAD HOUSE.

hogshead, well up to the top, as all poultry houses should be ventilated at the highest point so that the birds do not get into a draught, as this soon gives them cold.

Two perches may be fixed at about six or eight inches from the soil bottom. These should be moveable so that they may be taken out and cleansed thoroughly, as the ends form hiding places for vermin, from which it is otherwise very difficult to dislodge them.

The nest box should be just inside the opening so that it may be got at easily, and this should have a top so that the hen may get right inside when she lays her eggs.

The front should be boarded and a hole cut at the bottom, level with the dirt floor. A door which runs up and down in a groove might be made so as to let down over the opening, and so shut the fowls up securely that foxes, &c., cannot get at them when they have gone to roost.

In the summer it should have a wire door—a frame covered with strong wire, so that the opening is secured, but allowing the fresh air to get in.

To roof the hogshead a piece of roofing felt or canvas, well tarred, should be nailed on, and if any very wide cracks are found in the tub these should first be pasted up with brown paper and well tarred, so as to make the house quite weather tight, and additional slips might also be pasted inside, so as to ensure that all is quite watertight as well. If paper is put inside it should have a good coating of lime wash, as this will prevent vermin sheltering underneath it.

only requires tarring once in three years, and does not harbour vermin like the ordinary felt, and the germs of disease which are harboured by the old sort of felt need not be feared if the German felt is used.

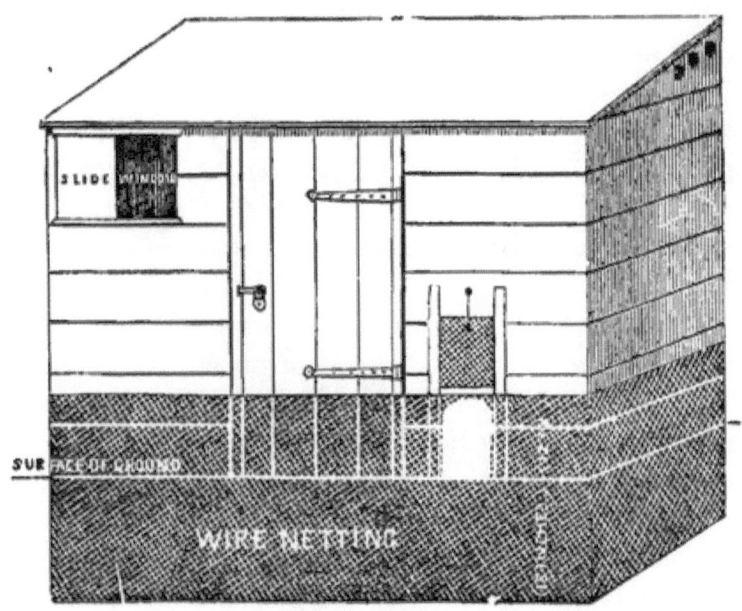

LEAN-TO HOUSE.
Showing wire netting above and below ground for keeping out rats, &c.

Feather edge boards are not so good for roofing purposes as these will not keep out wet without the felt to make them watertight, and when felt is used the ridges cut the felt through, so it is much better to use flat boards for the roofing. The boards should be well-seasoned and perfectly dry when they are put on, as if this is not looked to, when the sun shines on the roof the boards shrink, and sometimes pull the felt away, and so the good condition of the roof is destroyed.

One-and-a-half or two inch quartering is strong enough for the frame work, and for a small house even lighter wood than this would be strong enough, and the sides must be either tarred or painted, so as to preserve the wood.

Houses may be made so that they can be carried from place to place, or they may be made so that they lean against a wall. But whatever position they occupy care must be taken to well cover the floor with moss peat litter, as this is a deodorizer, and keeps the bottom of the house nice and dry.

Where rats are found they should be prevented getting into the house by strips of wire netting being put down in the ground, about 12 inches below the surface. This will prevent burrowing under the boards, and be an effectual safeguard against rats, and any house may be made rat-proof in this way.

Inside the house perches should be fixed so that the ends drop into a socket which keeps them about 15 to 18 inches above the floor of the house. Heavy birds should never roost higher than this, and light ones should never have perches higher than two feet. These should always be moveable, as if they are nailed the red bugs get underneath the ends and are most destructive to the comfort and health of the fowls, as they suck their blood when they are on the perches at night.

The perches should be paraffined two or three times during the summer to kill these, and bark should under no consideration be left on the perches.

Perches for fowls should be made quite flat, and about two inches wide, the sharp edges being bevelled off. Where round perches are used the pressure upon the breast-bone causes many of the chickens to have crooked breasts.

There should be quite a clear 15 inches between each perch, as if this is not allowed the birds are apt to peck each other.

The nests should be placed so that the front of each box faces the darkest part of the house. Some persons reverse matters, but experience clearly proves that a hen takes more readily to the nest when it is shaded from the light.

Poultry houses must *always* be ventilated, and to do this effectually the opening should be made at the topmost point of the building at either end.

This is important, because the birds should never be allowed to roost in a draught; and the vapour and ammonia from the excrement rise to the top of the house and are carried out by the rush of pure air.

This is one reason why the perches should be kept low, so that the foul air may rise and be swept out by this, the only proper method of ventilation.

Of course the opening for the fowls to go in and out should be fitted with a sliding frame, which should be covered with wire, as this also admits air and helps to purify the house, especially during the hot days of summer when all possible ventilation is needed.

The window, which should be made in every fowl house, should be made so that it might be opened or shut, according to the weather, fowls being very fond of light, which always has a tendency to benefit the health and well-being of living things.

It is not so necessary to keep fowls warm in fowl houses at night. The cooler they are kept the more eggs are produced during the winter months. Shelter from wind and wet is all they require. Fowls, as a rule, will lay as many more eggs in an open shed as they will produce in a warm brick building during the winter months. In fact they cannot have too much ventilation, as long as they do not sit in a draught. I always leave my doors or windows open at night even in the coldest weather. If fowls have a warm house at night they should have a warm, sheltered run during the day, as if they do not they feel the cold so when they run out first thing in the morning. I visit some thousands of poultry yards in the year during my lectures through the country. The warmer the houses—whatever breed is kept—I find the less number of eggs produced. Fowls should never be huddled together: too many birds in one house means disaster, and often disease.

In putting the houses together it is well to use screws as far as possible, so that the buildings may easily be taken to pieces. The sides might be made so that each one is a piece, as this makes it quite easy to transport them flat from place to place, and where possible they might also be made with a hinge, so that in an emergency they might be propped up so as to form additional shelter in wet weather.

Of course, after all, some may like rather to buy their houses, and plenty of good, reliable buildings may be obtained of dealers in such articles. The names of some of the makers may be found in the advertisement pages of this book.

Where people live in the country they will, in many parts, frequently have sheds or outhouses that will be useful for poultry, but for town dwellers this is almost out of the question, and we know that, generally, such poultry-keepers have to provide their houses in one or other of the ways I have mentioned. A cheap way of housing two or three small pens of fowls is to erect one long house and divide it into three parts, leaving a passage so that the attendant may attend to each section.

Smaller houses also may be made with wooden bottoms and mounted on wheels. These houses are very useful, especially to farmers, as by using them poultry may be moved from place to place. These houses are most useful, as during the autumn fowls should be put out in the fields, so that they may pick up grubs and beetles and wire worms, besides many most destructive insects which all make the best of food for fowls.

Fowls always do well upon entirely fresh ground, and by turning them out thus they will pick up their living for two months or more of the year, which is a great consideration as they eat up a good deal of waste grain and clear the fields of a great many most injurious things.

Then the young chickens should be put out in the grass fields, away from the farm yard, where they can pick up an abundance of insect life, get one-half of their living, and while growing faster and thriving well do the grass a good deal of good.

To hop farmers this form of insect clearing is especially valuable, and these should coop hens and chickens all over the hop fields.

The hens should be put into coops and the little chickens allowed to roam over the entire ground, and they will clear off a good deal of the insect life which is so abundant, as many insects fall off the bine and crawl up again if there is no means of clearing them off when they are crawling upon the ground.

Green fly, spiders, and grubs, as also the wire worm at the roots of the bine itself are all found in large numbers, and the chickens will scratch round the roots and get the wire worms out, and yet do no damage to the roots.

RUNS.

And now I turn to another part of this all important question, viz., the question of runs. It must ever be a fact that no amount of care can ever compensate for lack of space in poultry-keeping, but it is wonderful how much may be done in small runs even, when care is used to keep the birds clean and healthy.

A run seven feet wide and from five to seven yards long will be large enough for from six to eight fowls, but there should always be a part covered in so that a covered run is available.

This covered part provides shade from the sun in summer, and protection from wet and cold during winter. To protect fowls effectually from the cold winds, part of the run should be boarded up, or hurdles thatched with straw may be placed against the wire to make it warm and cosy for the birds.

The bottom of the covered run should be covered with quite dry earth, dry leaves or loose straw, and among this a few grains of corn should be sprinkled which will cause them to scratch, giving them employment, and circulating their blood.

This little exercise is most valuable and will ensure good health and laying results in confined runs, especially during the winter months.

A perch should be put in the covered run, as birds like to sit on these and clean their plumage. If this is provided they clean themselves more and do not pluck their feathers so much, nor do they huddle together in groups, and even in the open it is well to put up a perch, as anything that separates the birds gives them health and vigour. This should always be placed in such a position as to ensure plenty of sun, and afford good shelter from cold, wet and winds.

It is very unwise to herd fowls together in large flocks. Each pen should be kept separately and then one large run into which doors from all the pens open, and the birds should be let out one pen at a time for a few hours at various periods during the day.

Every pen will in this way get a good run and after a day or two they will go in and out of the pen with very little driving, as they get accustomed to the routine.

From seven to thirty birds is the very highest number that should be kept in one pen, while in breeding pens the number should never exceed 15.

To successfully plan out, say an acre of ground, it is well to divide it right across the middle. Then the houses and small runs should be put in the warmest positions and have a slide door through which the fowls might run into the large grass run.

If no grass is growing in confined runs they should be swept well, especially in hot and dry weather, and in very wet weather the top should be taken off so as to keep them as firm as possible. Even the grass run should be swept well and rolled two or three times a year after heavy rains, as this will make them harder and firmer, so that the fowls will not be able to scratch up the grass by the roots.

The foregoing is the very best and most economical method of keeping poultry, and one which has ever produced the very best results.

Brahmas and Cochins may be kept in a run with wire about three or four feet high, although for all other breeds it should be five to six feet high, and for breeds that are inveterate flyers even higher and over the top if the birds are to be kept in.

It is sometimes necessary to cut the flight feathers of one wing of the birds to prevent them flying. The flight feathers should be cut just underneath the first rows of small feathers, leaving about two of the long feathers at the end. When done in this way the appearance of the bird is not spoiled.

Of course it will be understood that the more comfortable the run can be made the better the fowls will like it, and any increased expenses will be compensated for by the extra number of eggs obtained in the winter.

Where a covered run is provided a plentiful supply of ashes and dust should be kept in a dry spot, just where the sun shines. A little fall also should be made so that the water may drain off freely. Some people dig the whole of the run over, but this should never be done, a small square place where the fowls may scratch, say in one corner, would provide scratching exercise, which is most beneficial. Corn should be buried here and the fowls will soon find it out and scratch it up.

To avoid a battle between cocks, where two or three pens of birds are kept, a board partition, about three feet high, should be put against the netting next the ground, as the cocks fight through the netting and injure themselves very much.

The question of farmers' fowls is one of the utmost importance, as they have so many facilities for the advantageous keeping of poultry, and I am glad to know that the farmers are everywhere beginning to realise the great advantages to be gained by the pursuit of this most profitable undertaking, especially as these practical men have found out how much really good food for fowls may be gathered up by the birds if they are turned down in the fields.

FARMER'S HOUSE ON WHEELS.

In order to make it possible for the birds to be moved easily from point to point over the farm, it is well to have houses upon wheels, like those shewn in the illustration. If a farmer has houses he might use these and have a sort of carriage or cradle constructed, to which the horse might be hooked, and so mounted on this the houses might be drawn about from place to place.

A good many houses are made with nest boxes outside, and great care must be taken that these are not knocked off as they are drawn through the gateways. They are usually fixed about one-and-a-half feet from the ground, and it would be better where the houses are likely to be used in the way mentioned, to fix these nest boxes at the end of the house, so that they are not exposed to danger. Farmers are beginning to find out what a source of profit poultry-keeping may be made.

New laid eggs ought not to cost the farmer more than a ¼d. each all the year round.

Where farmers are keeping pace with the times they feed and treat their birds properly, and the splendid supplies of insect food make it abundantly possible for them to gain the best of results.

Whenever a field is being ploughed up the farmer should have the houses removed into the field, so that the birds can follow the plough and pick up the worms, grubs, &c., which are thrown out on the turned up soil. This will enable them to get almost their whole living, and this insect food is the very best fowls can have.

I have known 150 birds that were kept in three houses and I have known when they have followed the plough they have not eaten 4lb. weight of corn in a day, so satisfying is this insect food.

It always seems to me that it is far better to let the fowls clear up the waste upon the farms than to leave it for rooks and wild birds to consume, as out of these no profit can ever be gained, and the rooks will also come again and eat the seed corn, as it is impossible to really pen these. Fowls can be easily managed and kept within bounds, and so the clearing is done, and growing crops left undamaged. Farmers should kill off many of the rooks and put chickens into the fields, as these would soon clear off the vermin.

There is no reason why farmers should not keep fowls in the farmyard as they do now, but larger numbers should be kept and spread over the fields.

Sometimes corn is very cheap. I have known farmers keep all their corn and buy in a lot of fowls who feed upon the wheat, and so consume it, and by so doing they have gained a good profit to reward them for their enterprise.

I have heard farmers say if they cannot get £2 per quarter for corn they give it to the fowls, and so make 10/- per quarter more for all the fowls eat.

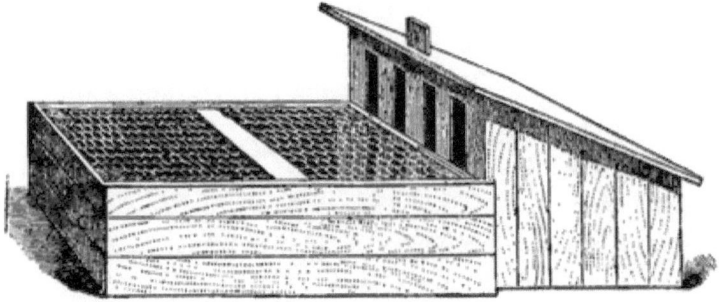

SMALL RUN.

I am constantly meeting with people who say they cannot keep poultry because they have not sufficient houses or runs

Houses may be made quite easily, about three feet in front, sloping down to two feet at the back, and from three feet to five feet long, and two feet six inches to three feet wide. The top should be boarded, the back and two ends being covered with felt, and for the front small mesh wire may be used. Chickens may be kept in these runs when they have the hen or foster mother, and continue in them until they commence laying.

Then these low places may be used for little chickens if necessary and also for laying hens out in the fields.

Then when not in use for either of these purposes they may be put alongside the fowl houses and used as covered runs, and in a variety of ways they become a sort of "hold all" to the poultry-keeper. One or two perches length ways, resting upon the quartering, two inches from the ground, will afford the fowls a resting-place, and they will sit here and sun themselves, for nothing is more beneficial or healthful for fowls than plenty of fresh air.

My readers will understand that these covered runs answer for sleeping purposes during the night as well as shelter at other times, and the fowls should have their liberty to run where they like during the day, and go in and out as they please.

It will therefore be seen that the providing of fowl houses and runs, although if gone into on an elaborate scale may be made expensive, may also be so managed as to make it possible for the poorest to make poultry pay.

MOSS PEAT.

Moss Peat a permanent benefit to fowls and owners—Lime and dust, danger and dirt—Moss Peat a deodoriser—German *versus* English moss peat.

MANY poultry-keepers who have only a few fowls look after them themselves, and, of course, to this class of poultry-keepers anything that will lessen labour and make the work of tending them pleasant is most welcome.

In many cases ladies take an interest in their fowls, and don't mind putting their hands to the work of tending them.

The greatest objection has, however, been felt in many instances to the work of cleaning out the fowl houses, owing to the really bad condition some of them have been allowed to get in, owing to the insufficient amount of litter and in some cases of the lack of suitable material for this purpose.

The poultry houses are generally limewashed, and in the towns or on the outskirts of towns these are generally low pitched erections—so built as not to be visible from the windows of the dwelling houses near.

This fact, of course, renders it very difficult for the poultry houses to be thoroughly swept and cleaned out.

To avoid having to do this often some people have used

dry earth, cinder ashes, and in some cases lime, to put on the bottom of the houses. These have not always had the best effect, and, in fact, the lime has in some instances proved itself most dangerous where it has not been mixed with peat moss, as when the fowls flap their wings, the lime flies up, and sometimes gets in their eyes, causing great irritation, and cases have been known where a fowl has done itself great injury through the scratching of the eye in this way.

In some cases the feet may be damp after running out, and if they tread in upon the dry lime this adheres to the damp feet and so when scratching themselves they make bad matters worse, and increase, instead of allaying the irritation. The eye is scratched right out sometimes, but in any case the scratching makes the eyes very tender, especially in crested birds.

And when all this is done there is always a faint smell from excrement, as there is nothing in these things to kill this.

Moss Peat is the best thing to use in the fowl houses, for many reasons.

The first and foremost of these is that it is a deodoriser. If it is spread from three to five inches thick on the ground of the fowl house, it will form a nice bottom, and if turned over occasionally it destroys the smell, and so keeps the house sweet and clean.

And not only this, but because it is absorbent, it keeps the bottom dry. The fowls run in with wet feet and soon they are nice and dry and warm, and this is a very great consideration and has a great influence on the health of the birds.

To ensure this, however, great care must be taken to see that the floor of the house is well raised so that the surface water from outside does not drain in underneath it and make it wet, as this destroys every advantage and only serves to increase the discomfort of the fowls.

Peat moss, if it is to be of benefit to the fowls must be *dry*, and when the weather is cold during the autumn and winter months some grain should be thrown into the moss so as to give them the scratching exercise which is so beneficial to them.

Fowls are very fond of dusting themselves, and they can have nothing better for this purpose than moss peat, and if a dozen fowls are turned into a house with a nice dry moss peat bottom, from four to seven of them would dust themselves in it.

Moss peat is one of the most useful things that poultry-keepers could have for the purpose I have named, as it not only saves a great deal of trouble in cleaning the houses out, but it also keeps them nice and sweet and fresh, so that the offensive smells that were once so frequent wherever poultry was kept have almost entirely been got rid of wherever this moss peat is kept.

Then again the peat is soft and spongy, and if a hen drops an egg from the perch it is very rarely broken, and when the birds jump down off the perches it is soft and nice for them, and avoids any possibility of bumble foot or affections of a kindred nature which fowls often suffer from, owing to some blow received when they fly down from any high point.

Fowls are very fond of it, and will often scratch a hole and lay their eggs in it in preference to the nests, and the clean comfortable houses make all the difference to the laying results.

And there is another side to the question. The moss peat not only absorbs much of the goodness contained in the excrement, such as the greater part of the ammonia, but it also retains it and after about six months, if the peat is carefully cleared out this makes most valuable manure and is excellent for all kinds of garden and farming ground.

Some of my readers may feel puzzled, and wonder how the peat can possibly be sweet when the excrement is still contained in it, but I can assure them that the smell does not exist, and so the houses are freed from the noxious vapours that might otherwise have filled the atmosphere. Some of my own houses are not cleaned out more than twice a year, or at the most three times, and they keep perfectly sweet, and thousands of visitors, who look round my pens at St. Mary Cray, express their astonishment at the very sweet, clean, and dry condition of the poultry houses, and I know very many who have had like experience with myself, and found it most valuable and efficacious. And it must be remembered that anything which renders the air in which the birds sleep purer is valuable upon the score of health, as pure air means often times purer blood and greatly increased vitality.

I generally use German Moss Peat in preference to the English, the latter being not quite so light and loose, but if any reader lives where the English is sold, it will, of course, be cheaper for them to buy this, although it will not last so long in the fowl house.

Farmers are, of course, often in possession of a good deal of short stuff that answers for litter, and where this is so, of course, it is not necessary or advisable to buy moss peat. There are cases where even, although none of the chaff and dust are forthcoming, short horse manure which makes a very good bottom, may be used. Of course the dust and chaff which come mixed together from the thrashing machine make good litter, and this should be spread six or eight inches thick over the floor of the house, but a barrow load or two of horse manure, fresh every week and stirred over occasionally forms a very good substitute for the dust.

Of course one great thing is to provide scratching exercise for the fowls and any litter should be chosen with this end in view, as the birds scratch it over and so hide much of the excrement from view.

I never recommend poultry people to spend a shilling where sixpence would do.

Moss peat is also a splendid thing for putting in the bottom of coops. It is especially valuable for putting into the chicken coops, as the little things run in upon it and so dry their little feet, oftentimes avoiding cramp and other affections, and in pens where fowls are put to be prepared for the show pen it is peculiarly valuable, it being dry and clean, and so the plumage is at its best when the show time comes.

One golden rule I would again emphasise, and that is that wherever moss peat is used it must always be kept dry, and then the very best results will be obtained, and wherever poultry-keepers are troubled with complaints respecting smells from fowl houses they will find the introduction of moss peat a sure remedy for the evil.

FEEDING.

Past mismanagement and its results—Soft food and how to mix it—Meat for fowls—Eggs without shells and how to avoid them—Feeding with troughs—Stimulants for sluggish fowls—Grit, maize, and egg shells, hemp seed and boiled grain—Fish diet and fishy eggs bring "fishy" financial results—Herbs and green food for fowls.

THE FEEDING of poultry has grown into a very interesting and, in some respects, difficult subject. A good deal of sound information has been given, and great pains taken, to shew how one form of diet, more than another, helps the birds under certain circumstances to produce just the eggs, and to be ready for market at a certain season, when they are most valuable.

Of course the old idea was that fowls were fed if they were given a meal of hard corn two or three times a day. And even this was not of the best quality, and the very mistaken policy was pursued of giving the fowls any poor, thin corn that was useless for every other purpose, and which was, in reality, useless for that.

Tail or poor thin corn should never be given to poultry whole; if given at all it should be ground and given in the form of meal, as it is more satisfying if given in this form, there being so much husk that the nutriment, which is always small, can be extracted so much more quickly if this be done.

Many people are so foolish as never to give their laying fowls meal, as they consider this wasting valuable food, but this idea is a very mistaken one, as fowls fed once a day on meal will produce, at least, thirty or forty eggs more per bird during the year, in comparison with others in exactly similar conditions, but which are fed on hard grain, and it must be remembered that these eggs would be produced during the winter months, just at a time when eggs are most valuable.

One reason why soft food in the morning is most beneficial to fowls is that the hard corn takes a certain time to soak in the crop and gizzard, but the soft meal passes into the system immediately, and the fowl is nourished at once, so that no time is lost and the flesh or eggs are produced with less exertion than if hard corn were given.

It will be seen, therefore, that it pays best to give the soft meal once a day, viz., in the morning, and this may consist of almost any kind of meal, such as barley meal, oatmeal or buckwheat meal, and either of these might be mixed with middlings or sharps. The quantity of sharps used depends greatly upon the other meal used, but one part of barley meal, with one part of fine and one of coarse sharps makes a very good mixture. This is sometimes a little inclined to be sticky, and to avoid this a little poultry biscuit meal should be used, and pea meal may be used occasionally with the sharps, for a change.

Whatever food is given to laying hens a good deal of bran should be mixed with it, especially in spring and summer, when the birds are breeding, as there is in this a good deal of bone-making material, which is very good and strengthening for the breeding stock, more than there is in the flour alone.

Hot water should always be used for mixing the meal or hot skim milk is better where it can be obtained, and during the winter months the food should be given warm, as this helps them in very many ways. Care should be taken not to make the food too wet or sloppy, as it is not so good for the fowls when it is sticky and clings to their beaks.

Fat or scraps from the table are very good for mixing with the meal, and in the winter if there are not very many scraps it is a good plan to buy some liver, lights, paunch or tripe to boil up for the fowls. A sheep's paunch may be had for twopence, and the tripe—nine to eighteen pounds—may be bought for one shilling, and this should be given to the fowls the last thing before going to roost, as they will greatly enjoy it, and eat ravenously of it.

It should never be given, however, before the corn, or the fowls will probably shew some preference for this, and eat the meat and leave the corn, &c. After the lights have been boiled the water might be used to mix the meal, as this water has a good deal of the goodness of the meat in it.

Some people would not have time to boil and prepare the lights, and these might use granulated meat in the soft food as this does not require boiling. Boiling water should be poured over the granulatsd meat first and then it might be mixed with the meal when it is hot.

Vegetable refuse, such as small potatoes and cabbages, and pieces of fat meat may also be used, as when these are mixed up with good meal they make first rate food. Turnips, mangold wurtzel, in fact nearly all vegetables may be used in the same way, especially during the winter months, when green food is scarce, and they should be thrown down so that they might peck at them raw—or they might be boiled.

During the autumn and winter the fowls should have their morning meal as hot as they can eat it, and it is well to give them warm water to drink first thing in the morning when the weather is cold, as after drinking cold water, they will often stand moping about on one foot, whereas the warm water seems to revive the whole system on a cold morning.

Poultry powders (as advertised at end of book) should be used in the soft food three or four times a week. commencing not later than the last week in August or first week in September, as that helps them through their moult, and brings one or two year old hens on to lay through the winter as well as the young pullets. When hens stop laying, or are not doing well in the summer a little poultry powder should at once be given for about a week, as this pulls them round, and they commence laying almost at once.

This should be discontinued when the fowls come on to full lay during the summer months as it is not necessary.

It is a very wise thing to drive the birds back into the house for three or four hours after a warm meal if they have no sheltered run. After the first few mornings there will be little trouble in driving the birds in, as they get accustomed to the kind of thing, and they will run into the house again as soon as they have finished their breakfast. They should be fastened in with the wire door, so that air and light may enter, and the place made and kept comfortable. The better plan, however, is to have attached to every house a covered run where the fowls may run in and be sheltered from wind and weather, and get plenty of scratching exercise. In these covered runs they might be fed, and so be protected from the cold winds which are likely to do them great harm on cold and windy mornings.

If these rules are carefully observed there is no reason why eggs should not be produced all the year round.

Biscuit meal is one of the very best foods to use, and it can be given alone or occasionally with other meals mixed with it. When biscuit meal is not used a little oyster shell, mixed with the meals already mentioned helps them very much, as it not only furnishes material for making the shells, but assists also in promoting better digestion, and thus is far superior to the old mortar.

If fowls do not have lime in some form or other the oviducts of the laying hens become very much weakened, and this results oftentimes in birds laying a number of eggs without shells at all. When this happens the yolk, &c., are apt to break before the fowls can pass them, and fowls die, or are badly ruptured for life, but more often they are found dead on the nest, or underneath the perch next morning.

In the breeding season flint dust should be used, as this is very beneficial, helping the egg organs and causing the chickens to hatch out much better, as this makes the egg shells stronger and more brittle.

A little salt should be put into the soft food occasionally to flavour it.

The following table will show the proportions of flesh-forming, &c., ingredients contained in wheat, barley, and other grain, &c., used for feeding poultry. It was, I believe, originally published in the *Poultry Diary*, but the copy given is taken from L. Wright's *Book of Poultry*.

There is in every 100 parts, by weight of	Flesh-forming material like gluten, &c.	Warmth-giving and fattening material, viz:—		Bone-making materials or mineral substances.	Husk or Fibre.	Water.
		Fat or Oil	Starch.			
Beans and Peas	25	2	48	2	8	15
Oatmeal	18	6	63	2	2	9
Middlings, Thirds, or Fine Sharps	18	6	53	5	4	14
Oats	15	6	47	2	·20	10
Wheat	12	3	70	2	1	12
Buckwheat	12	6	58	1½	11	11½
Barley	11	2	60	2	14	11
Indian Corn	11	8	65	1	5	10
Hempseed	10	21	45	2	14	8
Rice	7	a trace	80	a trace	...	13
Potatoes	6¼	...	41	2	...	50¼
Milk	4½	3	5	¾	...	85¾

So far I have confined my remarks principally to the best foods for fowls, but, perhaps, a not less important subject is when and how to feed them, and in what quantities. To safely judge this, one must take a great personal interest in their poultry.

Some writers lay down certain definite rules as to feeding and a suitable allowance per head, and although this system is very good in theory, yet in practice it is not always the best. The amount of food should be judged by daily experience, as one fowl will eat twice as much as another, and two birds will sometimes eat as much as six others. The birds vary very much in their feeding capacities. Some people weigh out the food; this, too, is bad policy as they had better never stint the birds.

The golden rule in feeding poultry is never to give the birds one morsel more than they will eat up quickly, and which they will run after if thrown a good distance, as then they eat their food with a relish, which is most helpful to them in many ways. No food should be left lying about the yards or runs, or even left in troughs, as the very sight of such food turns the fowls against it, as well as attracting sparrows, mice, rats, &c., and when rats once get into a poultry yard they often kill the little chickens also in addition to stealing the food. When fowls leave their food they should be made to miss a meal, and they will soon find the lost appetite, and the rest given clears the system, and in many cases this does the birds a great deal of good.

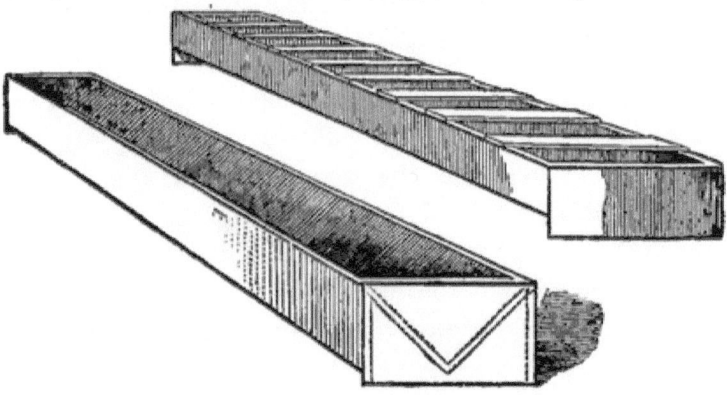

FEEDING TROUGHS.

If there is a dry piece of grass or gravel the fowls should be fed on it; but where there is a covered shed or outbuilding with a lot of loose stuff at the bottom, a good deal of the corn should be thrown into the covered up part as this gives the birds scratching exercise, which is especially valuable, because it brings health, vigour, and vitality to the birds in the cold weather. Where farmers constantly feed their fowls in the farmyard they might always throw the corn among the loose stuff, &c., so that the birds might scratch for it, and continually get the much-needed exercise.

In bad weather the meal should be given in troughs, unless a very clean, dry place can be had, otherwise the dirt sticks to the food and makes it very injurious to the fowls.

Where birds are kept in confined runs the soft food should always be given in troughs, as these ensure that the food is quite clean and the fowls relish it more. Another advantage gained by putting the food into troughs is that as soon as the birds have had enough the troughs can be taken away, and so no waste food is left.

During the spring and summer the fowls should be let out of the house for half an hour or more before giving them their breakfast, as this sharpens their appetite and they are ready for a good breakfast when the time comes. During the winter months, and more especially in October, when it is so chilly in the mornings, and many of the old birds are moulting, poultry require very generous treatment, and during this period they are better for a little good stimulating food, such as hempseed, &c.

Poultry powders are most useful at these times, and are most beneficial all through the moulting season, both for general health and egg-production during the winter months, as they strengthen every organ of the body, so that the fowls produce a large number of eggs, and are not weakened, as they do not over stimulate the body, as much of the stuff does that is sold for making fowls lay well.

And more than this, these powders impart vigour to the birds, and the combs become red, the plumage has a beautiful gloss upon it, and a marked difference, which is the result of vigorous health, soon makes itself visible in the appearance and general condition of the fowls before the powders have been used for ten days.

They have now been used for many years with good results for rearing chickens, turkeys, pheasants, and early ducklings by hundreds of breeders.

Of course these little details of careful attention mean a little time and expense, but the results pay well for them, as when they are thoroughly well looked after and fed on warm stimulating food they will often lay while they are moulting.

One of the very important things almost universally neglected by poultry-keepers is the providing of a good supply of sharp grit, for without it the fowls are quite unable to digest or grind their food.

A miller cannot grind corn without stones, and it is the same with poultry, and if they fail in getting a sufficient supply of small sharp stone grit in some form, they suffer in health, and become martyrs to all the evils of indigestion.

Sharp grit is to poultry what teeth are to human beings and animals, because instead of masticating the food with the mouth as these do, the food passes into the crop and gizzard, where the grit forms material by which it is ground up and thoroughly masticated before it passes into the system.

I have had thousands of fowls for post-mortem examination during the last fourteen years, and a large majority of these have been killed through not having had a sufficient supply of sharp grit.

The liver is affected first, and then the other organs soon follow and very quickly the whole internal organism becomes affected, and in many cases entirely ruined.

When birds begin to go wrong they will not pick up the small stones, &c., in which case all the sharp grit should be mixed with the meal, and forced down their throats, when, as a rule, they will soon be all right, their aversion to the grit only being the result of their weak condition.

Some people use round shingle, which is sent from the seaside. This material is quite useless, as it is ground so smooth by the action of the waves that it has no sharp edges left to do the work of grinding and masticating the food, for grit, which chickens need a good supply of always, *cannot be too sharp*.

It is a good plan to give the fowls egg shells; but they must be broken up very small before being given to the fowls, as if this is not done the benefit gained by the fowls eating the shell—because of this latter helping them to form the shell for new eggs—is over-shadowed by the risk of egg eating if great care is not taken to break it up very small.

The sharp grit which may be scraped up in the hollows of country roads after a heavy rain is very good for poultry. Ordinary road scrapings are also very good for poultry, but the grit I have mentioned is very much the best, but where neither of these can be obtained, flint stones broken up small should be given, as grit they *must* have in one form or another.

White crockeryware or glass can be broken up small and given to them, the largest of this being no larger than a threepenny piece.

Fourteen pounds of grit broken with a hammer out of solid black flints go further than a whole half hundredweight of ordinary grit that has been run through a machine, and sad to say a great deal of the grit that is sold at the present day is machine broken, and more than half as useless as the sea shingle I have condemned in this chapter, this oftentimes being the shingle run through a mill and called flint grit.

People only waste their money when they invest in such stuff for their birds, but it is sold at a cheaper rate and anything cheap attracts a certain class of very short-sighted people.

A very common mistake made by poultry-keepers is that of feeding their birds upon maize.

Too much maize is not good for fowls, as it brings on liver disease sooner than anything I know. It makes the birds too fat internally and also makes blood too fast.

Fowls that are fed liberally upon it are lined with yellow fat, especially in the abdomen, sometimes to the thickness of half an inch. The consequence of all this is that the egg organs become so weak that the hens lay eggs without shells.

And these are not the worst effects of feeding on maize, as birds that are so treated are generally in a very weak condition, and so they are susceptible to many other affections and diseases, especially cold and roup.

It is not always liver disease that actually kills them, but because of the derangement of that organ the birds get into such a state that diseases soon lay hold upon them, and overcome them, because the birds are too weak to withstand the ravages of the disease.

In some instances where I have found cases of roup that have been found incurable, I have found on examination that the liver was diseased, being full of tuberculous matter and white spots upon it.

Sometimes these spots are only as large as a pin's head.

In most cases where roup has not yielded to treatment, I have found this tuberculous liver existing and in some instances tumour, the growth of which maize is very likely to stimulate.

In cases where only ordinary scrofula is coming on, tuberculous substances form at first in small yellow spots; and these grow so rapidly oftentimes that in a very short time they are a quarter of an inch through and the liver more than three times the ordinary size.

I have weighed a liver of from nine to eleven ounces, the ordinary weight being from $1\frac{3}{4}$ to $2\frac{3}{4}$ ounces.

Another cause of a great deal of liver disease is in-breeding.

More fowls die of this disease than all the others put together.

Insufficiency of small grit, feeding on Indian corn, inbreeding and bad ventilation are the four greatest foes to success in poultry yards.

I have known instances where farmers have used maize for years together, and it has had such a bad effect upon the progeny, that scarcely a chicken of all that were hatched lived. They died, many of them, when from four to seven days old, some living until they were from three to six weeks old.

Poultry-keepers use maize because it is a cheap food, and fowls seem to prefer it to any other, but they have to pay very dearly for their fancy, and only the bare sad facts will convince some of the danger of using too much.

A little maize for a change does not hurt the fowls, especially in cold weather, but as a regular diet it should never be used.

I use more wheat for feeding than any other grain, as that does not make so much fat internally as some other grains. Next to that, French buckwheat and barley, and a good deal of dari during the spring and summer.

Good oats make a splendid change, but they ought not to weigh less than forty to forty-two pounds to the bushel, if forty-four pounds so much the better.

Hemp-seed is also an excellent grain for the breeding season, especially for the male birds.

If this seed is given there will not be many unfertile eggs as it helps the male birds very much,

It is a very good thing to give the birds during the autumn when they are moulting, as it is very stimulating.

It is used largely for bringing young chickens into good condition for the show pen.

One rule must be ever borne in mind, and that is to change the grain so as to give the birds a little variation, as they like this and relish their food all the better for it.

From October to March, it is well to give corn softened by boiling it from fifteen to thirty minutes and standing the pot on one side till it soaks up the water in which it has been boiled, giving it to the fowls hot.

Care must be taken not to boil the grain too much, or the too much water, as it causes the corn to burst, and it then becomes very sticky, in which state the fowls are not at all partial to it, and a good deal is wasted in consequence.

Fowls may have as much boiled corn as they can eat, but they should always have a meal of hard corn to finish up with.

When meat is given to the fowls care should be taken to cut it into pieces of moderate size, just so that they can swallow it easily.

If given in large pieces one hen gets hold of a piece and runs away with it, and while she is trying to peck it to pieces the others eat all theirs and run to the large piece to secure a share of it, in which case the hen that got the large piece in the first instance oftentimes loses it altogether, or worse than that in her hurry she bolts the mass, and this brings about a stoppage between the crop and the gizzard, sometimes with fatal results.

The better plan, where a large number of birds are kept and are to be fed on meat, is to run the meat through an old sausage machine, which would mince it up so fine that nothing of the kind mentioned could possibly happen.

Where fowls are not able to run on grass, and are at the same time fed liberally, but not allowed a good supply of green food, their blood becomes very hot, especially during the months of spring.

It is well when this happens to use a little flour of sulphur (sometimes called powdered brimstone).

There are two sorts of this, dark and yellow : the yellow is the best for this purpose, and one heaped up tea spoonfuls sufficient for eight or ten fowls.

There is a very unfortunate result sometimes where brimstone is used, and that is the eggs have a strong taste.

To overcome this an equal quantity of common salt should be given with the sulphur as this will partly counteract the musty flavour caused by the sulphur.

It is better not to use this medicine too early in the spring, as it has a tendency to open the pores of the skin too much if it is given in cold weather, or when cold winds are blowing, which would result in the birds catching cold.

Fish is a very good food for stock birds. Where, however, the eggs are to be eaten this should never be used, or if the eggs are to be sold for eating, the customers will notice the musty and fishy taste, and they will think the eggs are not fresh ; and customers will fall off, and, of course, this would be fatal.

English people do not cultivate herbs as much as they should for the use of their poultry.

Two herbs are most useful in the poultry yard, but sad to say they are often trodden under foot and thrown upon the rubbish heap, or are rooted up altogether as most worthless things.

I mean stinging nettles and dandelions.

The stinging nettle has cooling properties which make its action upon the blood most beneficial.

When the fowls have them they do not catch cold after having them as they do sometimes with sulphur.

The nettles should be got when young; they can be cut short and boiled, and then mixed with the soft food, and the water they are boiled in will also do to mix with their food.

If time cannot be found to boil them they can be put into a vessel of some kind and boiling water poured on them. They should be covered over so that the steam cannot escape, then the liquid may be mixed with the meal. A little salt added would improve them, but the nettles should never be given to the fowls in an uncooked state, as they are not tender enough for fowls.

When given in this way they are both food and medicine.

It is rather difficult to gather nettles, but if a glove is put on and the stems cut off, the roots will sprout out again. Nettles are invaluable for fowls.

Dandelions are excellent for the liver. They will often put poultry right when everything else fails, especially when fowls are kept in confined runs. The leaves can be cut from the roots and cut into small pieces, and given in a raw state.

If roots of these two herbs are set in the autumn or winter (not later than February) they will grow anywhere if they are planted underneath the soil.

Nettles may be found by the side of the hedges, and dandelions by the road side or on any waste piece of ground. They have a yellow flower which grows on a round stem.

Where many fowls are kept, it is wise to grow cow cabbages, as these are very large if grown properly; one is sufficient to last fifty fowls a whole day and the fowls are particularly fond of them. Mangold wurtzel is also very good for them. It is well to cut them in half, then the fowls peck out the middle, leaving only the skin quite empty.

Of course those who live in towns and have but little space at their disposal, cannot grow cabbage or lettuce, but they might sow rape, mustard, maize, wheat, barley, oats or any kind of grain.

These can be grown in shallow trays filled with a little earth and manure, but the seed must be well watered.

These spring up very quickly and in the hot weather it is ready in a few days. By having seven boxes and sowing one every day this gives a daily supply of green food.

The maize springs up twice or three times from the one sowing. It can be either cut or the box placed in the run for the fowls to peck it off.

Of course the size of the boxes must vary according to the number of fowls kept; not more than two or three inches of soil is necessary in the boxes.

If the space is very limited, the boxes can be placed on the top of the fowl house, but always in the sun as much as possible.

This green food can only be grown during the summer months.

I would emphasize especially in the case of town poultry-keepers the importance of giving scratching exercise, as on this so much depends. Wherever birds are kept in confined runs, corn should be buried and the fowls would scratch this up, and be very much the better for the exertion.

WHICH ARE THE BEST FOWLS TO KEEP?

Strain, not breed, the index of excellence—Good crosses for profit—Sitting varieties and non-sitting varieties—where to keep one or the other for the best results.

THE question which forms the title of this chapter is not an easy one to answer. To endeavour to do so by naming certain breeds would be sure to lead to misunderstanding, and if not this, some very erroneous ideas perhaps about some other breeds that others might know had produced remarkable birds, so I think I may as well say straight out that apart from some general characteristics that distinguish breeds that there are good and bad birds of every breed.

With regard to the egg producing properties in fowls, great variation exists in different strains of the same breed, and I have often known one bird lay well while another of the same breed was anything but a good layer.

Of course, as in all questions of this kind, a great deal depends upon the place and circumstances in which the fowls are kept.

I consider Houdan-Orpington, Houdan-Indian Game, Houdan-Dorking, and Houdan-Leghorn stand at the top of the list for general qualities, winter laying and table qualities combined.

Game Dorkings are considered tip-top table birds by many writers and breeders, and I have myself proved them to be really excellent birds, but Houdan-Indian Game grow much quicker and are ready as spring chickens from eight to twelve days earlier, and the pullets will frequently lay a month or six weeks earlier if the birds are all six or seven months old.

I have made careful calculation and taking the extra number of eggs laid and the rapid growth of the chickens into consideration, I find these birds produce from ten to fifteen per cent. more upon the year's return than the Indian Game Dorking. A Houdan cock cannot be crossed with the wrong birds, for Houdans are the best birds of all the non-sitting varieties to be used for crossing. Houdan-Leghorns are marvellous layers, and although they are not big yet they make splendid table birds.

I find they will, taking the whole year through, lay as many eggs as any cross I have tried, because both breeds are non-sitting ones, but they are not such good table birds as the Houdan-Indian Game.

During the last few years I have tried an experiment, viz: crossing the Houdan cock with Buff Orpingtons.

The Buff Orpingtons have white legs and skins, while the legs of the Houdans are a mixture of blue and white.

When these two breeds are blended nearly all the chickens have white legs, and grow very fast, being ready for the table earlier than any cross I have ever tried. I have had them weigh 3lbs. 3ozs. at thirteen weeks old, and at four months and a fortnight, 5¼lbs. and up to 5¾lbs., from three-quarters to one pound each heavier than Game Dorkings hatched at the same time.

I consider the Houdan-Buff Orpington cross stands right at the head of the list for winter laying and table qualities combined.

The following crosses, viz.: Plymouth Rock-Brahma, Plymouth Rock-Langshan, Plymouth Rock-Cochin, and Plymouth Rock-Indian Game make good winter layers and nice table birds where the situation is cold and exposed to the north-east winds.

They also produce very fine brown and tinted eggs, and make excellent sitters, and can be depended upon for that purpose.

They also make the best of mothers, and can cover their chickens well from the cold east winds. The hens of these crosses are good for sending on a journey when broody, as the sight of the eggs usually brings them to the nest at once, and they forget they are in a strange place.

They are very valuable, therefore, for these purposes, as they may be relied upon.

I may point out also that these crosses may be kept either in confined runs or in an open space, and will not disappoint their owners. They are like young turkeys on the table—one will serve a good sized family.

When early chickens are required these crosses are the best to keep, as they come broody early in the season, and can be depended upon, as they have so much heat in themselves.

They can be set on goose, turkey, or duck eggs.

For general purposes I find Houdan cocks mated with Plymouth Rock, Langshan, Brahma or Cochin hens very good birds.

When the pullets are hatched from a good laying strain one is equal to the other.

They come so much alike it is hard to distinguish them from each other if placed side by side.

If bred from a good laying strain the results will not vary ten eggs per bird in the twelve months.

Of the five the Plymouth Rock or Orpington crosses are the best table fowls. They have more breast meat, and are usually free from feathers on the legs.

The laying results are just as good when a Minorca cock is used with the four breeds mentioned, but the cockerels are not quite such good table fowls, as they are not so full in the breast, but they are excellent in flavour and very white and juicy. As a rule the eggs are about the same size as if a Houdan cock had been used. The pullets from all these crosses will stand confinement well, or do well if they have an open range.

They cannot easily be put out of their place. Most of them lay a tinted egg, some quite brown, and these are large and consequently saleable anywhere.

Those who have given these crosses a fair trial have not been disappointed in them, as they are such good winter layers.

Some people object to keeping birds that come broody. To meet their requirements I would recommend a Houdan-Minorca or Houdan-Leghorn, or Houdan-Hamburgh cross (I, myself, have had the best results from Houdan-Leghorn) as the best to keep, as these birds are excellent layers of white shelled eggs. They stand confinement well, and if sheltered a little from the cold winds, eggs will be found in the nest all the year round.

I have always recommended in former editions of this book Golden Spangled Hamburgh-Cochin which are very handsome birds, more so than any other cross. They are extraordinary layers both winter and summer, and the eggs are of fair size, most of them being brown or tinted.

They make fair table birds, rather small, but of excellent flavour, but we now find that Houdan Buff Orpington are quite equal in laying qualities, and far superior in table qualities, but they are not quite such a pretty colour.

If good coloured birds are desired we recommend the Golden Poland to be crossed with the Buff Orpington hens, as the offspring is quite equal in colour and beauty to Hamburgh-Cochin.

The colour of this new cross is really magnificent, consisting of a rich buff over which dark green spots are scattered, and they have a small crest something like that usually found on the head of a half Houdan.

The Game-Dorking cross birds are excellent for the table but only moderate winter layers.

They come broody very often during the spring and summer.

Some people prefer the Plymouth Rock-Dorking to the Game Dorking, but the latter is of rather a better quality though not quite so large a bird.

The Game Plymouth Rock is a very good bird, and I prefer them to Game-Cochin as so much better table fowls are produced, although not better layers. They make good sitters and mothers, and may be trusted with valuable eggs.

These birds are very strong in the wing to cover their chickens from the cold winds, so this cross is a very good one for game-keepers.

Anyone who has a fancy for pure-bred birds, and whose place is damp, I recommend to keep Orpingtons and Wyandottes. These are better for that purpose because they have no feathers on their legs to hold the wet and dirt, and they are more active than Cochins and Brahmas.

Langshans are also very good for this purpose although I give Orpingtons and Wyandottes the preference if the place is cold and damp. They do not show the dirt and smoke as many other birds do, they stand confinement and lay a brown egg.

Wyandottes stand confinement fairly well, and are good layers of brown eggs, but they do not breed true to colour.

Golden Wyandottes I have found lay better through the Winter than the birds of any other breed except the Orpingtons, and both these breeds are about equal in laying qualities during the winter months, the Orpingtons excelling the Golden Wyandottes only in table qualities, and the eggs they lay are a trifle larger.

As a non-sitting breed Minorcas are excellent, I prefer them as a pure bird to the Houdan as they are not quite so subject to colds when in their pure state. They stand confinement well and will lay all through the winter months if sheltered from the cold winds.

The Minorca is one of the most popular of non-sitting varieties. They lay a fine white egg, and the chickens are hardy and grow fast.

Another remarkably hardy fowl is the Leghorn. These birds are excellent fowls as non-sitters, and are remarkably hardy, laying more eggs during the cold winter months than Minorcas. Leghorns are the hardiest non-sitting fowls I know of, especially the white variety. The chickens thrive anywhere, but the eggs are not quite so large, nor do they make such good table fowls, although in confinement they stand the cold much better than Minorcas.

Andalusians are excellent layers of large white eggs, but the birds are very difficult to breed true to colour—black, white and blue birds often appearing among them out of the same brood.

They stand confinement well and if they have shelter they lay during the winter months.

Dorkings are not so good to keep in confinement when in their pure state.

Hamburghs I do not recommend for keeping in confinement, as Leghorns are so much hardier and lay more eggs during the winter months.

The black variety is rather hardier than either the Golden or Silver Spangled, which come next. The pencilled varieties are not suitable, and should never be reared in confinement.

Game fowls also ought never to be kept in confinement if wanted for profit alone. Birds of every breed, if from a good laying strain and treated properly, will lay during the winter months, more or less. It is not birds of certain breeds so much as certain birds of each of the breeds that make good laying strains and layers.

I have had two birds of the same breed running together and treated in the same way, one laid 260 and the other only 90 eggs in the twelve months.

For tropical climates the non-sitting varieties, viz.: Hamburghs, Houdans, Minorcas, Leghorns, and their crosses are the most suitable, while for colder and more changeable situations hardy, feather-legged birds such as Cochins, Brahmas, Langshans, Plymouth Rocks, Orpingtons, and their crosses are better.

We find in certain parts of Africa and other very variable climates that where there is very little green food, Missionaries and others who have had experience find no birds half so good as Orpingtons.

The chickens of this breed have bred where chickens of other breeds with less vitality and stamina have died, and I have had many letters to the effect that for these rough and ready conditions of life Orpingtons are excellent.

I have received many letters also from Australia, New Zealand and Africa stating that the writers had never known birds lay so many eggs in twelve months in these climates as the Black and Buff Orpingtons, so that it will be seen that for each several set of circumstances it is always wise of poultry-keepers to select carefully the birds best suited to their surroundings and requirements.

HOW TO BREED AND WHAT TO BREED FROM.

Good birds kept shews truest economy—Fertile eggs: how to ensure—Artificial incubation—Incubators; their defects and disappointing results—Foster mothers—Sitting and hatching.

ONE of the most important details in the plans of a successful poultry-keeper is that part in which he decides on what birds he will keep and breed from.

It is always wise to make a rule never to set an egg from an inferior layer or sickly bird.

If on the other hand fowls are required for the table only good-bodied birds should be selected, with long deep breasts, and these bred from with a cock of some good table variety. Careful selection is an all-important thing. It does not matter how many breeds a hen may have in her; if she is a good layer, and mated with a pure male bird the result will be good, as the pullets will lay from a month, six weeks and sometimes two months earlier than they would if the hen had been mated with a cross-bred or mongrel male bird.

I would impress upon my readers the great importance of *always* breeding from pure male birds, whatever kind of hens are used, whether they be mongrels, first crosses or pure hens of another variety, as these produce eggs just in the autumn and early part of the winter when eggs are most valuable, and at the same tims it saves so much food, &c., as the pullets do not cost so much to keep, because they begin to lay sooner and turn the food into eggs.

Where fowls are kept principally for laying it is an easy matter to detect the best laying hens, as these are sharp-looking, intelligent birds with bright eyes, and a nice sleek-looking head. They are generally out first in the morning and go to roost late at night, and are usually scratching and roaming about during the day, covering more ground than a bad layer.

If my readers will refer to the engravings of heads given they will see at a glance the difference in the appearance of the eyes and head generally of the two birds and so save a great deal of trouble and expense, as ten good layers will produce more eggs than thirty bad ones during the winter months at about one-third the cost.

It is always best to have a pure bred cock, as most pure breeds have some distinctive quality that it is well to introduce into cross-bred or mongrel birds.

A bad hen only spoils the birds bred from her eggs, while the cock if he is bad spoils the progeny from all the hens he is running with, and his influence is far-reaching beyond that of the hen, so it is important that of all the birds the male bird of a breeding pen should be pure.

It has been a question that has been many times debated how many hens to put with one cock so that the eggs may be relied upon as being fertile.

LIGHT BRAHMA.
GOOD LAYER.

LIGHT BRAHMA.
BAD LAYER.

BLACK ORPINGTON.
GOOD LAYER.

BLACK ORPINGTON.
BAD LAYER.

CROSS-BRED HAMBURGH-BRAHMA.
GOOD LAYER.

CROSS-BRED HAMBURGH-BRAHMA.
BAD LAYER.

Of course here again individual selection must be made. Birds of certain breeds and certain birds of each breed will take more or less hens according to his capabilities and the space they have to roam over.

As a rule a Cochin will take from four to six hens. A Brahma from six to nine hens, while the cocks of most other breeds eight hens with one cock or even up to fifteen will not be too many.

When fowls have a large range half as many more hens may be allotted to run with him and the eggs will prove more fertile, but I will deal more fully with this subject in the chapters on pure breeds and first crosses.

A heavy Cochin or Brahma, if he will breed, will not manage half as many hens as a smaller one. I have known as many as thirty hens running with one cock and early in the season all the eggs were fertile.

The subject of really proper mating is little understood by many poultry-keepers, and even some people who keep large numbers of birds are sadly deficient in their knowledge of how to keep and mate stock birds so as to ensure the best results.

For instance in some cases where quite a large number of birds are kept people sometimes put four hens with one cock, thinking to ensure fertile eggs in this way. Disappointment often is the outcome of this plan, while where seven or ten are put with one cock, nearly every egg is fertile.

Of course there are exceptions, but this most certainly is the rule.

The greatest secret of real success in keeping the stock up is the introduction continually of fresh blood into the breeding stock, as the chickens are never so strong and healthy where the parent birds are related.

ARTIFICIAL INCUBATION.

All in a piece with crossing and late hatching the adoption of the principle of artificial incubation is growing in importance, not only where large numbers of chickens are required, but also where a limited number are kept. Ladies who have time to attend to incubators find the work not only useful but very interesting. Cottagers frequently make their own incubators. Some of these answer very well, hatching as many as twelve chickens out of fifteen eggs.

The high prices charged for incubators prevent the working classes from investing in them to any extent, and we should hail with delight the advent of some cheaper machine that would do its work effectually.

I have tried the machines sent out by many makers, and have found that even where the principle has been good the machines vary very much, and many of them are almost useless, and yet to all appearance this is no fault of the makers.

Hearson's is the only machine I have found strictly reliable, and this I am bound to confess after having tried many; it most certainly is the best in the market up to the present.

Of course it may be quoted "There are as good fish in the sea as have ever been caught," and doubtless this is so, but the difficulty with most people is just where to drop on them.

I have heard very good accounts of Mr. Greenwood's machines, and I am told that the Bedford maker's machine hatches very well indeed, and stands nearest to Hearson's for results.

It is possible some one will bring out a machine to equal or even surpass Hearson's, but I have not met with one yet, although many advertise their productions as the best.

I have met with scores of people in my travels who have bought incubators and have placed eggs in them, and nearly every egg they have put in during the season has been spoiled, and in some cases I have known the machine burned up in despair, as not a single chicken has been hatched during the whole of the season.

In such cases as these it is not only the sacrifice of the first cost of the incubator, but the loss of precious time, so that the season has grown so advanced oftentimes that birds for the next season's egg production become out of the question, and so a whole season is wasted, and there are no pullets for laying nor any fowls for the table.

I have no wish to be hard on incubator makers, but several have been brought out and many machines sold, and I have never known of a single chicken having been hatched by them. I only mention this to warn poultry people against buying machines turned out by makers that have no reputation.

When people bring out an incubator they are much mistaken when they do not thoroughly test the machines before using them. They should be thoroughly tried in every way before they are sent out to the public, as if when poultry-keepers begin to use them and put in a sitting of valuable eggs, perhaps, and, after a most dismal failure sit down to think of a fresh setting of the old wide difference which has often existed between theory and practice, they are not likely to recommend others to adopt that particular make of incubator.

Two machines that are out, I am told, are working fairly well. Mr. Greenwood's machine that I have already mentioned, and Sharland's machine brought out at Oldham.

I cannot give this as actual experience, but as the opinion of breeders who have thoroughly tested the machines and found them most excellent and also that they work successfully.

I am a great deal more in favour of incubators now than I once was, and they are also very much improved and so are easily worked, as the principles upon which many of the machines are constructed are of a high scientific order, and where the incubator is reliable it saves a great deal of time that would otherwise be spent in getting together broody hens.

Another advantage is that the eggs may be put in quite fresh every day or two, as they are laid, where people breed from their own stock.

I may say that I always use Hearson's machine on my own place, and find it most successful.

In cases where fresh eggs are put into the drawer with others that have been in long enough to get nicely warm a piece of flannel or cotton wool should be put between them, as the cold eggs are apt to chill the others, especially if they have only been in a few days, or better still they may be put into the drying box for 12 or 15 hours to take the chill off. If eggs are in the incubator that are near hatching it does not hurt them.

It will be seen, therefore, that a really good incubator is a great boon to poultry-keepers, and although some people indulge in a silly superstition that chickens hatched in an incubator do not grow so large, nor do so well, it has been proved beyond all controversy that the birds do equally well if of the same stock and reared under the same conditions.

And another consideration must be borne in mind and that is that incubator-hatched chickens are not so liable to become infested with vermin as those hatched under hens. Hens are often found infested with vermin while sitting, and the chickens are often found attacked by these terrible pests as soon as they are hatched, if proper care is not taken to dust the hen thoroughly with the insect powder, specially prepared for this purpose.

I fancy there are more crippled chicks hatched with incubators than when a hen is used, but no chickens are killed by the incubator, as there are oftentimes when the hen tramples upon them, so I think one makes up for the other pretty well.

Incubators are a great convenience to the poultry-keeper as they save a good deal of time, can be worked at any period during the year, and very many, especially ladies, enjoy working them, and attending to them.

Where a new incubator is introduced it is better to test the machine by putting a few common eggs in, as this very frequently saves considerable disappointment with a new machine, as they very often take a few days to get them into working order.

Where non-sitting breeds are kept a good incubator is found most useful.

FOSTER MOTHERS.

It naturally follows that where poultry-keepers hatch by incubators they want some system of artificial rearing for their chickens.

Some have tried bringing them up by hens, but the easiest plan is to rear them in a foster mother.

I have tried various machines made for the purpose, but find very few that are really satisfactory, and all might be very much improved.

Mr. Hearson's new foster mother is excellent for its purpose, and Mr. Greenwood also manufactures one which answers well, and I have tried these and find them most successful.

Miss Wilson, of Kendal, has introduced a small foster mother, which might be used to very good advantage for a small hatch of chickens when the weather is cold.

SITTING AND HATCHING.

There are many opinions as to the proper and most successful method of setting hens. Some persons prefer making the nest upon the ground in a damp situation, while others set their birds in as dry a place as possible.

I have always found it safe to imitate Nature as much as possible, for, as a rule, hens that choose their own nests bring off large broods.

If a hen that is sitting in a stolen nest is watched it will be observed that she chooses a dry secluded spot for the nest, and although the ground may be quite dry when the nest is first formed, the heat from her body draws a certain moisture from the soil which moistens the eggs. This is, of course, a very gradual moisture.

She also leaves the nest early in the morning to search for food, and as the grass is wet with dew her breast feathers also get wet, and in this state she returns to her eggs, and upon sitting again she damps them.

It will therefore be seen that Nature teaches that it is best to make the nest on the ground and to cover it in from the others.

Where it is possible a separate house should be provided for the sitting hens so that they are left to themselves and secure from interruption, but where this cannot be done the nest should be made in the house and so arranged that the front might be covered up with a piece of bagging, &c., which might be removed each morning when the hen is lifted off the nest.

The best way to make the nest is to scoop out a little earth from the floor, and then the earth in the hollow should be beaten down quite firm in the shape of the nest. Where no earth can be removed a few shovelfuls of soil should be obtained and moulded into the shape in an ordinary nest box.

It is easier to form the nest of soil than with a turf, and the soil should be damp, beaten down well with the hand. An old glove should be worn to protect the hand against thorns or broken glass, whichever might be in the soil. If the soil is damp it forms a nice even surface and holds well together.

The nest should be a quite round hollow, so that all the eggs are covered when the hen alters her position. The lowest point should, of course, be in the centre, so that the eggs roll and keep together again when the hen steps into the nest.

Plenty of room must be given, as when a bird is cramped in sitting a good many of the eggs are likely to get broken.

The hollow should be lined with fine hay at the bottom of the nest in very cold weather, but, before this is put in, a handful of slack lime should be sprinkled in the nest, as this prevents vermin from breeding there. Hay is much better than straw, as it sticks closer together, and therefore holds the warmth better, and where this is used the hen may be allowed more eggs. Straw is hollow and so conducts the cold air to the eggs, especially in frosty weather.

When fowls are set in a strange nest it is best to put them on their new nest at night unless very tame.

They should never be forced or hurried, but should be placed in front of the nest they are to occupy, with a few common eggs in it, when they will generally take to it at once, and if not disturbed again too soon they will stick to it and sit well.

Some hens *will not* sit in a strange nest, and the only thing that can be done with them is to patiently allow them to have their own way, or not to set them at all.

One way of making hens sit is to take the bird and let her stand in front of the nest, holding her in front of the breast by one hand, and then stroking her gently with the other from head to tail, just as one would stroke a cat or a dog, then place the left hand in the same position as the right one, with which the bird was held, and draw the fingers of the right hand underneath the beak and down the neck underneath. Nothing else will tame broody hens half as much as this treatment.

Hens that have travelled a journey or been removed should be put into a coop and fed well with hard corn and water. They should then be placed on the nest like this in the evening and covered in so that they are partly in the dark, and should be allowed to remain on the nest all the next day and taken off the day after.

This ensures that they will be well settled down before being disturbed.

For the first few days they should be fed in a coop or other small place, if not they become very wild and will not go back to the nest.

Broody hens should be handled very gently, and when they are being fed it is wise to put the coop so that the hen may see her nest with the eggs in it, as after she has finished feeding she will go straight on again.

Many people make a mistake when they have eggs from a distance by setting them immediately upon receipt. Eggs should always be allowed to stand 12, 15 or 20 hours to rest, before putting them under the hen or into the incubator.

I cannot give the exact number of eggs that should be allowed each hen, as both hens and eggs differ so much in size; and a great deal depends on the state of the weather, but for fair-sized hens about thirteen ordinary eggs will be sufficient in the early spring, but a larger number may be given if the hen be set in warmer weather.

I have set twenty-four eggs under one hen, and hatched out twenty-three chickens, but this is far too many as a rule, and if any doubt is felt as to the right number to give to each hen it is always best to be on the safe side and give one less than give too many, for if a hen has too many eggs she may let a different one get cold every time she turns them—as a good sitting hen turns her eggs twice or three times in twenty-four hours—and thus spoil the whole batch.

When the nest is made without soil or turf the outer skin of the egg becomes very dry during the last week of incubation, and the chickens usually hatch out very badly, and often half do not crack the shell. To avoid this it is better to moisten the eggs slightly by dipping them into warm water during the last few days.

In moderately cold weather cold water will do to wet the eggs, but in real cold weather warm water must be used. I find it best to dip them in warm water and let them remain in one or two seconds each day for the last three or five days of incubation.

Should the hen break one of the eggs the contents should be removed immediately, and if any portion of the yolk, &c., is on the other eggs it should be washed off with warm water at once, and if very much soiled a small nail brush and a little soap should be used and the eggs thoroughly rinsed to cleanse them effectually. If the contents of one egg is allowed to dry on the shell of another it stops the pores in the shell, thus preventing the passage of air to the chick, which it must be understood is alive and breathing at least two days before it is hatched.

The sitting hen should be lifted off the nest every morning, and about the third morning she will rise up ready to be lifted off when the attendant goes to her.

Care must be used in lifting the hen, and this is best done by placing a hand under each wing to make quite sure no eggs are lodged there; and then take hold of the legs with the fingers, and lift steadily, letting the wings rest on the wrists.

In cold weather the hen should not be allowed to stop off the nest more than fifteen minutes, but in warm weather she may be off from forty to sixty minutes. When the hen is off, the nest should be covered to prevent other hens going to it, and in frosty weather it is well to cover up the eggs with a piece of flannel or wadding to prevent their being chilled, but this should only be done in the very severest weather, as the more air the eggs get the stronger the chickens will hatch out.

A supply of dust and ashes must be kept in a dry place for the hen to clean herself with, and food and water must, of course, be placed so that she may help herself. As sitting hens go a long time between each meal it is best to feed them on some sort of hard corn, such as maize and barley in cold weather, and wheat and barley in the hot weather, as this lasts much longer than soft food. Sometimes a hen will lose her appetite when sitting; if this should occur she ought to have a little hempseed, soaked bread and pieces of meat.

She must be tempted with these, as if she does not eat well she cannot sit her time and the whole sitting of eggs will consequently be spoiled.

It is always wise to examine the eggs about the eighth day to see if they have chicks in them. This may easily be done by taking the small end of the egg in the right hand and just holding it with the tips of the fingers, and the large end in the left. Hold it so that the light is concentrated upon the egg, and the egg should be turned gently round before a small lamp or candle in a dark room.

If there is a chicken in the egg there will be a dark spot near the middle, about ¾ in. from the large end, while an unfertile egg will look quite clear.

When the eggs have brown shells it is rather more difficult to tell, but if there is any doubt they should be left under the hens two or three days more and then tried again.

Unfertile eggs should always be removed from under the hens as this gives the others a better opportunity, and where a large number of chickens are hatched it is well to set three or four hens on the same day, and if many eggs are unfertile those found with chickens in, after testing, may be given to two hens, while the other hen is turned off or supplied with some fresh eggs, as it does them no harm to sit for a month or even six weeks if they are fed well and taken off every day.

This might be done all through the season, and by this means trouble is saved, and each hen will have a good brood instead of wasting time and energy with only a few chickens.

The eggs that are set should always be marked in ink with the date they are put under the hen, so that they may be easily distinguished. It is best to mark them on the large end, as if it is put in any other position the black marks interfere with the testing of the eggs.

The unfertile eggs that are taken away may be boiled hard and chopped up for the chickens, as they are quite as sweet and good as many French eggs that are sold and used.

When the hen is hatching I find it best to remove the chickens every two or three hours, that is when the little things are dry, and it is well to accustom the hen to having a hand put under her, or she will be restless and spiteful when the chickens are removed, and perhaps crush some of them or the hatching eggs.

As soon as the chicks are removed they should be placed in a box in wadding before the fire until they are all hatched. When the last chicken has appeared and been put into the box the hen should be let out for a good run and feed, for, as a rule, they do not come off the nest for two days before hatching. After a good feed and run the chickens should be put into a coop, and when the hen sees them she will walk in and brood them quietly.

If the hen is at all wild and restless it is better to leave her quietly alone when hatching, as if she is disturbed she is likely to flutter about and trample her chicks to death.

When the eggs are fresh they will often hatch in nineteen and a half days if the hen sits close and has plenty of heat in her body, but if at the close of twenty-one days the eggs are not chipped, a small hole, about the size of a sixpence should be made with a pen knife. If the chicken is alive the skin next to the shell will be white, if the chicken is dead it is a dark colour.

After the incision is made the egg should be turned gently round to ascertain where the chicken's beak lies. As soon as this is ascertained a small hole should be broken just at that point.

In any case put it under the hen at once; if no blood appears the chicken is very soon out of the shell.

Thousands of chickens die in the shell for want of a little help in this way, as when the beak lies in a slanting position against the shell, and the egg being oval, when the chick endeavours to free itself the beak slides. After making the hole in the shell, should any blood appear it will be several hours before the chick is out, as during that time the chick will draw up the blood into its body and be quite prepared to leave the shell even if before it is looked at the egg shell is not already empty.

CHICKEN REARING.

There are many methods of rearing chickens and I have tried most of them and found them all answer more or less although, I think, the following is the description of the best and simplest method.

When all the chickens are hatched they should be put into a coop with the hen, where they can get as much liberty as possible. If they are not cooped on or near grass they must be provided with a supply of green food, which should be chopped up small, and the more they have of this the better they will thrive.

Many kinds of coops are used but the best is made with match boarding, the size being according to that of the fowl.

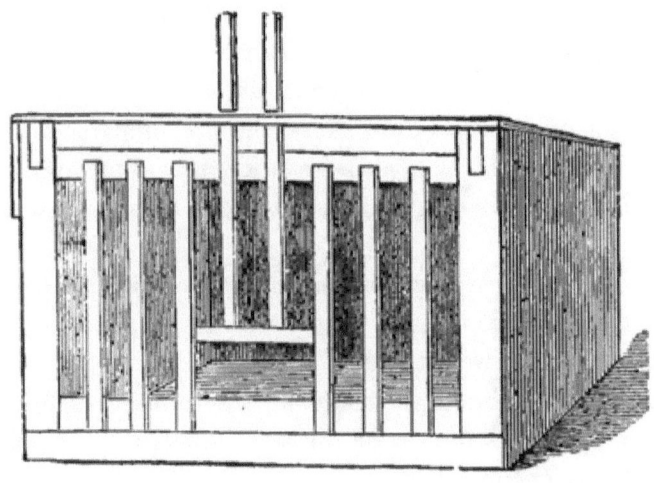

CHICKEN COOP.

A coop two feet square—or as some people prefer them two feet six inches—is large enough for any hen. This is quite heavy enough too, because if coops are very large they cannot be carried through doorways or about the place.

A six-inch board should be nailed along the top of the front part of the coop, and the pins or bars should run from this to the ground, and not cross ways. The bars should be about 2½ or 2¾ inches apart so as to give the chicks plenty of room to get through.

A little door may be made in the middle about a foot wide, worked with hinges, or a better way is to arrange for one or two bars to fit into sockets so that they may be withdrawn at any time, and so answer for the door. It is well also to put a board three or four inches wide at each front corner, as this prevents the draught cutting in.

This kind of coop will be found very light and may be easily carried about and will last for years if well tarred or painted, and kept out of the wet when not in use.

There are many elaborate coops and more expensive than those I have mentioned for those who are prepared to buy them, but there are also ways of providing even less expensive coops which may be made out of soap boxes or tea chests.

To make these weather tight, the cracks should be pasted up with stiff brown paper on the outside, and the strips should be well tarred.

The flat top should be made into a roof by nailing an extra piece of wood on it on the slant towards the back so that the water runs off.

I have used coops of this description for many years and have always found them answer well as they are very snug and warm.

I have always found it best to use coops with bottoms to them in very cold weather, and on these bottoms a little moss peat should *always* be used, so that the chicken's feet do not come into contact with bare boards. Chickens would be better on the bare ground than on boards or concrete without any peat or short stuff to keep their little feet warm.

If the poultry-keeper has only a limited space at his disposal in which to bring up his chickens, bottoms should always be put to the coops, as where the chickens run constantly, the ground gets very stale, and so is not suitable for the purpose. Of course where they are put out in grass fields or orchards where there is plenty of room to move them about it is better to have no bottoms to the coops, and the chickens will do better upon the ground, especially if the soil is chalk, gravel or sand.

Cramp is caused through imperfect circulation of the blood in the legs and feet, or in other words the blood gets chilled as it passed through the legs and feet.

If the cramp is not checked the toes refuse to do their proper work and become doubled under the feet. When they get to this stage they soon begin to look rough in plumage, which denotes that the cramp has got upwards into the body, and in bad cases the birds are quite unable to walk.

I have known cases where more than half the early broods die with cramp, and this is very discouraging after all the trouble of hatching them out, and it must be remembered that it is the early chickens that are oftentimes the most valuable—whether they are cross or pure-bred.

Whenever chickens show the first symptoms of cramp it is well to catch them at once and rub their legs with a little turpentine, or in bad cases spirits of arnica. This will soak in very quickly and then a little vaseline should be rubbed on the legs and feet, as this supples them and makes them nice and pliable. Then the legs should be wrapped in cotton wool, as this will keep them warm, and the blood will soon circulate quite freely again. (For directions as to binding, see chapter on cramp).

There are cases where chickens are born with their toes turned under, and when this is the case the splints, as recommended in the chapter on cramp, should be used in the same way.

Where chickens are kept under glass after they are a fortnight old, they are very subject to cramp and other diseases, and indeed it is not good for chickens to be kept under glass at all. They should have their full liberty, if possible, however cold the weather.

If there is a shed or cover of any sort that they can go under, when they like, so much the better.

When the weather is very cold or wet the front of the coop should be covered with an old sack or piece of bagging at night, but in moderately cold weather they do just as well without even this.

Newly-hatched chickens do not require food or water for twenty-four or thirty hours after they are hatched. After this, however, they will want something moist and nourishing. Hard-boiled eggs chopped up fine, and mixed with groats, or coarse oatmeal, form the best food for the first day or two.

The hen should always have a feed all to herself of plenty of corn before the chickens are fed, as if this is not done she will be likely to eat up all the food intended for them.

If the chickens do not eat the second day they should be carefully fed once or twice with a few small pieces of egg and groats, and after this they will look out for themselves.

A supply of clean water must always be kept in a shallow pan, where the chickens can get it.

When the chickens are two or three days old they should be fed outside the coop on a board or sack, and it is a very good plan to sprinkle a little fine flint grit on the sack, as this clings to the food and so serves as sharp grit, with which they must be well supplied from the very beginning.

After chickens are two or three days old the egg may be discontinued, and the food may consist of dry groats and biscuit meal, and in cold weather a little hemp seed.

The biscuit meal should be moistened with hot water, and not made too wet, as if this is not attended to the food is likely to bring on diarrhœa.

A little soaked bread may be given now and then, this always being soaked in cold water or cold milk, and if a little finely-chopped meat is added, this helps them wonderfully.

Chickens cannot be fed too frequently when they are young. They may have food every hour from sunrise to sunset, if possible, until they are a fortnight old, but only as much as they will clear up, as no food must be left lying about, or they will become dainty.

After the chicks are a fortnight old every two hours will be sufficient up to a month, after which they may be fed every three or four hours.

A mixture of meals is very good for feeding chickens, such as a blending together of buckwheat meal, barley and maize meal, locust meal and sharps, when they are growing large.

This frequent feeding is, of course, for chickens in confinement, as when they get a wide range, especially after the middle of April, in a field or orchard, they pick up a good many insects, and so do not require so much other food.

Chickens thrive best when fed on groats, but as these are rather expensive it is best to give them biscuit meal when they are a week or a little more old, and this may be varied occasionally by the use of a little other meal, such as buckwheat meal, ground maize, oats, &c. The meal should always be given to them warm in cold weather.

Bone meal is excellent for young chickens, as it prevents leg weakness, and they grow so much finer, especially the male birds. It is a cheap meal, as they do not require much of it, and it can be used with any other meal to the proportion of about a pound of bone meal to ten or thirteen pounds of any other, and more if necessary.

Rice may be used for a change, but it should be boiled, it may be obtained cheap with the husk on. Potatoes, &c., are also a very good food for them, and as they are generally fond of these things it is well to give them plenty, for they will eat and enjoy them when they do not seem to care for meal.

It is best to feed the chickens with grain for the evening meal, and this should consist of groats for the first two or three weeks, and afterwards of any other grain except maize, which must be kept out of their way until they are about six weeks old, as it is too much for them to digest. It will be a great advantage to the chicks if the hard corn is boiled occasionally, as described. For the first fortnight, or longer, if the weather is cold, the hen should be kept in the coop, but after this period she may be let out with the chickens to roam at will.

Cottagers, however, should always keep the hen in the coop, and let the little ones run where they like, when they will not fly to be an annoyance to the neighbours by getting into their gardens. This should be borne in mind by others as well as cottagers, and it will always be found better to place the coop in the middle of the kitchen garden, as the chicks will pick up a good many worms, insects, &c., and thus prevent these damaging the crops, but they must, of course, be removed as soon as they begin to scratch, and younger ones put into their place.

Gardeners complain oftentimes if chickens are allowed in the garden, but if only small chickens are put there no harm, but a great deal of good will result, as small insects, &c., will be cleared off, especially wire worms and slugs.

The hen should have charge of the chicks until they are about six weeks old, after which they will be able to take care of themselves, unless the weather is very severe.

Where it is possible, chicks should be allowed to roost out in a coop, or in an open shed, until a short time before commencing to lay, when they should be put into a house.

Where farmers have a lot of birds running about, it is always wise to provide a house in which the young pullets could be kept, away from the old hens, so that the young birds are not over-crowded.

Both hens and pullets would be the better, and both would produce more eggs, especially at the end of August, September, and October, in some cases double the number, if they are not allowed to crowd in together.

If chickens are fed in the manner I have described, they will not require much fattening before they are killed as they will be in first rate condition for table.

It is much the best plan to keep fowls in this way, for they may then be caught up and killed just as they are required, choosing the largest and best first, and leaving the others until they are in better condition, unless, of course, numbers are required for a good market, in which case all must be well fattened or they will not fetch a good price.

We often find that sufficient attention is not given to the chickens dusting themselves. When they droop their wings, and their feathers look rough, they should be caught and examined at once, especially round the head and under the wings and the abdomen, to see whether any vermin have collected on them, as if these pests are at work on the chickens they can never thrive.

Some people use lime to destroy them, but this is not a good thing, as it gets into the chickens' eyes and irritates them on the body very much.

Insect Powder, specially prepared for the purpose, should be used, as this kills the vermin and does not injure the chickens.

In some districts hundreds of chickens are lost through large ticks getting on the back of the head and literally extracting the life and stamina from the chickens. I remember one case that I knew of where out of a thousand hatched over eight hundred chickens were destroyed from this cause. Chickens should be examined for these; and where the nits are found, specially prepared ointment should at once be procured and applied.

Seven things should be strictly borne in mind and observed in connection with chicken rearing—

First—Feed so that there is not a kernel of corn or grain of soft food left, if so, it soon becomes sour, which not only turns the chickens against it, but the food causes rats to come after it into the runs. Second—A good supply of green food. Third—Always see that they have a good supply of sharp grit to digest their food, if not, they cannot thrive for long. Fourth—The dust bath is very essential. Fifth—See that they have plenty of ventilation in the sleeping house, and are not too thick on the ground. Sixth —Keep them scrupulously clean, especially when quite young. Lastly—When they are allowed water, let this be given and kept fresh.

If these seven rules are carried out success is sure to follow more or less.

Any green food will do for chickens if cut fine so that no large pieces are left, as sometimes when one of these is swallowed it causes a stoppage between the crop and gizzard, usually at the mouth of the latter, especially if the green food is of a tough nature, such as withered grass or dried cabbage leaves.

Sometimes hairs and pieces of soft wood get mixed with the soft food and the chicks are apt to swallow them. Anything of this nature blocks the passage to the gizzard entirely. I have had many sent to me for examination, and these simple things have caused death.

I have tried experiments for several years in rearing chickens without giving them water, and in many cases I have been very successful.

There is a good deal more trouble, however, attached to this than if water were supplied, as most of the grain has to be boiled.

It answers very well where table birds only are wanted, as chickens grow faster if all the corn is boiled and given warm, but if all stock birds were reared in this way they would in time become weak in their digestive organs.

Another method of rearing chickens in the cold and windy days of Winter and early Spring is as follows:—A small run should be made from three to five feet long, the width the same as the coop in which the hen or chickens are placed.

There should be a seven inch board each side, and one at the end, on which a small frame, covered with half-inch mesh wire, should be fastened, so as to cover in the run to prevent sparrows and other birds getting through to the food.

The two sides and end keep the wind away from the young chickens, and the wire at the top lets in the air without causing a draught.

In this way young chickens can be reared successfully in open fields all through the Winter.

Thousands of chickens are ruined through people attempting to bring them up in out-buildings, such as a pig sty, empty stable, or a barn, or loft.

A full description of the runs, &c., will be found in the chapter on houses and runs.

As I have before pointed out where chickens are kept shut up upon bare floors, cramp is almost inevitable, and after they have been kept from the fresh air for a time they become very tender, and susceptible to cold if put outside, and so many get congested lungs and cramp in the legs and toes as a consequence.

I have had my Buff and Black Orpington chickens out in the open through January, February, and early March, when it was coldest, there being sometimes fifteen to forty degrees of frost and snow upon the ground, and yet these chickens out in a bare open coop, and the wire runs with boards round, such as I have described, grew fast and did well, beginning to lay at four and a half months old.

PURE OR DISTINCT VARIETIES.

Plymouth Rocks—Minorcas—White Leghorns—Buff Leghorns—Black Leghorns — Creve Cœurs — Dorkings — Speckled Dorkings — Hamburghs — Scotch Greys—Game—Indian Game—Old English Game — Cochins — Houdans — Wyandottes—Golden Wyandottes—Buff Wyandottes — White Wyandottes—Langshans — Brahmas—Redcaps — Andalusians — Orpingtons — Rose Comb Orpingtons — White Orpingtons—Buff Orpingtons—Diamond Jubilee Orpingtons —Anconas.

IT is my intention to give in this chapter outlines merely of the pure or distinct breeds, just so that an amateur may be helped to distinguish one breed from another.

If I were to attempt a description of all the points of every pure breed, and full directions for mating birds for exhibition, &c., I should find this would take up more space than in a small handbook like this could be allowed.

All I can hope to do is to just state what are the best breeds to keep under certain circumstances.

Black and Buff Orpingtons, Golden Wyandottes, Buff White, and Brown Leghorns, Anconas, and Black Minorcas are the most popular varieties at the present time.

Buff Plymouth Rocks and Buff Wyandottes are both very much sought after; while among the newer breeds, Diamond Jubilee Orpingtons and Buff Dorkings, the merits that distinguish these from the quite ordinary races of fowls have made them popular, right at the outset, especially in certain directions.

The breed of the birds is not so much the distinction with regard to laying qualities; the point of variance of one bird from another is found in the strain. There are good and bad layers of every breed, but there are only good laying strains and bad ones, so that the most careful selection of individual birds, as well as breeds, is necessary if a good laying strain is to be built up.

No pure-bred pullet ought to lay before she is five or six months old, although where birds are from a good laying strain they will lay sometimes at four to four and a half months old, while on the other hand, unfortunately, many birds do not lay until they are eight, nine or ten months old, these latter, of course, not being from a good laying strain.

I always endeavour to prevent my pullets laying before they are six months old.

Until the pullets reach this age I always endeavour to keep them back if I notice they are reddening up at all, as it is too early in their lives, because nature must have time to do her work.

Another thing is that if they come on too early the eggs are very small.

After they have begun laying they should be carefully watched, and if they get on too fast they should not have the flesh food, which, under ordinary circumstances, serves to stimulate the birds to lay plenty of eggs, and they should have one food and another until suitable fare can be provided for them, and change from one run to another puts them back a good deal also.

On the other hand if they do not come on to lay at the proper time they require a stimulant, for it is only natural that where living things are not in their natural state they will sometimes require a little assistance.

PLYMOUTH ROCKS.

Plymouth Rocks have been a very popular breed, but during the last few years they have been somewhat superseded by Orpingtons and Wyandottes, although they are still kept very largely as they are good all-round birds.

I shall endeavour to point out the many excellences of the breed, and also seek to shew some of the points in which some people seem to think they fail.

One thing about Plymouth Rocks, that is most valuable, is that they are very hardy. They will stand confinement well, and the cold and damp does not affect them. Because of this they are good winter layers if they are fed and treated properly, and although they have a tendency to fatness this may be largely overcome if they are given plenty of scratching exercise, and are not allowed too much maize.

They come broody when the warm weather sets in, but they are easily checked if treated as described in the paragraph on broody coop. If they are required for sitting they make splendid sitters and good mothers. They have four toes on each foot, and are very strong in the wing, and they cover eggs or chickens very well.

The eggs laid by the Plymouth Rock are brown. The shade, however, varies considerably, some being dark while others are very pale. Sometimes purchasers are a little disappointed because the eggs vary in colour. It must be understood that the colour of the eggs has nothing whatever to do with the quality of the breed, but it is a singular fact that most people prefer the very dark brown eggs.

Plymouth Rock eggs are not large in proportion to the size of the birds themselves, though some hens lay larger eggs than others. Taking them all round the eggs are generally about the size of those laid by Brahmas, and are saleable in either town or country.

When set the Plymouth Rock eggs hatch out well, better generally than those of either Cochins or Brahmas.

One peculiarity about the chickens is that they do not appear to grow so fast during the first two months as those of many other breeds do, especially the cockerels, as these latter do not feather so quickly, even as the pullets.

But after the first two months they seem to get a start and to fill out very fast.

A good many of the cockerels come very light in colour, and are useless for breeding pure birds, but these rejected birds do famously for crossing purposes with any other breed.

There is also another disadvantage in breeding Plymouth Rocks, and that is that many of the pullets come black in plumage, and their legs are usually very dark, and the only point at which they may be distinguished from a clean-legged Langshan or Black Orpington is by the yellow of the feet which shews more clearly between the toes and

PLYMOUTH ROCK COCK.

PLYMOUTH ROCK HEN.

underneath the foot itself. These usually make the largest pullets and are good layers.

Some breeders mate a very light cock, with yellow legs and beak, with black hens to produce dark-coloured cockerels, with good evenly-marked plumage all through. It is not well to breed from a dark-coloured cockerel when the pullets or hens are dark; if so, many of the pullets will come black. This practice is almost out of date now as the proper lacing and leg colour are not so well obtained in this way.

Plymouth Rocks require great care in mating up if satisfactory results are to be gained, as if this is not given the results are often far from satisfactory.

Of course the mating of stock birds is the great point. It is not always those that have the best stock that breed the best birds for the show pen, or those which fetch a long price.

It is the way in which the birds are mated. Some things must be avoided, while others must be encouraged, and it is the best possible way of doing this that it is important to be quite clear about, and so I will try and shew how best to do this so as to breed good Plymouth Rocks.

If good birds are required, a cock should be chosen with red face and ear lobes, the latter free from streaks of white. The comb should be evenly serrated and standing erect, and the legs and beak yellow, if possible, the yellow legs being very important.

The breast and shoulders should be broad, and the bird should have a good carriage, the more evenly the cocks are marked the better.

Of course defects will arise. White feathers will appear in the tail, and this should be avoided, if possible, although it is very difficult to get a bird without some white in the tail.

The shade of the plumage, whether light or dark, is not so important as the evenness of the markings, this latter constituting the chief beauty of fine specimens.

In the hen the comb should stand erect and be firmly set to the head, and evenly serrated.

The plumage should be of two distinct colours, each feather being marked with a very light slate, almost white, and a very dark and more pronounced slate, and the more distinctly the shades are shown the better, as the light shade looks on a good bird a clear white against a very dark slate.

In those birds which are of a dark shade the dark markings look almost black, especially in the hens.

If the feathers are examined separately they will be found marked right to the quill with one bar of light and one of dark, alternately. The last bar or spot of white should just show, and the tip of the feather should be edged with the dark shade. When the markings are even the birds look as if they are beautifully spotted all over. The more evenly the hens are marked in this way the better, but the light markings must not run into the dark.

The hackles (neck feathers) should have finer markings, but they should be of the same shade as the other parts of the body.

The breast of the cock should be of the same colour as the hen's body, and the hackles and saddle should shew finer markings.

Some of the results of the careless mating of Plymouth Rocks are seen when the cockerels come very light or *vice versa* and some of the pullets black.

In mating, if some of the hens are of a dark shade, a light cock, with yellow legs and beak, should be used. Birds of this colour usually produce the best-marked pullets, but the cockerels from this mating will be very light.

It is very difficult to produce good pullets and cockerels from the same pen, unless one has a large number of stock birds to select from.

To produce good cockerels a medium shade cock must be mated with dark hens, but from this mating a few black pullets must be expected.

If the hens are of a light shade a dark cock may be mated with them, but owing to the various results to be obtained the greatest care must be taken in mating these birds, but one rule will be found absolute, and that is that a light-coloured cock, with bright yellow legs and beak, will produce the best marked pullets, and a dark shade cock the best coloured cockerels.

When chickens of this breed are brought up under trees, or in the shade, their plumage keeps a much brighter colour, as when exposed to the sun it tans very much.

During the summer months Plymouth Rock hens lose the yellow cast from their legs, in fact some become quite white, especially if they are allowed to sit. The legs become yellow again when they change their feathers, but not such a deep colour as when they are pullets. I do not mind a Rock hen having pale legs if I know the blood is right. The colour of the legs is not always a safe guide in choosing Plymouth Rocks, as many half-bred Rocks have much brighter legs than the pure ones, and purchasers of Plymouth Rocks should be most careful from whom they procure their stock.

If Plymouth Rocks are only required for table and eggs, the foregoing points may in some measure be lost sight of, and birds with short legs and an intelligent-looking head sought after.

I like to introduce fresh blood every year when eggs only are required, as this plan always pays in the end. The result of this will at once be seen in stronger chickens, and the pullets will lay earlier and the cockerels fledge faster.

The pullets usually commence laying when they are about six or seven months old. Very much depends upon how they are attended to when young, and whether they are bred from a good laying strain. I have known cases in which birds laid sixty eggs before they were eight months old, but these are exceptions, and this number is not an average one. I had a hen once that laid ten months out of the twelve, and the pullets bred from this hen laid when five months old. The cockerels were very short in the legs and broad in the breast, and this is a most useful type of bird, but at the present time longer legs are sought after in the show pen.

Plymouth Rocks are heavy birds and stand confinement well. They do not show the dirt, lay a brown egg, and are very hardy. They have no feathers on their legs and stand the cold weather very well.

I prefer Plymouth Rocks to Cochins, as they are more active and better table fowls, and I breed a large number of them every year, having from eight to ten strains of them unrelated.

Wherever table fowls are required this breed answers capitally, and ought to be kept, especially if cross-breeds are wanted, as they are most useful for crossing, and improve the cross birds very much.

As we have said before the greatest care must be used to shelter good specimens, or the sun will tan the plumage. Some shades tan more than others. The dark markings which people sometimes call black, fade and turn brown, especially in the cocks. It is noticed, of course, more particularly on the top of the back, and it is well to avoid exposure so as to make this impossible.

Sometimes when they are a rusty colour before the moult their new plumage will come quite a distinct colour, and make them fit for exhibition.

Plymouth Rocks are good birds for a town and do not show the dirt.

The Plymouth Rock chickens are easily distinguished from those of other breeds. When all are hatched out together they are very dark on the back—it may almost be called black—and light colour underneath.

The distinguishing mark is at the back of the head and is a small grey spot. The legs and beaks are usually very yellow. The chickens do not show the markings on their plumage until their feathers grow.

One vigorous Plymouth Rock cock may run with nine hens, and almost every egg will be fertile.

MINORCAS.

The Minorca is one of the most popular breeds of non-sitters in England. More of these birds are kept and bred than, perhaps, any other non-sitting breed. They are excellent for confined positions, and they can now be found in almost every town in England, as well as in many country places, and on farms.

I have experimented for many years with Minorcas, keeping them on different soils and trying them in both cold, exposed, and sheltered places. I have tried rearing them without putting them into a house or shed from the time they were hatched until they laid.

The Minorcas produce very fine eggs, and are indeed one of the breeds that lay the largest of eggs; some strains of Houdans lay as large eggs, but it is not general among them as it is with Minorcas, and there are strains also among the Creve Cœur Spanish and La Fleche that lay large eggs, but with Minorcas it is a characteristic of the breed itself.

The eggs of all the breeds that lay large eggs vary very much in size, the reason often being that the good layers begin to lay at an earlier age.

A pullet that commences laying at from four to five months old will not lay such a large egg as one that does not begin until she is six or seven months old.

Although Minorcas lay white eggs these are saleable both in town and country as they are generally a good size. They are, without exception, one of the best non-sitting breeds to keep where large eggs are required, and there are many thousands who keep fowls solely for egg production, and

BLACK MINORCA COCK.

BLACK MINORCA HEN.

who do not care in the least whether the fowls they keep are good table birds or not.

But although Minorcas are not looked upon as a good table fowl, yet they have very much the flavour and colour of the flesh of a turkey—and people are generally very fond of turkeys—indeed Minorcas have remarkably white flesh and no bird could be whiter as a table fowl. They are not so juicy as a Dorking, but their flesh is very much the same flavour.

A great deal may, of course, be done by breeding these birds up to a good size, and they may be got up to a large fowl in this way, and indeed they have been made so more than ever during the last few years.

I have known instances where, when birds have been bred for weight, they have been got up to 4½ to 5lbs. each at six or seven months old.

The cockerels are much larger, and they would not disappoint any nobleman if they appeared upon his dinner table.

Minorcas should be more extensively kept among all classes of breeders. I breed hundreds of them every year, as they are not only good in their pure state but they also make excellent layers when crossed with any other breed.

Minorca eggs hatch out generally very well, the cockerels fledging well and the pullets even more quickly. They are very strong, healthy, and easy to rear.

Minorcas are very active fowls, and scratch well for a living when they have their liberty, and yet if they are penned up closely they seem quite contented.

They have very nice black plumage, and the cocks especially have a splendid gloss upon their feathers, which adds to their beauty.

The cocks have very large erect single combs. The comb in the hens falls over to one side, and when they are bred for the show pen these falling-over combs are very long and should be evenly serrated. The serrations should be very wide and flat, and taper off to a point, and the comb in the cocks should stand well erect and be also evenly serrated.

When bred for exhibition they ought to carry their tails well out, that is to say, not too upright, if so they are called squirrel-tailed, and this is considered a fault in the show pen.

They should have dark legs, not blue like those of the Spanish; four toes on each foot, well spread out from each other; large white oval ear-lobes free from red spots.

The cock should have all these face points and the ear-lobes and legs should be the same in colour, &c., as those of the hen, only the comb should, of course, stand very erect—the more upright the better—while the ear-lobes should be much larger than the hen's, and of almond shape, not round, and should be free from wrinkles as much as possible and as soft as a kid glove.

Birds of this breed—like those of all others that have white ear-lobes and large combs—require preparing for the show pen. (Refer to chapter on this subject).

Sometimes a cockerel will be perfect in every other point, but his comb will hang over to one side, because it is of very fine substance, and so has not strength in itself to

WHITE MINORCA PULLET.

BROWN LEGHORN COCK.

stand up, and, of course, because of this he is totally unsuitable for the show pen. Such birds are usually killed, because some owners think they are of no use.

These birds, however, are oftentimes the finest of the flock, and yet they seem condemned because of their defective combs.

These cockerels make the best pullet breeders and produce birds with very fine combs, and just such birds as win in the show pen. They have quite a different appearance to the pullets bred from a cock that has a good erect comb, as many of the pullets bred from such cocks have heavy, thick, or what are called "fleshy" combs, which are too strong to fall over to one side of the face, and part of the comb goes over to the wrong side, making it fall half one side and half the other. These combs represent a fault in exhibition fowls.

Of course if Minorcas are not required for exhibition the falling over of the comb a little, or even a streak of white, is no detriment to the fowls, as these little defects amount to nothing when the fowls are only required for laying purposes.

Minorca chickens when hatched are white underneath and black on the upper part of the body.

When the feathers begin to grow the black covers the white. Sometimes white feathers remain in them for three months, but they usually shed them before that time.

I have not written upon the White Minorcas as the points are the same, only their plumage is white instead of black They ought not to show a coloured feather of any kind. The comb, wattles, face, and ear-lobes should be just the same, and the legs white. For my own part I like black much the best.

An active Minorca cock can run with from seven to ten hens of the same breed in a confined run. Twelve to fifteen hens would not be too many when the birds have a large range.

LEGHORNS.

Much has been said in favour of this breed during the last six years, both as layers and hardy birds. They cannot be spoken too highly of, although they are small. There is not much of them, so that they are not very good birds for table purposes, and in addition to this their skin is rather yellow, and they lay white eggs.

Their good qualities, however, far outweigh their failings, for they are very hardy and stand confinement well. They will thrive even in the back yards of towns and lay all through the winter if properly housed and fed.

They are easily reared as chickens fledge fast and mature early.

They commence laying at from five to six months old, although the former age is too early. If they lay under five months old they usually commence shedding their feathers like old hens, but they get over it quickly and soon come on to lay again.

Leghorn chickens may be hatched any time from January to September. They are beautifully shaped birds and often take the eye in preference to the larger breeds as they are very active, and when allowed their liberty they range a long way from home, but do not lay away, as birds of many other

WHITE LEGHORN COCK.

WHITE LEGHORN PULLET.

breeds do, if they have proper accommodation in the roosting house.

There are six varieties of Leghorns, viz., Brown, White, Black, Buff, Pile, and Duckwing Leghorns. I can only recommend four varieties, viz., Brown, White, Buff, and Black, as I have found these always the best. The Pile and Duckwing being bred for exhibition are more fancy varieties and do not breed true to colour, although splendid layers.

The Brown Leghorns I have found very good layers, but the White are, if anything, a trifle better, in fact I have found them stand my cold place as well as any other pure-bred birds. The White lay a rather larger egg than the Brown, and the hens are a little bigger.

The Brown look rather the best in a confined run as they do not show the dirt, and they stand confinement quite as well as the White. All varieties of Leghorns stand confinement well.

I do not recommend White Leghorns to be kept in thickly populated towns or manufacturing districts, as the plumage becomes very dirty when they are kept in close confinement, although even there they prove themselves wonderful layers.

The cocks of the Brown variety are very handsome, much the same colour as a black breasted Red Game Cock. The hen's hackle feathers should be well marked brown, edged with black. These are the hens to breed from if good birds are required.

The egg table of the Leghorn varies very much, just as is the case with many other of the breeds. Sometimes they will lay as many as 250 eggs each in the year, while some birds, kept under the same conditions, will not lay more than seventy to a hundred all told. When I meet with a pen of good laying birds I always endeavour to keep them up, or even a single fowl if a good layer. I encourage the owner to breed from them or buy the birds myself.

Leghorn eggs are usually very fertile and hatch out well. One cock may run with from eight to twelve hens in the open, or with from six to eight in a confined run, but when they have a grass field to roam over as many as fifteen hens would not be too many. Leghorns are non-sitters, and when properly tended give good value for the food they eat. They are birds that ought to be more encouraged in our country.

I can recommend Leghorns as the best breed to keep if only eggs are required for home consumption, either in confinement or in an open range. The White, Brown, Black, and Buff varieties are my favourites, as these varieties of Leghorns keep free from disease more than any birds I have ever kept, except, perhaps, Cochins.

Leghorn eggs are not quite so large as those laid by Black Minorcas, but the combs are not so quickly cut with the frost and cold winds as the Minorca's.

Leghorns are still very popular, their laying qualities recommending them wherever they go, especially in cases where a pure non-sitting variety is required.

Small sprightly birds they must always be, although greatly improved in size in the new varieties. The great need of the poultry world to-day is birds that combine laying and table qualities, and, while holding their own as layers, as table birds they are eclipsed by the newer

BUFF LEGHORN COCK.

BUFF LEGHORN HEN.

varieties that are so superior in this respect, and, as the tendency is to concentrate, birds combining qualities that are only found singly or in part in other varieties, must, of necessity, come rapidly to the front, as is the case at the present time in regard to new kinds that have been introduced.

BUFF LEGHORNS.

Buff Leghorns have become very popular during the past few years. They are of that lovely buff colour which always takes the eye of the public, but it is difficult to breed them all true to colour.

At present many of them come a very pale buff and not the nice deep colour they should be. They are marvellous layers and their eggs are about the same size as Leghorn eggs generally. There is a great demand both for eggs and birds, and good bred fowls of this variety will realize much higher prices than any of the others, as they are very difficult to breed for exhibition.

The tail in the male birds is the most difficult point to get right, as in most of the male birds this comes quite white, or the centre of the feather is white, while the edge is brown. The chickens are quite as hardy as those of the brown and white varieties. There is a great demand for birds of this breed for crossing purposes.

The head points of all classes of Leghorn hens should be single combs lying over to one side, evenly serrated. In the Buff and White the beak should be yellow, but in the brown rather a dark horn, although a few are found with yellow beaks.

Red face and white ear-lobes should be found in all varieties. The tail should be carried rather high, and the birds should stand rather short on the legs and have a small compact body. The head points of the male birds are exactly the same as those of the hens, only the combs are larger, also standing erect and the serrates wider apart, and these latter should be wide at the base, coming off to a point at the top.

The plumage of the White variety should be pure white throughout, and that of the Brown much the same colour as that of the black breasted Red Game.

The Buff variety should, of course, be a beautiful buff colour right throughout, but good specimens of the male birds are few and far between. All classes should have yellow legs and four toes on each foot.

BLACK LEGHORNS.

Black Leghorns have the same head points with yellow legs, but with black plumage throughout, although a few are inclined to show white in the sickle feathers of the tail.

Some people prefer them to any other variety of Leghorns, but their legs are more liable to become dark or spotted down the front instead of a bright yellow.

CREVE CŒURS.

The birds of this breed are very much the same style as Houdans, but the colour is different, Creves being quite black and a trifle larger, and lay about the same sized eggs as Houdans, and about the same number.

The cocks of this breed should weigh from seven to eight pounds when fully developed, and have a large comb

CREVE CŒUR COCK.

CREVE CŒUR HEN.

divided in the middle like two horns. The wattles are long and the top-knot ought to be large as well as the whiskers and bib.

The hens are non-sitters and good layers, they have top-knots, &c., the same as the cocks, but the combs and wattles are much smaller. The legs are blue, with four toes on each foot.

Creve Cœurs are not much known in this country and where they are known they are valued both for their table and laying qualities, for they are fine table birds.

DORKINGS.

There are six varieties of this breed, viz., Coloured, Silver Grey, Cuckoo, Buff, Speckled and White. A full description of the speckled variety will be found further on in the book. The White also is very little known and less appreciated.

All four of the more generally known varieties resemble each other in having deep square bodies with broad breasts and short white legs, with five toes on each foot. The comb should be single and evenly serrated, in the coloured and silver grey, while the white and cuckoo should have double or rose combs.

The Coloured or Dark Dorkings are very large birds, the cocks weighing from 8½ to 11 lbs., and the hens seven or eight pounds. The breast and tail of the cocks should be black, the hackle and saddle feathers being grey and black, the upper and lower part of the wing being a greyish white, while the middle bar should be black.

The feathers on the top part of the hen's back should be very dark, each feather showing a light-brown stripe in the centre. The breast is of a reddish brown shade. The tail should be black, and the hackle feathers striped grey and black.

The silver grey resemble the coloured in shape but are not quite so large. The cock's plumage is also much the same as that of the coloured, but the hackles, saddle, and shoulders are much lighter, and more of a silvery shade, while the tail and breast are black.

The hen's back should be a delicate pale grey, the breast being of a light-brown shade, rather paler than that of the robin and the hackles striped white and black, and very bright. Both varieties are very popular and grow increasingly so.

Cuckoo Dorkings are smaller than the coloured, but are very handsome, each feather being a greyish-white, tipped with slate at the end. They are kept the least of any of the Dorkings, being very delicate, there being great difficulty in procuring fresh blood. They resemble Plymouth Rocks in colour very much.

White Dorkings are about the same size as the cuckoo variety, but rather longer in the leg, and these also are rather delicate unless they have a good open range.

As is generally known Dorkings carry a large quantity of white meat, and as they are the best birds for table purposes, as regards quality, they command the highest prices in the London Markets.

They are not good layers in confinement, and most people find them delicate to bring up, although I myself have never found any difficulty in rearing them; but the chickens

SILVER-GREY DORKING COCK.

SILVER-GREY DORKING HEN.

always do better if they have a good open space with short grass to roam over, and not too thick upon the ground.

No fowls require the constant introduction of fresh blood more than Dorkings, and unless a change of blood is frequently brought in it will be found that the eggs and chickens get smaller every year.

SPECKLED DORKINGS.

Few of my modern readers know anything about the original Speckled Dorkings as they are called. These birds were shown, and cups given for them, forty-five to fifty years ago.

As I before observed this variety has almost died out; in fact, at last I only knew two people among all my extensive range of poultry-keeping friends who kept Speckled Dorkings distinct. One was a clergyman in Lincolnshire, who had them from his father who had won a cup for them in his young days. The son always kept a few for the sake of the remembrances that they brought him of his father, and he so loved them that he said he could get nothing better. We exchanged blood, he having some birds from my yard.

I have long been fond of all sorts of poultry, and have a weakness for birds of the Speckled Dorking colour, having kept them so many years, but now that Speckled Dorkings are revived people must not think they are a new variety, because they are only an old one revived.

There are rose and single combed birds of this variety, just as there used once to be of Coloured Dorkings. They have the Dorking five toes on each foot, white legs, long, deep bodies, beautiful white skin and flesh, exactly the same as the other Dorkings, but are not so big.

In the course of a few years I hope to get them up quite as heavy as the others, and perhaps heavier than the White Dorkings, and considerably heavier than the Cuckoo Dorkings.

The colour to my mind is very startling, being a mixture of brown, black and white.

In the single comb variety the comb should be erect and well serrated, but the serrations should be rather small. The face should be red, but the ear-lobes, not noticed as in other Dorkings whether they be red or white. The beak should be a dark horn colour, eye hazel or brown, well curved, long, deep breast, evenly mottled all over, shewing well the three distinct colours.

The wings should shew white flight feathers, and the top part of the shoulder should be the same colour as the breast, and the hackles and saddle should be the same, only the long tapering feathers should be rather bright in colour. The sickle feathers should be principally white, and the tail should be carried well back. The hen should have a comb lying over to one side, but evenly serrated, and an even colour all through, that is to say with a mixture of brown, white, and black, giving the bird a very handsome appearance. The tail should be of the same colour.

The rose comb birds should be exactly the same as the single in shape and colour, differing only, of course, in the comb.

This latter should be evenly serrated all over, what some people call full of "work," with a nice spike at the back,

COLOURED DORKING HEN.

not necessarily long. I may say the chickens of this variety feather very rapidly and lay more eggs in the twelve months than any other Dorking variety I have ever kept.

BUFF DORKING.

The Buff Dorking is quite a new variety, and is also quite a new variety of Dorkings altogether. There are a few in England, but I claim the honour of bringing this new variety out. No doubt in a few years they will become very popular as they lay far more eggs than the other Dorkings. The bodies should be buff entirely, as Buff Orpington, Buff Rock, &c., but they have much more black in their tails at present. They are big birds and have the five toes on each foot. The chickens are very hardy and grow faster than either of the other Dorkings except, perhaps, the speckled variety.

HAMBURGHS.

There are five varieties of Hamburghs, viz., Silver-pencilled, Golden-pencilled, Golden-spangled, Silver-spangled, and Black.

With the exception of the black, which only differs in being a little larger, all the varieties of Hamburghs resemble each other in having nice white ear-lobes, rose combs ending in a point behind, and small, but somewhat plump, bodies, with blue legs, and four toes on each foot. They are also non-sitters

In the silver-pencilled variety the hens are evenly pencilled nearly all over the body, the only part not marked being the hackle feathers, which are almost white. The cocks are nearly pure white, the exception being the tail, which is black, slightly edged with white, also the feathers on the lower part of the body between the ends of the wings and the thighs, which are evenly pencilled, and some of the wing feathers, which are slightly touched with black.

The golden-pencilled are marked in exactly the same way, but with rich brown colouring on the feathers in place of white.

In the silver-spangled variety the hen should be spangled on the breast, back, saddle, and thighs, the tail and wing flights being white with black spots on the ends. The neck hackles should be striped black and white.

The cock's breast is spangled and the hackles and tail white, each tail feather being tipped at the end with black. The back and wings should be grey and white, with a few dark feathers, the wing being marked with three distinct bars of black.

The golden-spangled birds are marked nearly in the same way, but the feathers are coloured rich brown instead of white, the cock's tail being pure black. They are often known as "Moonies" or pheasant birds, especially in the Midland counties.

The black birds have pure black feathers, which look quite a metallic green in the sun. They appear to have a slight touch of the Spanish build, from which breed they, no doubt, obtain the extra size.

Hamburghs are well known on account of their laying qualities. They lay medium sized white eggs, which do not sell well for market. Although the birds are small they make fair table fowls, as they are plump and the flesh is white and tender.

SILVER-SPANGLED HAMBURGH COCK.

Hamburghs do best with a large range, but if shut up securely and kept clean they will thrive well in confinement.

These fowls are kept largely in England and still retain quite a reputation as layers. I have tried them against Leghorns for the last fifteen years, but Leghorns should have the preference for several reasons. The first is that Leghorns are much hardier when kept in open situations, and exposed to cold and wet. The second is that they lay better during the winter months, producing larger eggs, which make a better price than Hamburgh eggs do. The third is that the chickens are much hardier and can be reared with much less trouble, not being so subject to colds during the winter months when the weather is changeable.

Hamburgh chickens ought never to be brought up with chickens of other breeds, as if they are they never do so well. They must never be allowed out in the damp grass early in the morning, and if reared in confinement they must be kept very clean.

SCOTCH GREYS.

This breed is very little known in England, although the birds are good useful fowls. In Scotland they are very popular, and are thought a good deal of. In colour they are much the same as Plymouth Rocks, but the markings are finer, and the dark markings of the feathers are of a lighter shade than those on the Rocks, and the lighter markings not so light. In well bred Scotch Greys the markings are very even and of two shades of grey, one light and the other dark, so that if a single feather is examined it will be found that the bars of light and dark shades run right down to the stem of the feather.

The markings are so distinct that many of our English breeders have crossed them with the Plymouth Rocks to get the even markings of the Greys into their birds.

Scotch Greys are very hardy, with fairly short white legs, broad in the breast, skin very white, and are fair table fowls. The chickens grow fast and are very hardy. A few of the cockerels are a little delicate but this is where they have been in-bred too much. If bred from a good laying strain the pullets will commence laying when from six to seven months old, and make good layers of fair sized white eggs, although some of them will hatch out black.

They stand confinement fairly well, and are good sitters and mothers, and can be crossed with any other variety.

If the owners of Scotch Greys wish to increase the number of eggs, and do not mind white shells, the best breeds to use for crossing are Houdan, Minorca, or Leghorn cocks, the first-named being best. When crossed with either of these breeds they make excellent layers, and will produce from thirty to fifty eggs each more than in their pure state in twelve months, and also commence laying earlier.

When a Leghorn cock is used many of the pullets commence when five months old. When the Houdan cock is crossed the best table fowls are produced. When the Minorca cock is mated the eggs are a little larger than those from the other crosses. When a White Leghorn cock is used most of the pullets come white; if the Houdan most of them come black, with small top-knots; if the Minorca sixteen out of twenty come black.

The laying results from these crosses are marvellous. If table fowls for market and good winter layers of tinted eggs

SCOTCH GREY COCK.

are required I recommend a Buff Orpington cock to be crossed, as when these cross birds reach the London markets they are bought up at once, as their legs and skins are so very white.

If brown eggs are required I recommend an Orpington cock to be used. I breed a large number of this cross.

If the birds are required for pheasant rearing I prefer the Indian Game Cock to be mated with the Scotch Grey, as the pullets from this cross are hardy and good winter layers, and are excellent sitters and mothers. If the two latter crosses are tried in the North of Scotland the egg list there would be doubled in the winter.

I have had pullets of the Scotch Grey cross commence laying at five months old. If this breed were only better known in England the birds would be kept largely, as they are a very favourite fowl of the Scottish poultry-keepers.

GAME.

All the Game varieties resemble each other in having a sharp, strong beak, and intelligent eye, and a very bold appearance, strong legs, varying in length according to variety, but all the game birds are splendid for the table, and if any could be best it is the Indian Game. All the varieties of Game have four claws on each foot, with broad firm breasts, and the general appearance of the birds should be firm and hard, this being caused by the feathers being very short, and strong, and lying close to the body, and each having either single or pea combs which, of course, correspond in the sexes of either breed.

Some people cut off the comb and wattles of the cock birds when they are from five to seven months old. This is called "dubbing," and is done because it is thought the birds are less liable to hurt each other if they get fighting. This is a thing I neither do myself nor recommend to others, as I much prefer the birds in their natural state.

There are so many Game varieties that it would not be possible for me to describe them all in this book, but the most common of all the varieties is the black breasted red, the cock of which should have a black breast and tail, while the lower part of the body should be black also. The hackle and saddle feathers are of a rich brown-red colour, the upper part of the wing is of a deep red, with black edging, the centre part being black and at the end a reddish brown, something like the colour of the hackles. The hen's back and wings should be brown and the under part of the body rather lighter. The hackles are striped black and brown. I have found the birds of this variety both the best layers and the most popular of them all.

Game fowls are fairly good birds to keep when they have a good range, as they search well for their own living and are very hardy. The hens are not good layers in confinement and only in exceptional instances where birds are bred from a good laying strain are really good laying results obtained.

The average Game hens only lay fairly well if they have a good range, but they are good sitters and mothers, and will defend their brood against anything, but they are spiteful to chickens belonging to other hens.

The Game make much better table birds than one would expect, as they are very plump and fit to kill any time, but I should not recommend this breed to any one desirous of

BLACK RED GAME COCK.

INDIAN GAME COCK.

INDIAN GAME HEN.

keeping fowls for profit in small, confined runs, nor at all, unless they have a wood or field for them to run over, in which case they would practically take care of themselves.

INDIAN GAME.

The Indian Game variety has been very popular in England for table purposes during the last few years. They are used more particularly for crossing purposes so as to produce good table birds. The hens are far better layers than the ordinary Game, and lay a brown egg.

The birds themselves are of a beautiful mottled colour much the same as that of a pheasant. The legs are of a bright yellow colour and the plumage is a mixture of very dark brown, almost black, and a lighter shade, giving the bird a beautiful pencilled appearance. They have a deeper cut of meat upon the breast than birds of any other variety, and this is what makes them so popular as table birds, and more especially the cocks for crossing purposes.

The feathers lie very close and tight like those of any other variety of Game. Indian Game fowls should have a very strong beak and head, and the hens make good sitters and mothers.

They do not have a single comb like the ordinary Game, but a pea or treble comb, much like that of a Brahma, only in the male birds it is larger. The face and ear-lobes should be red, and the plumage dark in the cocks, almost a dark-brown, which makes them appear almost black when viewed from a distance, and the legs should be quite yellow. Those who breed for the market should never be without Indian Game blood in their yards.

OLD ENGLISH GAME.

The Old English Game variety is again becoming very fashionable. They have a fine deep breast, and small bones, and have proved themselves the best layers of any of the Game varieties I have had during the last season. They should have white legs, although one will come occasionally with yellow legs. There are various colours and shades but I prefer the black breasted red. These latter are very much like the black breasted red modern in colour, but have a much longer tail and more of it, and the hackles are thick and long, whereas in modern Game they are shorter and finer.

Old English Game hens lay white or cream-coloured eggs, about the same size as those laid by modern Game and I am very pleased that people are taking them up, as they are a good old-fashioned fowl which I can heartily recommend for many good and useful purposes.

COCHINS.

All varieties of this breed should have four claws on each foot, and the legs should be yellow, fairly short, and feathered down to the end of the middle toe with a great deal of fluffy feathering on the thigh which should meet the leg feathers, so that there is no vacancy between. The comb should be single, rather short, and standing erect, the breast appearing very broad, and the general attitude of the fowls rather leaning forward. The cocks ought to weigh from eight to eleven pounds, and the hens from six and a half to nine pounds.

BUFF COCHIN COCK.

PARTRIDGE COCHIN COCK.

The colours most commonly kept are the buff, white, and partridge, but black and cuckoo Cockins are frequently met with. I prefer the buff and partridge varieties and I only keep these.

The Buff Cochins differ a good deal in shade, some being of a pale lemon colour, while others are much darker. The cock's feathers should be very glossy and of a rich brown-red colour on the wings and back.

Partridge hens are pencilled something like a partridge, but are rather darker. The feathers on the body are pencilled, and those on the neck are black and brown tinged delicately round the edges with light brown. The cock should have black feathers on the breast and under part of the body and red on the wing and back.

Cochins are often disliked on account of their bad table qualities, and their tendency to want to sit; but in spite of these failings they are very good fowls for anybody to keep who has only a small space at their disposal and that perhaps in a cold and damp situation, as these birds stand confinement well and are very hardy.

I have known disease to go through every breed in the poultry yard with the exception of Cochins; and even Brahmas will take diseases that will not touch Cochins.

As chickens they are hardy, and may be hatched all through the winter, although they fledge very slowly.

In breeding, care should be taken to select a young cock hatched about April or May, as then they are more active, and do not grow so large, and by breeding in this way as many chickens may be hatched from two broods as would be obtained from four if this precaution is not taken.

The best varieties for keeping in confinement are the buff and partridge. The latter are first rate layers, and will lay well in winter, as their feathers being long and strong they can stand any sort of weather. They lay a good-sized egg, very rich in flavour, the white being thicker and more glutinous than that of any other fowl, except that of the Game, and the colour of the shell being quite brown they sell well and command a good price in any market.

These birds are also very valuable for crossing, and may be crossed with any other fowls; but I recommend non-sitters, as Cochins are so often broody, and I have known farmers, who have crossed Cochins and Dorkings to obtain good table birds and have been tormented with broody hens.

Care should be taken in selecting birds to cross with Cochins to choose those with short legs and plenty of breast meat, or otherwise the half-bred birds will be very lanky.

Cochins require careful feeding, as when fed entirely on corn they will only lay a few eggs and then become broody, and although they make good sitters and mothers, they are a nuisance when so often broody. They are also very liable to fatty accumulation internally which, of course, stops their laying, and often causes death by apoplexy. Cochins are condemned by some people but they are favourites of mine.

HOUDANS.

The Houdan is of all the French varieties the one most generally known in this country and holds in France about the same position as the Dorking does in Englrnd.

The birds are much the same shape as those of the Dorking varieties, and are first-rate table fowls, having small

HOUDAN COCK.

HOUDAN HEN.

bones, short legs, and plenty of very white and rich meat on the breast.

They are, however, much better layers than Dorkings as they produce large numbers of fine white eggs during the year, and stand confinement fairly well.

The hens are non-sitters and should have black feathers tipped with white, the markings being as regular as possible.

The best cocks weigh from six to eight pounds when developed, and are the same colour as the hens on the breast, although they are darker on the back, with greenish black feathers in the tail.

Birds of both sexes have fair-sized crests, with feathers round the ears and under the beak, known as "whiskers" or "bib."

The cocks have large combs, opening in the middle, similar in shape to an oak leaf, of that shape known as leaf combs. The hens have combs of the same shape, but smaller. All the birds have short legs of a blue white colour with a few white spots upon them, and five claws on each foot.

It will be seen, therefore, by the above description that Houdans are very fine fowls to keep for crossing purposes when a supply of eggs is wanted and also for producing chickens for the table. I recommend the Houdan as far superior when crossed to anything it can ever be in its pure state; and that they take a very high position as an all-round bird for crossing.

WYANDOTTES.

This is one of the most popular in England of the breeds introduced from America. There are four varieties—Silver, White, Golden, and Buff.

Opinions vary, and some praise Wyandottes while others are disgusted with them. I have found them excellent layers, and there are not many of all the varieties that surpass them in this direction, indeed they may be classed among our best layers.

The eggs are tinted or brown and rather small—some would call them of medium size—and the fowls are fairly hardy, will stand confinement well, and make fair table birds, as they are short and compact, and very full in the breast. The birds of this breed have yellow skins which is all against them as table birds. The hens make good sitters and mothers, and will often lay in the coop before the chickens are three weeks old. If the hens are not required for sitting they are easily checked, as three days in the broody coop is usually sufficient to bring them on to lay again, and they will often commence laying before the seven days are past. The hens should be laced all over, both breast and back, with white and black, and both cocks and hens should have rose combs, rather small with a peak or spike over the back of the head, pointing downwards towards the neck, the face and earlobes being red.

In most specimens the beak is a dark horn streaked with yellow, but some good specimens have a perfectly yellow beak. The legs should be of a bright yellow and free from

SILVER WYANDOTTE COCK.

SILVER WYANDOTTE HEN.

feathers, with four claws on each foot, well spread out from each other, and tails black.

The cocks are much the same colour as a dark Brahma Cock, the saddle and hackles being white, evenly striped with black. The back and wings are of a silvery white slightly edged with black. Many of the cocks come with black breasts, but they should always be laced on the breasts quite evenly or, as some people term it, mottled.

Wyandottes have become very popular during the last few years as they are good layers. When this breed is mated to produce exhibition birds or for good marking in the pullets, a cock with a good laced breast should be used, and a mixture of white in his fluff feathers, as, if a bird of this kind be selected, well marked pullets may be expected. It is rather difficult to get a nice shaped comb with a good peak at the back in the cocks, but it is an important point. One thing will be found difficult to overcome, viz., that so many of the pullets come very light in the breast.

GOLDEN WYANDOTTES.

This variety came in some years after the introduction of the Silver Wyandotte, and they certainly are very taking birds.

I am very fond of them myself, as they are extraordinary winter layers of brown eggs which are, however, rather small. The colour of the bird is very striking, being black and brown laced, and I go in very largely for them.

The skin of these Wyandottes, however, have a yellow cast, just the same as that of the Silver, and they cannot be bred true to colour, that is to say one breeds a good many fairly good specimens.

They produce some of the best winter layers we have ever known. The points are as follows: Cock birds should have a rose comb, fitting nicely to the head with a peak at the back, pointing downwards; short curved beak of a dark horn or yellow colour; hazel eyes, red face and ear-lobes, wattles of a fair length, hackles very full, reaching well down in the shoulders. The colour of the feathers should be golden brown, edged with black. The hackles should not be too light in colour, and the saddle feathers should match them if possible. The shoulder or middle of the wing should be of a deep red colour, while the flights of the wings should be brown, edged with black, the underneath part of the wing is black, but should be well tucked under the saddle feathers, leading from the shoulder and not showing. At the end of the wing should be two rows of spangled brown and black. The breast laced, if possible right up to the throat, the centre of the feathers brown or buff, while the edge of the feathers is black, the tail should be black, not large, but a fair size; legs yellow, four toes on each foot, well spread out from each other. The hens or pullets should be evenly marked right throughout, but the hackles should be darker in proportion to the other part of the bird's body. Each feather should be brown in the centre, with a black edge all round. Each flight feather should be brown, edged with black, so that when the wing is closed it looks like little black marks on each feather. They should have a rose comb, which should be small and neat, fitting close to the head, red face, dark horn beak, striped with yellow. Broad in the breast, fairly short

GOLDEN WYANDOTTE COCK.

GOLDEN WYANDOTTE HEN.

WHITE WYANDOTTE COCK.

upon the legs, which should be yellow. Four toes on each foot.

BUFF WYANDOTTES.

Buff Wyandottes are of the same character and shape in every respect, only they have a buff body, but many of them come with a little black round their hackles and tail, which is a fault, however, as show specimens must be buff throughout.

They are handsome birds and good winter layers. The Buff Wyandotte variety is quite a recent introduction from America, from whence all the Wyandotte varieties have originated, but they have been bred differently, because they are practically a mongrel bird, and the first specimens were got together from various parts, and had a little Shanghai blood in them, and several other breeds were crossed with them, among them Game.

Notwithstanding all this, however, they have proved themselves splendid layers and hardy fowls, and the eggs are of a fair size, brown or tinted. Golden Wyandottes are improving every year, and the best specimens are making a long figure.

We are living in days when anything that is a buff colour will sell, particularly if the birds are good layers. There is one thing, they have yellow legs and skin, as most of the American varieties have, and which some people do not object to, although a good many do. I can recommend these birds heartily as they are good winter layers.

WHITE WYANDOTTES.

This is also a white variety of Wyandottes, which are of the same character. They, too, have rose combs and yellow legs, and four toes on each foot. They are sports from the Silver Wyandottes, are very hardy and strong, and good winter layers. They should be pure white, and are a little bigger than either of the other varieties.

I have kept them for some time and like them exceedingly. It would, however, be quite impossible for me to enter fully into their merits in this little work.

LANGSHANS.

Though this breed was once so much ridiculed the birds are now great favourites and one of the leading varieties now they are better known. Langshans are indeed good all-round fowls for table, hardy in bringing up, but they should never be killed before they are six or eight months old, as up to this age they are deficient in breast meat, but after that time they are like young turkeys, and the pullets are splendid layers of brown eggs, which are saleable anywhere.

They are good birds to breed, excellent sitters and mothers, and they stand confinement well, do not show the dirt, and are good foragers, if they have their liberty.

They have a beautiful green black gloss on their plumage. A black fowl is much easier to breed than birds of any other colour. There is in the Langshan just what is wanted by many, viz., laying and table qualities combined, and also great beauty.

If breeders would only keep to breeding from the best layers and make this a special point it would be a grand thing.

Langshans have more tail than Cochins and black legs, slightly feathered down to the outside toe, not the middle one which should be quite free from feathers.

LANGSHAN COCK.

LANGSHAN HEN.

Very thick fluff (vulture hocked) is a fault in Langshans, especially in the cocks. These latter are generally rather long in the leg and should be broad in the chest, carrying themselves very erect. The combs should be evenly serrated and erect in the cocks, and the same in the hens, but the hen's combs are sometimes a little inclined to one side, although this is not a serious fault, and they should also have very red ear-lobes. They often have a few light feathers on their feet, but these ought to breed out, although birds showing them are frequently passed in the show pen. They should have four toes on each foot. Sometimes the male bird throws a few red feathers on the neck and saddle.

If a cock is a very active bird he can run with from seven to nine hens in a confined run, in cases where a larger range, say a grass field, can be provided ten or twelve hens would not be too many, and, as a rule, eleven eggs out of thirteen will be fertile.

If birds are being bred for exhibition a less number of hens should run with the cock, as the birds used for this purpose are heavier, and it is not well to run more than six to eight hens. The hens fledge fairly well, the cockerels being rather backward, but all the birds are very hardy.

Langshan chickens are black on the back when first hatched, and a whitish yellow on the underneath part and round the head. The first feathers sometimes come tipped with white but these pass away in the first moult.

BRAHMAS.

There are two varieties of this breed, viz., the light and dark. Both are of large size, and should present a broad, substantial appearance. The cocks weigh from 8½ to 10 lbs., and the hens from six to nine pounds. The legs are yellow, and should be short and well feathered down to the tip of the middle claw. The comb should be small and set close to the head, and is what is called a pea or triple comb, having the appearance of being cut down or rounded off like three small peas, the one in the centre being the largest.

In Light Brahmas the plumage of both cocks and hens should be of a white colour all over, with the exception of the hackle feathers which are striped white and black, and the tail feathers which are black, slightly edged with white, and the saddle feathers streaked with black, but the best specimens are white all over.

In dark Brahmas the cock's breast, tail, leg feathers, and under part of the body should be pure black. The upper part of the wing is of a greyish white, the centre being black and lower part white, tipped at the end with black.

The hackle, back and saddle feathers are of a greyish white and black. The hen's hackle feathers should be black, edged with silvery white, and the body should be pencilled all over, even to the end of the tail. To breed well-laced pullets a cockerel should be used that has light markings on the breast.

Brahmas are very good fowls to keep in confinement as they are very hardy and do well in a small space. They are good layers of brown eggs in the winter months; but in spring and summer they are often broody, and as they make good sitters and mothers it is often well for people who keep non-sitting varieties and wish to hatch a few chickens

DARK BRAHMA COCK.

LIGHT BRAHMA COCK.

LIGHT BRAHMA HEN.

to keep a few Brahmas, as they may then be sure of a broody hen sooner or later.

If this breed is especially bred for laying only, these birds make excellent layers. I have known them lay from 130 to 170 eggs each in twelve months while the show Brahmas have not averaged forty each.

A good laying strain of this breed will come up to the Rocks, and also the Langshans, and they will lay from thirty to forty eggs without missing a day. I have known several specimens that have not come broody the whole of the year. They do not make as good table birds as the Rocks and Langshans when they are pure, but they are equal for crossing purposes. Brahmas breed rather better than Cochins, eleven out of thirteen eggs usually being fertile. This is, of course, a consideration. I was years procuring a good laying strain of dark Brahmas. If Brahmas are bred for laying only they do not disappoint their keepers. If they average 110 per bird that is what may be called very good, but all depends upon the treatment the birds receive.

When they become broody and are not required for sitting purposes they ought to be shut up at once in the coop mentioned, then they will come on to lay again in a few days. The Brahma is a good fowl to cross with other breeds, particularly when birds are to be fattened for market as they put on fat very quickly. Looking over my egg book I find that some of my Dark Brahmas have laid 170 eggs each in 12 months.

REDCAPS.

This is a very old breed, though it is well known in many parts of the country, being best known in Yorkshire, Derbyshire, and Staffordshire. In Yorkshire the farmers call them "mooney" fowls, and in Staffordshire pheasant fowls. I have known better layers from the latter place than from either of the others, although I have tried all three.

I have found Redcaps good layers of fair sized white eggs, and one pullet I have known laid 70 eggs in 70 days. Of course the laying strains vary very much, but the birds do well either in an open range or in confinement. The chickens are rather delicate, and consequently difficult to rear, and where they are brought up with large numbers of other chickens they usually succumb at an early age so that if Redcaps are to be reared successfully they must be brought up by themselves.

If only a brood or two are required and a little care is bestowed on these for the first three or four weeks they will grow and feather well, both cockerels and pullets, and make fair table birds with white skins and blue legs, four toes on each foot, free from feathers on legs and feet. The plumage is very much the same colour as that of the Golden Spangled Hamburgh, being a reddish brown with a tip of black something like a half moon.

Hamburghs have more of a spangle and are also much brighter in colour, and have smaller combs. Redcaps should have red ear-lobes and very large rose combs.

When the chickens are first hatched they are of a light buff colour underneath, and have two stripes on the back,

RED CAP COCK.

light and dark brown. These come occasionally rather buff, and only show a dark stripe at the back of the head, and others are almost black. They are very pretty as chickens.

The cockerels may be distinguished from the pullets when hatched, or at least in a week or two as they have such a large comb. The cockerels are ready for the table when about four months old if fed and attended to well.

ANDALUSIANS.

This is a favourite breed with some fanciers, and especially poultry-keepers who require large numbers of eggs, as they are excellent layers of very fine eggs.

Their plumage is different in colour to that of other varieties being slate colour, and when the hens are properly marked they are very handsome. The ground colour is rather a light slate, each feather edged with a very dark shade. They look as if they are pencilled. The neck hackles are very much darker than the body, the ear-lobes white, face red, and single combs lying over to one side, the legs rather a blue slate, and four toes on each foot. The cock has face and ear-lobes similar to the hen, the comb being single and standing erect and evenly serrated, and well set to the head.

Their backs should be dark, almost black, and the breast more the colour of the hen and these latter should be laced all over, and especially upon the breast with light and dark shades, of blue sufficiently pronounced as to form a contrast.

Andalusians do not breed true to colour, some come black and others white and a few a very light slate with no pencilling.

Those who do not understand the breed when buying a sitting of eggs must not be surprised if three or four different coloured chickens are produced, as some come black, some white, and others blue, and occasionally a few speckled ones will appear.

The reason for their not breeding true to colour is that they originate from Black and White Minorcas. They are excellent layers of large white eggs, and if the birds are sheltered from the cold winds they will lay in the winter, spring and summer months in abundance. The chicks do fairly well, the pullets thriving best and also feathering better than the cockerels. They usually commence laying at from five to six and a-half months old. One cock may run with seven to ten hens.

ORPINGTONS.

This breed is one which the author originated in 1886, and sent out to the public. They have spread more quickly than any other variety, as they can be found in all parts of the world.

The Orpingtons have filled up the vacancy that existed in the poultry world, as there never has been any breed of bird to answer the description of the Orpingtons, which are good winter layers of brown eggs, excellent table birds, combined at the same time with a handsome appearance, and are very easy to breed, the chickens fledging quickly and growing fast.

ANDALUSIAN COCK.

ANDALUSIAN HEN.

The hens are good sitters and mothers, but are not so troublesome as many of the sitting varieties when not required for that purpose. They are free from feathers on the leg, and have a beautiful black glossy plumage, therefore do not show the dirt when brought up in towns, like many other varieties. They stand confinement and lay through the severest of wintry weather, producing a beautiful brown egg, just the kind to command a ready sale in town or country. If required for table they are very satisfactory, being an excellent flavour, and the breast meat remarkably white, the cockerels growing to an immense size. It is said they have the finest skin of any breed in existence.

The birds fatten up quickly for table when young. They breed quite as true as other varieties. The plumage is very glossy in both sexes, but more particularly in the cocks. The sheen should be much the same colour as that of a good Langshan; single comb, evenly serrated in both sexes, standing erect in the cock, not large, but neat, very deep and long in the breast, red face, black legs, not too long, white toe-nails, four toes on each foot, well spread out from each other. The hen's comb may fall a little to one side if it is evenly serrated and without folds in it, but for the show pen these should have quite erect combs.

Some of the pullets come with rather a large comb and in some cases it falls on one side the same as it does in many other breeds. These birds are all right for breeding from for utility, because, as a rule, they are excellent layers, but I do not recommend them to breed from for exhibition though many of them would produce birds fit for show if they were mated carefully. It is not always those who have the best stock birds that produce the choicest specimens; there is a great art in mating the birds. The male birds should always be fully developed in the points where the hens are deficient. For instance, if the hens have very large combs, the cock should have rather a small one, or one strongly set on the head, and if the hens are a good shape, but lack brightness of colour, the male bird should have an extra brilliant gloss upon its feathers, though it may not be such a fine-shaped bird. It is always best to make them up with an unrelated strain. I have many distinct strains of this breed quite unrelated, but there is no difficulty in procuring fresh blood from almost any place in England, as there are many thousands of breeders of this variety situated in different parts of the world. When one is buying eggs, if he does not know the owner of the birds, he is liable to get the eggs from brothers and sisters, because in many cases a person will have a sitting of eggs one year and keep one cock and kill the other male birds, and then breed from the pullets, which are, of course, brothers and sisters. In this case the chickens are liable to come very weak, not only in this variety, but it applies alike to all breeds. There is nothing like having fresh blood, if healthy vigorous birds, and good laying hens are required. The Orpingtons have been known to lay as many as from 30 to 65 eggs without missing a single day. They have laid all through the winter, where it has been cold, wet, and very dirty. The pullets are usually in full lay at six months, many of them at five months. They are splendid birds to breed from, no matter whether the soil is

SINGLE COMB ORPINGTON COCK.

SINGLE COMB ORPINGTON PULLET.

wet or heavy, and they will do well in confinement or when they have a large range.

I knew a lady who had six Orpington pullets one winter, and she said the six birds averaged four eggs a day right through the winter. Another gentleman had 14 pullets and they averaged over 70 eggs per week during the winter. As far as my own experience goes the laying results of the Orpingtons have been better than any other of my pure breeds up to 1895, when in the very severe January and February the Buff Orpingtons beat them entirely in laying. Of course I am referring more particularly to the laying results during the winter months.

At the present day no breed of fowl is used more for crossing with mongrel hens and pure birds of other varieties than Orpington cockerels. I have heard many breeders say that it was quite a job to keep any cockerels for their own domestic use as so many farmers and cottagers want them to improve their stock.

The illustration of this variety will give my readers a good idea of what the breed is, as it is a true representation of one of my best specimens.

THE ORPINGTON—STANDARD.

It being the intention of the Club to fully develop and maintain good laying and table properties, therefore in judging this variety attention should be strongly directed to points indicating these qualities.

COCK.

Plumage.—Close, black throughout, with a " green ' sheen or lustre upon it, free from coloured feathers.

Head.—Small, neat, fairly full over the eye, carried erect.

Comb.—Medium size, erect, evenly serrated, free from side sprigs.

Face, Earlobes, and Wattles.—Red.

Beak.—Black, strong and nicely curved.

Eye.—Black, with dark brown iris, full, bright, and intelligent.

Shape.—Cobby and compact.

Breast.—Broad, deep, and full, carried well forward, long straight breast bone.

Back.—Short, with broad shoulders.

Saddle.—Rising slightly.

Tail.—Medium size, flowing and inclined backward.

Hackles.—Full, both neck and saddle.

Legs and Feet.—Black, strong, short; four claws on each foot, with white nails; sole of feet, white.

Skin.—White, thin, and fine in texture.

Flesh.—White and firm.

Carriage.—Erect and graceful.

Weight.—Between 9 and 10 lbs., when fully matured.

HEN.

Plumage, Head, Comb, Face, Beak, Eye, Breast, Legs and Feet, Skin, Flesh and Carriage.—Same as in the Cock.

Tail.—Medium size, inclined backward and upward.

Cushion.—Small, but sufficient to give the back a short and graceful curved appearance.

Weight.—About 7 or 8 lbs., when fully matured.

POINTS FOR JUDGING.

Plumage and Condition	10
Head	5
Comb	7
Face	5
Beak	3
Eye	5
Shape	15
Breast	10
Tail	5
Saddle or Cushion and Back	5
Legs and Feet	5
Skin and Flesh	5
Carriage	10
Weight	10
	100

DISQUALIFICATIONS.

The slightest feather or fluff on legs or feet.
Yellow skin.
Yellow in legs or feet.
Long legs.

ROSE-COMBED ORPINGTONS.

This variety is exactly the same colour as the Orpingtons and much the same in shape, the only thing they differ in is they have a very neat rose comb. The pullets breed remarkably true, not two out of a hundred will come with mis-marked feathers, though occasionally one will crop up with a little feather on the leg. All the chickens do not come with a rose comb. Wyandottes, Hamburghs, in fact every breed with rose combs are liable to throw single combs. Sometimes there may be thirty birds bred and not one come with a single comb, and I have known as many as three out of ten come with a single comb. This variety stands right away from any other breed, as they are large black birds with rose combs, and there is no other large breed similar to them. This is why so many poultry fanciers and keepers in England take them up in preference to any other variety. In Australia and New Zealand the Rose-Combed Orpington is very popular. I am told it is one of the leading breeds, both in the show pen and for egg and table purposes. They are splendid winter layers of brown eggs, quite equal to the Orpingtons in laying and table qualities, and the pullets usually commence to lay rather earlier. I have had this variety lay at four months and a fortnight old, when they have been hatched in the middle of winter. I found one pullet sitting upon 19 eggs which she had laid away before she was six months old. Many of them are in full lay at five months old, and they are usually all in full lay at 6½ months old if they are managed properly when young. I have known old specimens of this breed to lay over 250 eggs in the year, and the greatest number of these have been produced in the autumn and winter when eggs are most required and command a good price.

Their plumage is a beautiful black, with a green lustre upon it, both in the hens and cocks, but especially in the latter. They make splendid sitters and mothers.

I may mention the chickens are like those of every other black variety, that is to say, they are black on the back and

ROSE-COMB ORPINGTON COCK.

white underneath and round the head when first hatched. Novices often get put out very much when they find chickens from black birds come black and white, but it is a law of nature and cannot be altered. Those which have most white on when hatched as a rule turn out a beautiful metallic green sheen when they become full grown, and are usually marked as the best birds. As chickens, Rose-combed Orpingtons are very hardy and can be brought up in cold and damp places. They fledge well and grow fast. Sometimes they will throw white feathers in the wings, but these usually drop out in the chicken moult. They rapidly grow into good table birds, as they have a fine deep breast and will stand confinement well. In fact they cannot be put in the wrong place. Another thing in their favour is they do not show the dirt in confined runs in towns. I can strongly recommend them as one of the best all-round fowls for both town and country.

The plumage is black throughout in both cocks and hens, with rose combs set close to the head, with a small peak at the back, not turning down like that of a Wyandotte, but keeping quite straight out. Red face and ear-lobes, dark or hazel eyes, black, nicely curved beak, black legs, white toe-nails, four toes on each foot. The cock's tail should be full and flowing, with very fine hangers or sickle feathers, with a beautiful metallic green lustre on them. The tail should be carried fairly well back, but more upright than that of a Langshan. If carried too near the neck it is a fault. The brilliant gloss should always be aimed at when mating these birds. If the male bird has a large comb, put it with hens which have small combs. If the hens lack gloss on their plumage, mate them with cocks which have a few red feathers in their hackles. Whenever a cock shows red feathers he usually produces pullets of a good bright colour. The illustration gives a true representation of what the best specimens of this variety are like.

WHITE ORPINGTONS.

This variety is of a more recent date than the black. They are considerably smaller than the black variety and take rather a different shape to the single and Rose-combed Orpingtons.

There is the same difficulty with these birds as there is with all other white varieties, that is, although they may do well in a confined run in towns, the plumage shows the dirt and they never look nice and bright, but where they can have a nice grass run or a field to roam over they always look nice.

As layers they can hold their own with almost any other breed, the egg being of a nice cream colour, not quite white, of a good size. A few often come broody, and they make fair sitters and mothers when they are allowed to sit. White Leghorns are considered one of the best breeds for laying purposes of the non-sitting varieties, and the White Orpingtons lay about the same number of eggs taking the whole year through, but they do not breed so true as the former, as some of them are liable to throw dark feathers, while in others a few brown ones will crop up, but this is now rare. I only mention it so that those who take up the breed may not be disappointed when they find the White Orpingtons do not breed quite true to colour. The chickens grow remarkably fast, and feather as quickly as young

WHITE ORPINGTON COCK.

WHITE ORPINGTON HEN.

partridges. The cockerels can be killed at a very early age; though they are not large, the skin is as white as that of a Dorking, and the legs are the same colour.

The pullets will lay at five months old, but most of them are in full lay at six and a half months old. To those requiring white birds of a good laying variety, combined with a handsome appearance generally, I can strongly recommend the White Orpingtons. A great many of the aristocracy have taken up this breed in preference to White Dorkings.

The following are the points to be sought after in selecting good specimens of this variety :—neat rose-comb, white beak, red face, white plumage throughout, white legs, four toes on each foot. The cocks should carry their tails fairly well back, much in the same way as a Dorking, only the tails are a trifle smaller and are carried higher than those of the latter. This is what the male birds ought to be bred to, and the points of the hen are just the same, only the combs and tails are smaller.

The cocks are splendid for crossing with White Leghorns, Light Brahmas, or White Dorkings, that is if the owner wishes to keep the stock birds white, and at the same time does not wish the laying qualities to go down.

It must be understood that new breeds are usually excellent layers, because in making them up there is fresh blood blended together. I have heard it remarked by many poultry-keepers that they always try and have every new variety which comes out as they always lay well.

There are two varieties of the White Orpington, the single and the rose comb. The two varieties are identical in character in every way, excepting the comb. In ordering eggs or birds they should be careful to state which —the rose-comb or the single variety—they wish for.

BUFF ORPINGTONS.

Whilst writing upon this variety I am reminded it is eleven years since the Black Orpingtons were introduced. It was at the Dairy Show, in 1894, that this variety made their first appearance. As the Buff Orpingtons have now been before the public some years, I am able to give my readers some idea of how poultry-keepers are taking them up. Thousands of sittings of eggs have been sold and many hundreds of birds. No breed or variety of fowl up to the time Black Orpingtons were brought out ever took so well in England as they did, but the Buffs have sold off quicker in the time even than the Blacks.

Some of my readers may say, Why bring out the Buffs when the Blacks took so well, is it not overdoing it? Not in the least. No one ever complains of a florist bringing out new varieties of flowers, particularly if the colour is more attractive than the old varieties. So with Buff Orpingtons. They are the same shape as the Blacks, but the colour is quite different. It was eight and a half years before the birds were ready to bring out to the public.

I commenced making them when I brought out the Black and the White Orpingtons. In introducing both the latter varieties I mentioned to the public how they were made, and I will do the same with the Buffs. First I mated Golden Spangled Hamburgh Cocks with coloured Dorking hens of good size and from the best laying strains

SINGLE COMB BUFF ORPINGTON COCK.

SINGLE COMB BUFF ORPINGTON HEN.

obtainable. These produced many pullets of a reddish Brown colour which I mated with a Buff Cochin Cock. The Hamburghs are extraordinary layers but are rather delicate to rear as chickens. The Dorking is a splendid table bird, with a very long breast, and when crossed with the Hamburgh will produce wonderful layers. Buff Cochins become very broody and have a great deal of leg feathering. When bred from a good laying strain, however, they make extraordinary winter layers, often producing twenty-eight eggs each per month during winter. When mated with the Hamburgh and Dorking Cross they produce quick growing birds with splendid laying and table qualities. The chickens are so hardy they can be reared in the cold frosty weather.

On the 5th January, 1894 (during which month my readers will remember we had some very severe frosts), I had chickens of this variety hatched out, and they were put in small coops right out in the open, with no shelter whatever except just a thin bag over the front of the coops at night. The snow was simply swept away from the front of the coops.

Some of the pullets began to lay when they were four months and five days old. Those hatched in January were laying in May. Pullets at four months and three weeks old weighed 5lbs. each, and several cockerels at the same age turned the scale at over 6lbs. each, one at 6½lbs. They have been tried in the bleak open fens and marshy parts of Lincolnshire, and their owners find the cold weather does not affect them in the slightest, they appear to grow right before the other chickens. I have also had many letters during the past twelve months from those who have tried this variety, saying they never had chickens grow so fast, and they also feather well, particularly the pullets.

Occasionally some of the chickens will show a little leg feathering, and some will come yellow-legged instead of white, and a fifth toe occasionally will crop up. Some will also throw a few black feathers in the neck instead of coming a beautiful buff all through. I mention this so that those who go in for these birds will not be disappointed. People who come to my farm and see hundreds of the chickens running about are quite struck with them, and often pass the remark, " How uniform in shape and colour they all look." It is only when one gets close up to them a few of the coloured feathers are noticed.

Those cockerels which do come with a little leg feathering or yellow legs do very well for crossing with other varieties, just as well as those which come with clean legs. The pullets which do not come true to colour make quite as good layers as the better specimens. Taking them on the whole they pay well to keep, as the birds are so useful for all round purposes. Those which come true to type and colour are very valuable, and there is a great demand for them, as they are quite different to any breed which has yet been brought out in England. This is the first Buff variety which has yet been brought out with white legs and skin. Nineteen people out of every twenty who see Buff birds are struck with the colour. One reason why Buff Cochins have not taken better than they have in England is because of the long feathers upon their legs and their broody propensities. I have noticed for the last 30 years when a

Dorking has been crossed with a Cochin what splendid chickens have been produced. Cochins are the hardiest breed which has been introduced into this country. This I have proved over and over again. I have known contagious disease break out in various poultry yards, which has seized every other variety upon the place except the Cochins.

Buff Orpingtons, if hatched early, will come on broody fairly early, but will not trouble one so much as several other varieties, because they have Hamburgh blood in them. If allowed to sit, they make splendid sitters and mothers, and often come on to lay when the chickens are from 18 to 21 days old, and take care of their little family at the same time.

Buff is one of the most difficult colours to breed, that is to get a real good Buff all through. It will often fade a great deal in the sun during the summer.

Care has to be taken in mating these birds. If the pullets are a little black in the hackles, but quite clean in the legs and of a good shape, they may be bred from, but should be mated with a cockerel perfectly free from any black in the hackles.

I have known people give from 10/- to 30/- each for fowls which have been bred from good stock and mate them together, and produce better birds than other pens which have cost five guineas each bird. The great secret in breeding good fowls lies in mating them together properly, but there are hundreds of people who do not appear to realize this fact. Both the cocks and hens of this variety should have broad breasts, be fairly short upon the legs, which should be white, and very intelligent looking eyes. This is the standard of the Buff Orpingtons for my readers to refer to.

Cock.	Colour, even Buff throughout, either light or dark shade. Tail, Buff preferable, Black or White allowed, if body Buff (as it is most difficult to produce a Buff tail), points ...	40
Type or Shape.	Body very compact, with broad and deep breast, short back, hackles rather long, full saddle, well up to tail, latter compact, carried well up with plenty of hangers, points ...	25
Legs.	White, free from feathers, fairly short, plenty of substance, four toes on each foot, toes well spread out, points	15
Head.	Comb, medium, firmly set upon head, evenly serrated and straight, free from side spikes, points	10
Beak.	White, or light brown colour, well curved, Eye brown, earlobes and face red, wattles medium, points	10
		100

Weight, eight to ten pounds. Skin and flesh white.

DISQUALIFICATIONS.

Feathers on legs. Five toes. Legs other than white. Crooked breast. Comb on one side.

HENS.

Shape. Body very compact with broad and deep breast, short back. Nice curve from neck to tail. Base of neck rather thick, tail fairly high.

ROSE-COMB BUFF ORPINGTON COCK.

ROSE-COMB BUFF ORPINGTON HEN.

LEGS. White, free from feathers, short, otherwise same as cocks.

HEAD. Comb evenly serrated, standing erect, preferred free from wrinkles and side spikes.

Weight, six to eight pounds. Other points same as the cocks.

ROSECOMBS.

Rose-combed Buff only differ by having a neat rose comb, well set upon the head, with small spike at back, slightly curved.

I have mentioned a few may come with yellow legs, and it often happens the best coloured birds turn out like this.

Occasionally a male bird may have a few white feathers in his tail, but they are more inclined to come with black than white, particularly in the sickle feathers. If a person breeds a nice shaped bird, good colour throughout, including tail, and nice comb, he should have no difficulty whatever in selling it at a good price if he wishes to do so, say from 10/- to 10 guineas.

The Rose-Combed Buff Orpingtons are exactly the same shape and colour as the single-combed variety. Some prefer one and some the other, but the rose-combed birds were always favourites of mine.

It must be understood, however, all rose-combed fowls are liable to throw single combs. Even Hamburghs, which have been out nearly a century, will do this, because the rose comb is a freak of nature in the first place.

If a person has got a good rose-comb cock, and single-combed pullets which have been bred from rose-combed stock, and mates them together, as a rule they will produce the neatest rose combs. It is very seldom we get birds with rose combs bred from single-combed birds.

Buff Orpingtons are not only good fowls for all round practical purposes, but they are also coming up well as a show bird, so they really combine the three qualities, viz., laying and table and exhibition points.

Many of our old breeders say it is impossible to combine these three, but my experience is it is quite possible. Many of my best layers among the Black Orpingtons have won prizes in England, Ireland, and Scotland. The Buff and Black Orpingtons are the two finest birds in all our exhibitions.

DIAMOND JUBILEE ORPINGTONS.

It has been my aim to produce breeds suitable for using for the production of eggs and fowls as articles of food, and these as handsome as it was possible to make them, and in the Diamond Jubilee fowls I think I have succeeded almost beyond my own always sanguine expectations.

The Diamond Jubilee Orpingtons are in reality, so far as colour is concerned, a revival of the old Speckled Dorking, which was in my estimation one of the prettiest birds I have ever known.

Forty years ago it was quite a common thing to put Dorking Cocks down in farmyards, and so a good many birds of this colour are to be found up and down the country.

I had, however, because I have always admired them so, kept some of these birds as nearly pure as possible. They had been inbred to a very large extent, and almost so much so as to spoil the colour. I found out, however, during my

DIAMOND JUBILEE ORPINGTON COCK.

travels, a clergyman, whose father had kept Speckled Dorkings, and because of this the son had always kept a lot. He was anxious to get fresh blood, as he too had to resort to inbreeding, to keep the colour. We therefore exchanged some of our stock, and as all practical breeders will know to good advantage too.

When crossing I found the progeny came very much larger, and the laying qualities were revived and improved.

About ten years ago I had begun experimenting by crossing Hamburghs and Cochins, so that these Diamond Jubilee birds are made very much in the same way as the Buff Orpingtons, only that a Speckled Dorking is used instead of a Coloured Dorking. The colour is brown, black, white, and the old Speckled Dorking colour is preserved beautifully in this new breed. They should have four toes on each foot, and have perfectly white legs, light horn or white beak, a deep body, long breast bone, and skin and flesh very white, either the single or rose comb variety.

In the hens the tail and wings should have a good deal of white, and underneath the flights they should be white. The tail should be carried fairly well back, and the single comb birds should have erect combs. The cocks should have red face, and the breast should be the same colour as the hen's body. The hackles and saddle and back on the top should be a bright red, with feathers streaked with white and black. The long wing flights should be white, and also the greater part of the tail.

Sometimes five toes will appear, and such little faults as dark or yellow legs will occasionally crop up, and a bird will come brown, but all these very seldom.

Of course proper mating will soon make these faults impossible, and it will be found that these Diamond Jubilee Orpingtons will worthily follow in the train of those other Orpingtons that have gained a world-wide fame.

ANCONAS.

The Anconas are quite a new variety of fowls. The name has been known in England many years, but not in connection with this breed of fowls which some people say was introduced from Ancona in Northern Italy, and not made in England.

It matters little, however, where they originated from as they are evidently one of the best non-sitting varieties for laying purposes that England has ever possessed.

One gentleman brought some of them from Ancona, in Italy, but it must be remembered that Leghorn blood also comes from Italy, only the birds have been improved.

Of course anybody who went to Italy and picked up birds here and there might get one of these birds, which are of very distinct colour and of the Leghorn stamp of fowls, and then call them by any name they chose. Some Ancona breeders declare they are not of Leghorn extraction, but I am certain they are.

I have as perfect Anconas as one would wish to see, which have been bred from Black and White Leghorns, and these birds have never seen Italy, nor their parents either.

They can either be got by crossing Black and White Leghorns, or bred from sports from Leghorns, but however

ANCONA COCK.

produced, because they are a new breed, they are quite sure to be good layers, and they will become popular, as people like something fresh.

Many poultry-breeders are surprised that I am taking up Anconas as I have brought out so many new varieties myself, but if I find anything is good I take it up at once, and it is surprising how quickly people are taking Anconas up. There is one thing about them and that is their striking colour. Most of my readers will know what the appearance of the Houdan is like, black and speckled, and know how striking the colour is.

The Ancona cocks have large combs which should be just like a Leghorn's, well set on the head and with large serrations; white ear-lobes, which should be considerably smaller than those of the Leghorn, long wattles, yellow beak, streaked sometimes with a darker shade, face red, eye brown or hazel, and yellow legs, or these latter in some cases a little mottled or with a few streaks, with four toes on each foot well spread apart.

The plumage should be speckled black and white, and free from red feathers and the carriage very upright. They should be compact birds and with tail carried rather high; they have an alert appearance and are very nervous.

The hens are just the same colour as cocks, the comb should be over to one side, and the more evenly marked the better. In breeding if hens or pullets are light in colour they should have a dark cock mated with them, or *vice versa*.

Anconas breed fairly true to colour. I have known them lay over 100 eggs by the time they were nine months old, and altogether they have proved themselves extraordinary layers, and the two year old birds lay very large eggs according to their size.

Anconas stand confinement well and are very good birds to range far away for food if they have their liberty. The cockerels are splendid birds for turning down among cross birds where people go in for eggs, and I can recommend them very highly. Although they are a new breed I have several strains unrelated.

BANTAMS.

Bantams not useless—Juvenile interest awakened and results in after life—Favourite varieties—Mistakes and Pleasures—Hints as to management.

THESE small birds are often looked upon as useless by many, and even those who keep the larger breeds. The day of small things should not be despised, as small beginnings often produce large endings. There are many large breeders of the present day who only commenced with a pair of Bantams, and trace their success and love of poultry to their parents allowing them to keep these pets. I think it so nice to allow a boy or girl to keep a few fowls; and Bantams can be kept where the larger breeds cannot.

Young people must have something to do in their spare time; and if parents do not find it for them, they will for themselves, and not always in the best direction. It would be well for parents to study their children a little more in this respect, as it gives young people a love for their homes, whether the pets are fowls, pigeons, or rabbits. I have kept all three, and the former not only gave me much pleasure in looking after them, but also paid for their food, and a little over. I always had an eye to pleasure and profit combined. Bantams usually give young people a great deal of pleasure. Many people keep them all their lives, and make a study of them. If a cockerel and pullet are purchased, they will soon breed a pen of birds. A dog kennel, or large box, will serve as a roosting house, or a little house 2ft. 6in. square would be large enough for a cock and four hens. Game Bantams are kept more than any variety, especially the black-breasted reds.

The Duckwing and Pile are favourites with many. The colour of the birds should be much the same as the Game fowls of these varieties. If persons are desirous of keeping good specimens, it is well for them to go to a good show, or to where the best Bantams can be found. It is always advisable to prepare Bantams for the show pen, especially the black rose-comb, as birds of this variety require great care. Refer to the chapter on "Preparation for the Show Pen."

BLACK ROSE-COMB.

This variety is spreading rapidly, and is becoming one of the favourites in the Bantam fancy. They are my favourites as they are not only very pretty little birds, but such good layers and very hardy. Being black they do not show the dirt when kept in the back yards of towns. Many of our leading fanciers first started by keeping a pair of these birds. I always like to encourage young people in keeping these pets. Birds of this breed should have nothing but black feathers, with a splendid gloss on their plumage, especially the male birds. Both sexes should have a neat rose comb, red face, free from spots or streaks of white, and small white ear-lobes, free from wrinkles and red spots, black legs, four

ROSE-COMB BLACK BANTAMS.

ROSE-COMB WHITE BANTAMS.

toes on each foot. The cocks should be very full in the breast, and have a fine flowing tail. The smaller they are the better, if they are compact and well-shaped. Where so many make a mistake in breeding Bantams is they hatch them out too early in the season. If they are not required for the show pen until November, May or early June is the best time to hatch them out. If for the summer shows, they may be hatched out early. The smallest Bantams I ever bred were hatched in the month of September. I have found this variety the best layers of any Bantams, and also of the largest eggs according to the size of the bird. They can be kept in a very small pen, if required. One male bird may run with about three or four hens. In all cases where they have not a grass run they ought to be supplied with green food. Nothing is better than watercresses where they can be procured reasonably, and chopped grass and dandelion. The chickens hatch out strong. When first hatched they are black on the back and a light colour underneath. Occasionally they throw white feathers in their wings, but usually shed them in their chicken moult.

WHITE ROSE-COMB.

These are the same shape, and have the same characteristics as the black, differing only in the colour of legs and plumage, which are both white.

T

CROSS-BRED FOWLS.

Cross-bred Fowls: what they really are—The utility and great value of the system, and the advantages accruing therefrom—Crossing and re-crossing Houdan-Orpington—Houdan-Minorca—Houdan-Leghorn — Houdan-Indian Game — Minorca-Langshan — Leghorn - Plymouth Rock — Dorking - Brahma — Indian Game-Plymouth Rock — Indian Game - Dorking — Indian Game-Buff Orpington—Buff Orpington-Dorking—Orpington-Dorking — White Orpington-Light Brahma—Orpington-Brahma—Leghorn-Orpington

BEFORE proceeding to give a description of cross-bred fowls I wish to make it quite clear what they really are, for I often hear birds that are sheer mongrels called cross-breds.

What is called a first cross is a bird obtained by crossing two pure bred fowls of different varieties mated together, say a Dorking and Game, and if their offspring are crossed again, the chickens are called a second cross if a pure male bird is used. If first cross hens are bred from with a pure cock the progeny will be second cross birds.

For instance, if a hen of Rock and Langshan cross is mated with a Dorking Cock her offspring have three breeds in them, half Dorking, a quarter Langshan, and a quarter Plymouth Rock, and if these are bred from again the progeny may very properly be called mongrels unless a pure cock is used, in which case they are half-bred fowls.

The question is often asked, Why not breed from cross-bred cockerels? The principal reasons are—1st, the chickens bred from them eat a great deal more; 2nd, they do not lay so early by six weeks and sometimes three months, and altogether they do not show such good qualities as the first crosses, although, of course, there are exceptions. I proved that first-cross pullets were best by having some first-cross and some mongrel birds hatched at the same time and all brought up together, when I found that the first-cross pullets laid from a month to three months earlier than the in-bred mongrels.

There are many opinions as to the advisability of breeding and keeping cross-bred fowls, for while one eminent author will write, "Cross your fowls as much as possible; you cannot have too many breeds mixed;" another will say, "Pure-bred fowls are best, as, while some of them average 170 to 200 eggs per bird in the year, cross-breds will only lay 80 to 120 in the same time." My own experience has been that first-cross fowls, or selected mongrels, or cross-bred hens (if they are good layers) mated with a pure-bred cock, are much the best for general purposes if people study economy. If a pure hen will lay from 120 to 130 eggs in a year, and she is mated with a pure cock of another breed, and the cock has been bred from a hen which laid about the same number of eggs in the time, the offspring will produce from 150 to 190 eggs in a year, for in cross birds the qualities of two pure-bred fowls are blended together. For instance, in half-bred Hamburghs and Cochins, there is part of the hardiness and size of the Cochin, and part of the plumpness, non-sitting and wonderful laying qualities of the Hamburghs; and besides this, cross-breds are generally larger and hardier, on account of fresh blood being introduced. I do not wish to run down pure fowls in any way, for without them, of course, no cross could be produced; but I do most decidedly recommend a half-bred when only laying fowls are required, and have, therefore, written fully on some of the principal crosses I have tried. What I wish to make clear is this, that a person may often have from 20 to 50 hens running say in a farm yard, either mongrel birds or from pure cocks. In such cases, say ten of the best layers should be picked out and then a pure cock mated with them. Sometimes a person has no place in which to shut them up separately, in that case they should get two pure cocks and turn them down with the whole number. Farmers, and those who keep a large number of birds should use pure cocks every year, as by so doing they would save 25 per cent. more a year, and pullets uniform in shape and colour would be produced.

There are, of course, many I have not mentioned, but I have written on those I consider best. For instance, if it is more convenient, a Leghorn or Minorca cock may be used instead of Hamburgh or Spanish, or Creve Cœur in place of Houdan, or Brahma in place of Cochin, &c.

It would take too much space to describe in detail all the crosses that might be made with a Houdan cock, but if people have either Brahma, Cochin, Plymouth Rock, Orpington, Wyandotte, Langshan or even mongrel hens, the effect—as regards their laying qualities—of their mating with a Houdan cock would be in each case about equal, if all the hens were bred from good laying strains. The pullets from the Langshan, Plymouth Rock, Orpington, and particularly Indian Game and Dorking, would make the best table birds. Why I class all these together is that some people have Brahmas or other birds by them, and if they read that one variety is a good one to mate with the Houdan cock, they immediately conclude that breed alone is the one which should be used, while possibly the birds they have would, if crossed, produce equally good results, without giving them the further expense and trouble of buying in fresh birds. All the varieties mentioned are good sitters, while the Houdan is a non-sitting variety, so about one half of the pullets will want to sit.

If anyone has a taste for crossing, and still wishes to retain his pure-bred fowls, he may easily do so by letting two pure hens run with a cock of the same breed and four or six more of a different kind. I may mention that a Houdan cock, with two Houdan, two Minorcas, and two Orpington hens, answers very well, and that it is always best when crossing non-sitters to have a Langshan, Plymouth Rock, or Orpington, to be sure of a broody hen for sitting in the Spring.

The number of eggs I have given as being produced by certain crosses may seem very large, but it must be understood that it is only birds bred from the *very best* laying strains that will produce these numbers; and great attention must, of course, be paid to their feeding and management. Amateurs must, therefore, not be discouraged if their birds do not produce such numbers for the first year or two. Those, however, who give attention to the birds, and follow my instructions, will find an increase in the number of eggs they obtain every year.

I have known fowls lay from 100 to 275 eggs in a year, but the numbers vary according to the laying strains, and the way in which the birds are kept and managed. The owners must have practical knowledge, and this is obtained by closely watching the habits of the fowls. It is usually those who are fondest of their fowls that succeed the best in the end. A book may be a great help and guide, but this will not do all that is required in the poultry yard. Persons may get good advice from a book, but they must have practical experience if they want to do well and make their poultry pay.

HOUDAN-ORPINGTON.

Houdan and Creve Cœur cocks are very much the same in qualities, especially when used for crossing, as it is impossible to detect a Houdan cross from a Creve cross, and where it is more convenient to do so a Creve Cœur can always be used in place of the Houdan cock.

In former editions I recommended Cochins for this cross but the Orpingtons are better table birds, lay far more eggs, and have quite as strong constitutions as the Cochins.

The chickens from these crosses will hatch out well and fledge quickly, especially the pullets. They are very hardy, and will do well in cold or *wet* weather; while, as a rule, chickens cannot stand wet weather, but I have reared these chickens from a week old; and the death rate has been very low, some years not a single chicken dying after they are a week old, although they have never been inside the hen house, or had a shed to protect them from the wet and cold at night, living entirely in a coop until a short time before laying. They make good table birds, often being ready to kill when three months old, and are very plump and of good flavour, the skin on the body being very white. Seventeen out of every 20 pullets are black; sometimes they have white legs, but there are a few with black, while some of the pullets will come with a brown mottled breast, similar to that of a thrush, the groundwork being of a darker colour, particularly when they are bred with Buff, White, or Jubilee Orpingtons. The hens lay fine eggs, generally brown, some tinted, and a few white, that will command a good price in any market. They will do well in confinement or with a large run, are very healthy, and I have never had them suffer from anything except cramp.

For all-round birds, winter layers, and table birds combined, the Houdan-Orpington is *the* best of all the crosses I have tried out of over 100 different first crosses.

HOUDAN-MINORCA.

Both these are non-sitting varieties, and therefore the cross birds produce white eggs, and while I am describing the qualities of the Houdan-Minorca, I may mention that the Houdan-Andalusian answers the same purpose, as one can scarcely be told from the other.

The birds producing this cross can be mated either way. I prefer the Houdan cock, as the eggs are more fertile when crossed in this way. Houdan hens, having a crest and beard, are often a little timid, as they cannot see behind them, neither side face. Owing to this, rather a large proportion of the eggs are unfertile. If the Minorca cock is used eight Houdan hens are sufficient; if the Houdan cock with Minorca hens, ten to twelve, and in many cases fourteen hens are not too many if they have a good range. The eggs from this cross are very fertile. The chickens when hatched are dark or black on back, and yellowish-white underneath. The heads are usually black and white, and show a small top-knot and beard; they are fairly strong, fledge well, and grow fast. Most of the pullets come black, and make good-sized birds; they have blue or black legs. The cockerels usually have coloured feathers in their hackles and saddles, a kind of straw colour. They require to be removed from the pullets at an early age—about three months—as they become rather troublesome. They make fair table fowls, and the meat is of a superior flavour, but very white; not a popular fowl for the market unless hatched early and sold as spring chickens, then they make a good price, as they are very plump and have not much bone. This cross is noted for the size of the egg, being the finest for size of any cross. They are eggs that always command a good price in the market, notwithstanding they are white. A few of these mixed with smaller ones are often the means of obtaining a longer price for the small ones. Where fowls are kept for the purpose of selling eggs, I recommend some birds of this cross to be kept. In the number of eggs they differ very much according to the strain, from 105 to 220; I put the average down at 150 eggs per bird per annum. I have had them lay 240 in a year, but these are exceptions, not the rule. They will stand confinement well, and lay all through the winter months, especially if they can be sheltered from the cold winds. They are very active and want employment. They are fowls that will suit all classes of people, in town or country. They are non-sitters, but occasionally there is one that will want to sit, but they cannot be depended upon. As non-sitters I recommend Houdan-Minorcas, especially where only eggs are required and sitting varieties are not wanted. They are good foragers, hardy, easy to rear, and good layers.

HOUDAN-LEGHORN.

For a non-sitting cross this cannot be surpassed in number of eggs and hardiness of fowl. The birds may be brought up in small back yards, and will grow fast and feather well, giving but little trouble. They are remarkably active as chickens; when first hatched they are black on the back and yellowish-white underneath, and usually show a small top-knot, and a few come quite white. The cockerels ought to be killed off early, as they become very troublesome when they are from twelve to fifteen weeks old. If kept longer they ought to be separated from the pullets. They do not make large table fowls, but are very plump, have small bones, and the flesh is very white and juicy. I do not recommend them as a market table fowl, unless it is for early spring chickens, when they are not required so large. They stand the cold weather very well, and are ready for table earlier than the larger breeds. Some of the pullets commence to lay very early, sometimes at four months old. This is rather too early, as if they commence when from five and a half to six months old it is better for them, and the eggs are larger. These are white, of a medium size, a little larger than a Dorking's. A good proportion of the pullets come black, but sometimes a number of white are produced, and if brown Leghorn hens are used some have brown hackles, but all have black bodies. They are very compact fowls, and will work well for their living when they have an opportunity. They fly if they have their liberty, but if brought up in a wire pen they are very contented. Where eggs are required all the year round I strongly recommend the cross as a non-sitting breed, as they will stand any amount of damp and cold weather and they will not disappoint their keepers. If bred from a good laying strain they often lay 200 eggs each in a year, when kept in confined runs. They, of course, vary very much according to the method of management. The average is about 170 eggs each per annum. Some specimens have laid over 270 eggs in twelve months. The eggs from Leghorn hens with Houdan cocks running with them hatch remarkably well, very seldom less than nine chickens out of twelve eggs, and in many cases eleven or twelve. Leghorn hens are very good to breed from. It is much the best to run a Houdan cock with these hens; from seven to twelve of the latter to one male bird. For those who only require eggs, and especially if only for home consumption, a more profitable cross cannot be kept, if something is given them to scratch in so as to keep them employed.

The number of eggs produced by these birds is marvellous, and if six hens in their second year and six pullets can be kept, the owner would never be without eggs in the cold dark days of winter. This cross can be hatched very late in the season when it is necessary. July and August hatched chickens will often lay at the end of January and during February. I have known them to be hatched the last week in August, and in full lay the first week in January. This cross ought to be named the "Amateur's Friend," considering their good qualities, as they hatch out well, are very hardy as chickens, can be reared in small back yards, grow fast, fledge well, lay early and constantly, and cannot well be put in the wrong place. If they are allowed their liberty they travel long distances, but seldom lay away from home. This is one of the crosses I recommend to those about to start poultry-keeping, and to any who cannot spare much time in looking after their birds. If the birds in a breeding-pen have the advantage of a grass run, the eggs are more fertile, and a larger number of hens may be allowed with the male birds. Hamburghs can be used, and the results will be very much the same with a Houdan cock, only the eggs are not quite so large, although the laying results are about equal.

HOUDAN-INDIAN GAME.

This cross may be produced by running a cock of either breed. The best results are obtained when the Houdan male bird is used. From ten to twelve hens may be allowed to run with either male bird, providing the fowls have a good range. The chickens hatch out well, are remarkably hardy, fledge and grow very quickly. They have a great deal of breast meat, and can be killed any time after they are about twelve weeks old. Very often they do not require fattening, but can be killed straight from the yard unless required for market. The pullets make good winter layers of fair-sized eggs, especially if they have their liberty, and have a wood to range in. The eggs can usually be depended on all through the winter months; some are white, and some are tinted. If the Game cock is used many of the chickens come brown when first hatched; if they are crossed the other way they come black and white.

I may mention in finishing up the Houdan crosses that the pullets can be bred from again with cocks of other breeds, but they always have rather a mongrel appearance, as some come with a bib, while others have a top-knot.

MINORCA-LANGSHAN.

For a black cross-bred fowl I know nothing that will breed truer to colour than the Minorca-Langshan, or Langshan-Minorca, whichever way they are crossed. Ninety-nine out of every hundred come black, with a beautiful gloss on their plumage. All have black legs, with four toes on each foot. There may be one occasionally with five toes, but these are very rare. They are well shaped birds, and take the eye of those who are partial to black fowls. They are splendid layers either in confined runs or an open space, and they cannot well be put out of their place.

A Minorca cock may run with from seven to nine Langshan hens, or a small Langshan cock with about the same number of Minorca hens. The latter must be large and strong, if not the results will be unsatisfactory, and great care must be taken if success is to be gained when birds are mated in the latter way. It makes no difference in the colour and qualities of the offspring which ever way they are crossed. They hatch out well, and make strong chickens, the pullets fledging fairly well, while the cockerels are a little naked for a time. They lay good-sized tinted eggs, some being brown. They average from 150 to 170, and many will lay 200 in the year, usually commencing to lay when from 5½ to 6½ months old. About half of them become broody. They make good mothers, but are rather timid when sitting; they want handling gently. They make good table fowls, skin and flesh exceedingly white, of good flavour, and juicy. I do not know of a fowl a better flavour, but of course their black legs go against them in the market. The cockerels should be killed early, from 13 to 16 weeks old, if not they must be kept from the hens and pullets. The best laying hens of this cross may be kept until they are two or three years old. They do not get so fat internally as birds of many other crosses do.

This cross may be classed with some of the best layers, both winter and summer. They are excellent for confined runs, as they do not show the dirt. A few of them are slightly feathered on the legs. When first hatched, the chickens of this cross are black on the back and yellowish-white underneath. I strongly recommend them when large eggs are required all the year round. They are one of the most popular crosses we have in England, as they are excellent birds to breed from again. In shape and attitude they resemble the Minorca-Brahma and Minorca-Plymouth Rock. I have bred an immense number of them, usually keeping several pens of this cross. I cross both ways, one pen either way, but the most economical method is to mate a Langshan cock with Minorca hens, as more eggs are produced from the Minorca hens during the breeding season than from the Langshans.

If one wants a good-sized bird, brown eggs, and winter layers, they should use a Buff Orpington with the Langshan-Minorca pullets. If they are crossed with a Buff Orpington cock they come, most of them, with a black back and a beautiful mottled breast and hackles, and every pullet comes a good shape. If table birds are required to be bred from these pullets, mate with a Dorking cock.

LEGHORN-PLYMOUTH ROCK.

The Leghorn cock can run with from seven to nine Plymouth Rock hens if he is a strong bird, and ten eggs out of twelve will be fertile. Any variety of the Leghorn may be used. If the brown is used many of the pullets come that colour, and a few the colour of the Rock. If the white, there is a variety of colours, some quite white, some a mixture of white and drab, and a few the colour of the Rock. They make excellent layers of a fair sized tinted egg, saleable in market. I recommend this cross to be kept where birds are exposed to the cold east winds, or where there is a wet soil. They are very active and so hardy they cannot be put in the wrong place. They do as well in confined runs as in a grass field. For number of eggs and hardiness of fowl, there are few that will surpass this cross. Some pullets will lay over 100 eggs before they are 12 months' old, and in a few cases 120. Where birds are wanted for laying only, this is one of the best crosses that can be kept, and it will become one of the most prominent of the day for egg-production.

There are many specimens that lay 260 eggs in twelve months. These are, of course, bred from the best laying strains, and are all well looked after. The average number of eggs per annum is from 170 to 200. They can be hatched all the year round, if required. They are so hardy they fledge like partridges, many being fully fledged at three weeks old. There are a few of the cockerels a little backward in fledging.

I cannot recommend them as table fowls for the market, as their legs are a bright yellow, and many of the skins the same colour, which many people object to. The flesh is juicy, but with rather a yellow cast upon it, especially when good stock birds are bred from them. They are of a fair size, mature very quickly, and may be killed at three months old. If kept any longer they must be separated from the hens and pullets; if not they become very troublesome. The pullets are of a more uniform colour when the Rock cock is used, as many of them are marked like the Rock. The legs and beak are a much brighter yellow.

A large Rock cock should never be allowed to run with Leghorn hens; if so, many of the latter will be badly injured. Small compact cockerels should be used for this purpose. If the Rock cock is an active bird, not less than nine hens should run with him, rather over than under that number. It does not affect the size or colour of the eggs which way the birds are crossed. About five out of twelve of the pullets want to sit.

DORKING-BRAHMA.

This cross was once very popular but it is not now so much in vogue. The best way of crossing is to have a Dorking cock with from six to nine Brahma hens; either variety of Dorkings may be used for crossing; the coloured or silver grey are the best varieties to use, but the former is a little larger, and is more used for the table.

The chickens from this cross are healthy and strong, may be hatched early, grow very large and make good table birds. The cockerels should be killed off when they are from three to four months old, as, after this, they will not be fit to kill until they are six to eight months old, at which age they will be like young turkeys for size, and will realize good prices in the leading markets. They are a splendid cross for the Sussex fatteners, as they make up well, and always realize a good price in the London market. The pullets commence laying from seven to eight months old, and lay better than the pure Dorking, but are often broody.

If any are allowed to sit, care should be taken to select those that have four toes on each foot, as when the hens have five large claws on each foot, they break the eggs and kill the chickens when hatching out; if those with large feet are used for sitting, the young chickens that are hatched first should be removed while the others are hatching, and placed in wadding in a box or basket before the fire, to prevent their being trampled to death.

If desired, Cochins may also be crossed with the Dorking, the chickens from this cross will resemble the Brahma-Dorkings in many ways, but the cockerels grow a little longer in the leg. As a rule the pullets lay about the same, and most of them come a buff colour.

If the owners of cross-breeds, mentioned above, wish to do away with broody hens, and, at the same time, desire to have an increase in the number of eggs laid and retain delicacy of the flesh, I advise their running the cross-bred pullets with a Minorca or Houdan cock, using the Houdan if possible, as the colour of the legs is more suitable for table.

By breeding in this way there will not be half so many broody hens, and those that are broody will be more easily cured and commence laying much sooner; the chickens will be quite as hardy, grow shorter in the leg, feather earlier, have more breast meat, and only about two out of twenty will have blue or dark legs. The cockerels will be ready for table two weeks sooner, and the pullets will lay six weeks to two months earlier, laying, as a rule, when they are from five to six and a half months old. These birds are excellent for anyone with plenty of room, as they scratch and look well after their living; and about ten to twenty per cent., more would be realised by again crossing in this way than by breeding the first cross of Brahma-Dorkings or Cochin-Dorkings.

In selecting the birds for breeding the above, care should be taken to choose the hens that lay best, and a Houdan cock with as light-coloured legs as possible.

INDIAN GAME-PLYMOUTH ROCK.

This cross can be produced either way. A vigorous Indian Game cock can run with from eight to twelve Plymouth Rock hens. The chickens can be hatched all the year round, if required, and are very hardy and strong. They keep very free from cramp, fledge quickly and grow fast.

They make heavy table fowls, having a deep breast, but unfortunately many of them have yellow skins and legs, and occasionally a few have bronze legs, which is rather against them for the market. As they have such a deep cut on the breast they are a very favourite bird in spite of their yellow skin, but sell better in country town markets than in London. They can be killed very young, as early as 11 weeks old; from this age to six months they are always ready to kill when well attended to. The cockerels are rather long in the leg, but in this respect the pullets are very moderate; they have a good shaped body, and many of them come the colour of the Game hens, but when a Rock male bird is used 18 out of 20 come that colour.

A Rock cock may run with from eight to twelve Game hens, if they have a good range. This cross makes good autumn and winter layers of fair-sized tinted eggs. They are good sitters, and may be trusted with valuable eggs: not one or two in a hundred will fail. They are excellent mothers to their own chickens, but if other chickens of different sizes and ages are allowed to run with them, they will kill them, as they are so very spiteful. They will defend their own chickens from rats, stoats, hawks, cats, or dogs in the day time, if they have their liberty. Nothing comes amiss to them.

They are an excellent cross to keep where young pheasants are reared, as they can be depended on as sitters, and are very gentle mothers to their own little ones. They become broody early, so that they will usually hatch out chickens or ducks in January or early in February, and bring up their brood if required, and then sit again early enough for pheasants' eggs. They are a most valuable fowl for gamekeepers, or to those who have a large range for their poultry, and wish to have eggs in the autumn and winter months, they are also early sitters and good table fowls for home consumption. This is one of the best crosses to keep for these purposes.

INDIAN GAME-DORKING.

These birds may be crossed either by running a Game cock with ten Dorking hens, or a Dorking cock with seven Game hens. The chickens will hatch out well, are remarkably hardy, and feather well, often being fully-fledged at three weeks old. They make *very good* table birds, being ready to kill at ten or twelve weeks old; but they may be kept much longer, if required, as the breast meat does not waste away on the young cockerels after they are four months old, as in most other breeds, but, on the contrary, increases. If well fed they do not require fattening, but may be killed at a moment's notice, and will be found in splendid condition, the flesh being white and well-flavoured.

The pullets make fine birds, and lay a medium-sized egg, but very rich in flavour; they average about 100 to 125 eggs in the year according to the laying strain, being fair layers in autumn and winter, but poor in summer. Both parents being sitters they are often broody. They make good mothers where only a few chickens are reared; but, if many of different sizes are brought up together, they often kill them if they go in the wrong coops.

I do not recommend these birds to anyone with only a small yard, as they require a good open run, but for a gentleman with plenty of room, or a person who wishes to breed for the London markets they are just the birds, as they realise a good price for table purposes. They fatten up well when put into the fattening coop.

INDIAN GAME-BUFF ORPINGTON.

The Indian Game-Dorking cross is recommended by many breeders in England when table birds for profit are required.

My own experience has proved that from 15 to 25 per cent. can be saved during the autumn and winter by crossing the Indian Game with Buff Orpingtons in the room of Indian Game-Dorkings, because as most people know the Dorkings are not good layers as a rule, particularly during the winter months, when eggs are most required and most valuable.

Of course if the eggs are not laid it is impossible for people to hatch chickens for spring consumption.

As a rule fifteen Buff Orpingtons will lay more eggs than thirty Dorkings from 1st September to 1st January, just when eggs are most required for hatching birds for early spring, and the chickens grow faster.

Where poultry-keepers once try this cross they will never go back to Game-Dorking again. I have tried many experiments in crossing, but must confess that Indian Game-Buff Orpingtons come right to the top of the tree, and after all experience is the best teacher.

And another thing to be considered is the fact of Buff Orpingtons being so much easier to rear than Dorkings, and the pullets lay at least three months earlier than the Dorkings, and because of this I strongly recommend an Indian Game cock to be crossed with Buff Orpington hens, as the chickens from this cross grow fast and fledge quickly, and the pullets make excellent winter layers.

BUFF ORPINGTON-DORKING.

Many people have already got Dorkings and wish to keep them because they have white legs and are good table birds. In such cases I recommend a Buff Orpington cock to be mated with Dorking hens, as these cross birds are excellent for table, if a good, well-developed Orpington cock is used, and the offspring will equal pure Dorkings, and grow much faster, being ready for the table quicker, while the pullets make excellent winter layers.

ORPINGTON-DORKING.

This cross may be obtained either way. If active, a Black Orpington cock may run with from eight to eleven Dorking hens, that is if he is mated early in the season. This makes a vast difference, as Dorkings are not very early layers in the winter months, but at the same time are very partial to the male birds, so that many of the eggs are fertilised long before the hens commence to lay. It is much the safest way to use the Orpington cock if early chickens are required, as the cold winds do not affect the male birds of this breed so much as the Dorkings. There is not sufficient attention paid to male birds in breeding, especially early in the season, and yet this is chiefly where success or failure commences. Cocks for breeding in all cases should be strong, healthy and vigorous, and not brought up in glass houses or heated fowl-houses, as when such birds are mated with hens many early-hatched chickens are almost out of the question.

The Orpington hens lay much better in the winter than the Dorkings, so it is easy to obtain eggs from the Orpingtons. If it is very early in the season a Dorking cock should not have more than from six to eight hens, but if they have a large range they may have ten. Too much care cannot be bestowed on mating fowls for breeding purposes. The chickens hatch out remarkably strong from this cross, and can be hatched all the year round if required; the pullets fledge very quickly, also most of the cockerels, but about two or three in twenty are a little naked. The cockerels grow to a very large size, and if well fattened will run from eight to ten pounds each at the age of six or seven and a half months old. This cross not only produces large table fowls but the quality is excellent. I know no other cross to equal it, taking everything into consideration. As chickens they are remarkably hardy, and grow fast, even in cold weather; the legs are usually white if mated right.

The flesh is remarkably juicy and of excellent flavour, and if the birds are fed properly they will command the highest prices in the market.

Birds of this cross ought to be bred more for market and also home consumption. This will be done when the cross becomes better known, and there is an increasing demand for good table fowls in all the leading markets, especially in London, and good prizes given at shows for the best cross-bred birds. An Orpington cock that is selected for mating with Dorking hens should have a long deep breast (if pale in the legs so much the better), and good carriage;

plumage is nothing. When the Orpington cock is used, seventeen out of twenty will come black in plumage.

When the Dorking cock is used they come more of a mixture, and the legs are usually rather whiter in colour. The pullets are of excellent shape, and make good autumn and winter layers, most of them laying good-sized tinted eggs which are saleable anywhere.

This cross will stand confinement fairly well, but should not be kept a second year for laying as a rule, unless very good layers, as a few specimens have been. When kept in close confinement they frequently become very fat internally. These birds do well in a moderate run for the first year, but after the pullets have laid one year, that is when they are from eighteen to twenty months old, just before they commence their first adult moult, they will weigh from six to nine pounds each, and are in good condition for the table. They make excellent sitters and mothers, and come very broody in the season. March-hatched pullets will sometimes sit in December. They have a great deal of heat in their bodies, and can be set on Goose or Turkey eggs, if required. They are very quiet, and can usually be removed to a fresh nest, and can cover a large number of eggs. If it is cold, frosty weather, not less than thirteen eggs should be put under them; I do not put less than eighteen. I would recommend less rather than more to those who may not understand making the nest, as it is best to be on the safe side. I give this cross the preference for good table fowls, and some of the most useful breeds to keep.

No birds have been used for crossing purposes in farmyards and among ordinary stock so much during the last six years as Black Orpingtons. Thousands of them have been used all over England for this purpose ; indeed there are more hens and pullets crossed with Black Orpington cocks than of any other variety in spite of their black legs, as they have increased the size of the fowls and improved the eggs. Hucksters who have sent them to London markets from the Midland Counties say that they have got threepence a head more early in the season than they got for ordinary farmhouse birds of any other cross. At present there is a great demand for the Buff Orpingtons in the fattening country, because they are such quick growers. Farmers frequently order ten of them specially for crossing in one farmyard. They will become great favourites for this purpose, as they have white legs, skin and flesh, and are good layers, particularly in cold weather.

WHITE ORPINGTON-LIGHT BRAHMA.

Sometimes, when the owners of light Brahma fowls are satisfied with the laying results, and still a little disappointed in the cockerels for table purposes, there not being such a deep cut of meat on the breast as they would like, they often ask the question, "Can I still retain my white clean-looking fowls, and have as many eggs, and a little better table fowls ? I answer " Yes ; the White Orpington is just the fowl you require." When the White Orpington cock is used with light Brahma hens, the results are very satisfactory. The hens lay better, from 30 to 40 eggs more each in the year. The chickens grow faster, fledge quicker, lay about six weeks earlier, and the cockerels are much better table fowls. They will stand confinement moderately well, if required, but are better for a grass run. A white Orpington cock may run with from seven to nine Brahma hens. The chicks may be hatched out all the winter if required. Eighteen out of every twenty will have white legs and excellent flesh, fit for any market or nobleman's table.

ORPINGTON-BRAHMA.

When black Orpingtons and Brahmas are mated together they produce very large handsome birds, and most of the pullets come black. These latter are splendid winter layers of a large brown egg, and make excellent sitters and mothers. They can be sold at a good price early in the spring for sitting purposes, after they have been laying all through the winter. They are as good as Plymouth Rock-Brahmas for sending upon a journey, or for changing from place to place, as they are so quiet and docile. Birds of this cross can be set on Turkey or Goose eggs, or trusted with valuable pheasant's eggs, and they make large table birds, the flesh and skin are also very white.

As chickens they are remarkably hardy, they grow and fledge well, especially the pullets. Birds of this cross cannot be put in the wrong place, as they will stand the bleak cold winds and damp soils. Some of the cockerels, if fed well, will weigh from 7 to 9 lbs., when they are a little over six months old. This is a consideration when they are required for home consumption, but they are not a cross which would sell well as tip top table birds in the London markets. In the country town markets, especially in the north of England, no class would sell better, as they have such an immense frame. They are splendid birds for a novice to keep, who has not had experience, as they are so little trouble, and are so strong and hardy, both as chickens and adult birds. If they are kept the second year, care should be taken not to get them too fat internally, but when they moult out early in the autumn, after the first year's laying, they will often lay all through the second winter. When they lay late in the autumn it is wise to kill and eat them, as the smallest of them seldom weighs less than 6lbs. I have had some of them turn the scale at 8½lbs.

LEGHORN-ORPINGTON.

These breeds can be crossed either way. A Leghorn cock may run with from seven to ten hens. If they have a large range 15 hens will not be too many, and the eggs will be fertile. They make fair-sized birds, not large, and good layers of a brown or tinted egg. The chickens grow fast, and fledge well at a very early age. Many of the cockerels are ready to kill at three months old. If a white Leghorn is used some of the pullets will come white, but the greater part of them are black. If a brown Leghorn is used most of the pullets will come with black bodies and brown and black hackles. They are much the same in shape as a pure Dorking, the flesh being very white and juicy. In some instances it may be more convenient to use an Orpington cock with Leghorn hens. When this is the case, a small compact bird should be selected. If not, many of the hens get very much injured, and a number of the eggs will be unfertile. This cross can be bred from again with a Houdan cock, but they will lay white eggs. When brown eggs are required a dark Brahma should be used.

DISEASES.

Poultry subject to many diseases—Ignorance of many people respecting this fact and the result of same—"A stitch in time saves nine"—Warm comfortable houses the best preventive of disease—Roup—Liver Disease—Leg Weakness—Gapes—Cramp—Egg Eating—Egg Bound—Crop Bound—Soft Eggs—Comb Disease—Feather Eating—Consumption—Diarrhœa and Dysentery—Dropsy in the Abdomen—Inflammation of the Lungs—Vermin—Bumble Feet in Fowls—Enteritis.

POULTRY are subject to many diseases, and, as a rule, are much neglected when unwell, as they get abuse from their own companions, and the owner often says they must take their chance, live or die, and therefore, the poor sick birds are left with the healthy, and driven about and pecked till they pine and die unhelped and uncared for.

All poultry-keepers should be acquainted with the different diseases fowls are liable to, as, if the knowledge is not needed so much the better, while if the owner has sick birds it will often save pain to the fowls and loss to himself, if most diseases are treated at once, as many valuable fowls may be soon and easily cured that would die if left alone, and if proper precautions are taken it is possible to prevent the disease from spreading to the healthy fowls. " A stitch in time saves nine." Just so with the sick fowls. If the first is saved there is little doubt about the remaining ones. If it is anything very contagious it is best to kill and bury at once, unless birds are very valuable, in case it spreads.

Where a large number of poultry are kept it is well to have a small house by itself, so as to isolate the sick bird at once, as most diseases are infectious little or much. Any kind of house will do that is clean, free from draughts, and well ventilated at the top. The best thing for the floor is chaff or moss-peat, the latter having the preference, as it is a disinfectant, and also keeps the fowls warm and dry, and prevents any excrement from sticking to the feathers.

The house is better not heated, as diseases are often traced to artificially-warmed houses. Poultry should be kept as much as possible in one temperature, and, therefore, if the house is heated, the runs should correspond, being made as warm and snug as possible. This may appear unnecessary, but to those who have tried and studied it it remains a fact; for when fowls come out of a warm house on a cold morning they stick about close together and look miserable, while if it is a mild morning, or a warm run, they will be busy picking and scratching about and enjoying themselves. Fowls roosting out of doors do not feel the cold nearly so much, and also keep free from disease; but if roosting in a warm house the cold nips them very much, and they mope about and refuse to eat, which checks the growth of the chickens and the production of eggs in the older birds, and brings on diseases, and more especially cramp and roup.

One of the most important things to keep poultry in health is to keep their houses and runs perfectly clean. People who do not care for their fowls in this way often wonder why their birds do not lay, but the wonder is they live at all, and probably the only thing that saves their lives is the plentiful ventilation and pure air they get. In the country, about two people out of five keep their poultry in this way, but in the town it is different, as the sanitary authorities compel people to keep their birds clean, or otherwise they would be very offensive in a crowded neighbourhood. The houses should be limewashed at least once or twice a year.

I do not intend in this little work to go very scientifically into the matter of diseases, as it would take up too much space to fully describe all diseases fowls are subject to, but only to mention the most common, and to give the symptoms, and remedies I have found most efficacious in a simple way, so that even boys or girls may understand them, and treat their own fowls in a similar manner.

ROUP.

This disease is usually brought on by cold or sudden chill to which birds are liable on very hot days and cold nights, or by sitting in a draught when the fowls have not been used to it, or sleeping out of doors one night and in a nice warm house the next, getting wet and cold and then sitting in a draught, or the house closed up with a number of birds in it without sufficient ventilation, all these things will bring on cold or roup. More birds get roup from the latter cause than from all others put together. When fowls are accustomed to sleep in trees and are put direct into a warm house, or into a covered basket and sent on a railway journey, especially when sent to a show after sleeping out of doors, they are almost sure to return with roup.

When poultry are travelling by rail and are allowed to stand for hours on a draughty platform—especially when coming home from a show, after having been taken out of a crowded place, where it has been very hot, and the railway officials allow them to stand for hours on the platform in the middle of the night—some of them are sure to have roup. I have mentioned a few causes of this disease. It comes in three different forms. The first symptoms appear quite distinct from each other.

When a fowl first takes cold and the system is in good order, the first symptom is a little running at the nostrils. At first the discharge is clear water, but if neglected the mucus becomes thick and the nostrils stopped up, and it usually ends in roup. If not taken in time and treated properly the fowl soon begins to cough and sneeze. The running from the nostrils may last for a long time. I have known this to continue for three months and not lay the birds up. This discharge from the nostrils goes harder with chickens than with old hens, and if they do not get good attention it stops their growth. When the first symptoms appear they should be examined to see if the mouth and throat are free from white spots or ulcers, and with no rattling noise in the throat. Their nostrils should be squeezed so as to clear out all the mucus, by putting the fore-finger in the roof of the mouth, and the thumb over the nostrils. If the fore-finger is not put in the roof of the mouth the mucus may partly stop the breathing as it is pressed inwards instead of outwards. The nostrils should be washed afterwards with a little alum and water. It is well to dip a feather in the alum solution, and put down the fowl's throat. If it is a little sore or inflamed, the alum will do it good. Give one heaped-up teaspoonful of Roup Powder to six hens; chickens proportionately. The powder should be given in the morning meal. If they object to eat it then, mix it with about two handfuls of meal and throw down, a small quantity at a time, when they will run after it and swallow it greedily. If they refuse to eat it when given in this way they must have pills, as will be seen further on.

As a rule there is no difficulty in getting them to take it. When there is only a running at the nostrils, and no offensive smell, they may be allowed to run with the other fowls without any danger of them infecting the others. If this cold is neglected there is a very offensive smell from the fowl's breath, and a discharge from the nostrils, dried all round the outside, often preventing it from breathing, also thick saliva in the mouth, and if this is not stopped it soon turns to a thick mucus, and corrodes very fast, spreads down the throat, and causes the fowl to breathe very hard, and soon the worst symptoms of diphtheric roup are fully developed. In very bad cases a thick cheesy matter forms on the tongue, mouth, and down the throat. It grows very fast, so much so in bad cases that the tongue protrudes from the mouth, and the bird appears to be swallowing all the time. In some cases the mouth is clear to all appearance, and the fowls look quite healthy and eat well up to the hour of their death. The only symptoms which appear are, the bird opens its mouth to breathe, and if watched may be seen to try to throw something up from its throat, but in vain. In such a case the fowl should be caught (a second person usually is required to hold its mouth open), the opening of the trachea (that is the windpipe) should be worked up and down from the outside by the thumb and finger. The fowl's mouth should be held wide open, if not the opening cannot be seen, and hold the head quite still for a few seconds, and when the fowl breathes the opening of the windpipe can be seen. Then dip a feather in some Roup lotion. Do not strip the feather, but well saturate it with the lotion. It should be a small pointed feather, plucked or clipped from a fowl's wing. A tail feather will not answer this purpose. The opening is small, so care must be taken to put the feather right down the windpipe and not the throat or swallow. It may be put from two to four inches down the pipe. Give two or three twists round and draw it out slowly, and in most cases there will be little pieces of fungus adhering to the feather, a kind of whitish-yellow matter. It looks like crumbs of cheese.

In some cases it can be seen just at the top of the windpipe; sometimes it is half as large as a small pea, and in other cases it may not be larger than a pin's head, but in all cases it should be well saturated with the lotion with another feather. Then use the quill end of the same to rub off any white spots that may be seen at the top of windpipe or in the mouth. In most cases it will peel off very easily; if not it will the next morning. If a sharp instrument is used it may injure the fowl if it makes a slight struggle. It usually bleeds a little when removed. In some cases it grows again; if so, treat as before, and it will gradually get better. Always take care to burn the feather which has been used.

When the lotion has been used for a fowl's throat it is well afterwards to pour down half a teaspoonful of salad oil out of a small bottle, which saves time. Sometimes this scrofulous matter forms on the side of the mouth; occasionally it forces the mouth out so that from the outside it looks like a swelling. The lotion should be used in the same way, but it will require more of it. Sometimes it is necessary for a few drops to be dropped on or in, as in some cases when the fungus is removed there is a hole. In this case do not omit the salad oil, as stated previously. When the disease comes in the last two forms I have mentioned, or in a similar way, the fowls do not always have a discharge from the nostrils. It sometimes stops their laying, but does not appear to injure their health, unless in very bad cases. If neglected, it usually ends in death.

What is called canker in pigeons is much the same thing, and can be cured in the same way. If, however, the birds are not valuable and their mouths are filled up with fungus, it is best to kill and bury at once, the first loss is best. When birds have been penned up closely in coops in the London and other markets, they are the birds which usually spread the disease in poultry yards. Roup shows itself in quite a different form at times, viz., with a swelling in the face and round the eye. The first symptom is usually a little white foam round the eye, and the fowl will frequently scratch this with a toe nail. Sometimes before anything else is visible these symptoms will appear; at times the fowl's nostrils are quite dry, and at others there is a slight discharge with an offensive smell. Sometimes in the course of twelve hours the fowl's face has swollen to such an extent that the eye is completely closed up. When this is the case the face should be bathed at once with very warm water, using a sponge or piece of flannel. Bathe it for a short time, from two to five minutes, according to the condition. In all cases wipe the face quite dry; if not, more harm than good will be done, as the fowl is apt to take fresh cold. A little alum may be put in the water used for bathing the fowl's face with advantage. Painting with iodine directly after bathing is an excellent thing, as it draws the inflammation out very quickly. They must be very bad cases that the last remedy does not cure. Bathe twice a day.

The fowls should be out of the draught and yet have plenty of air in a fairly warm place, but not a heated one, unless they are very ill, when warmth is required. When they are recovering they should be hardened off a little at a time, particularly in cold weather, first put in a snug outhouse, then in an open shed. The first time they are allowed to go in a pen should be in the middle of the day; if not they may take cold again.

In some instances the swelling of the face does not go down, or only partly so, but becomes much harder. In such cases as these there is a hard, cheesy lump formed under the skin, which should be lanced carefully and squeezed, one finger being inside the fowl's mouth. Seven out of ten can be cured in this way. Sometimes it settles under the ball of the eye; in such cases the bird loses its sight.

Roup comes in three different forms, and whichever it comes in it can usually be cured. My advice is if the bird is not valuable kill it at once, but valuable birds should be treated at once as described, or isolate the bird from the others, especially if there are many kept. Treat the affected bird with roup powder, and add camphor to the water for the unaffected birds. If the fowls are free from liver disease, and inflammation can be kept from the lungs, not five in 100 will die if treated properly. It is always safe to give a spoonful of salad oil when a bird shows any of the symptoms mentioned.

When roup or any contagious disease breaks out, it is always well to give one teaspoonful of Epsom salts to every 10 or 12 birds, but if very bad, one teaspoonful to eight is not too much. It opens the pores of the skin, and they are liable to take cold, so that roup powder should be used at the same time, that will counteract it and prevents them taking cold.

If the bird is breathing hard, give a teaspoonful of salad oil, this may ease it considerably. If the rattling in the throat is very bad and the breathing very hard, the lungs should be painted with iodine, There is a place free from feathers just under each wing, where the lungs lie, and this spot should be painted over. The exact place to apply the iodine can easily be detected if the bird is watched as it breathes, as the movement of the lungs can be seen if the wings are held up. The iodine will soon give the bird relief, and ease the breathing considerably, unless there is tuberculous matter formed over the lung, which nothing will remove. In several cases I have taken from the lung of a dead bird a piece of matter 1½in. long by ½in. wide.

Stewed linseed is very strengthening to a sick bird. This should be put in cold water, over a slow fire, so that it does not boil too fast, but just simmer for half-an-hour. If a little lemon juice can be added, so much the better. Give the linseed as warm as the fowl can take it. A hen may take from three to six teaspoonfuls ; a cock seven to ten. If they have more it will not hurt them. The bird should be held under the left arm, in a position so that the feet cannot have any bearing ; otherwise the linseed cannot easily be given ; or the bird can be held between the operator's legs, with the fowl's body resting on its thighs, the legs hanging down, so that they cannot catch against anything ; give two roup pills, and fifteen birds out of twenty will be well in from three to seven days, if treated when the first symptoms appear. It is always the best to go into the fowl-house in the evening, especially in the autumn and winter months, just to see whether the fowls are all right. Should the fowls be blind in both eyes, they ought to have a little water poured down their throats with a tea-spoon, as they cannot see to drink. Even bad cases soon begin to recover if there is nothing but roup in the system. If they only partially recover, and do not eat after fifteen or twenty-one days' treatment, they usually have liver disease, or a tumour, for which there is no cure. I usually kill and bury them at once. If they are valuable fowls, it is well to give them two teaspoonfuls of cod liver oil each day.

It is well for those who are interested in poultry to try these experiments on common fowls, if time will permit, and especially if they think of keeping valuable poultry; if not, killing the first is usually cheapest in the end, especially if there are many birds left. The first symptoms of roup in young chickens are usually a slight running at the nostrils, roughness of the plumage, drooping of the wings, and loss of appetite. They usually drink a great deal of water, which makes them much worse, as it frequently gives them diarrhœa. It is well to put a small ball of camphor in the drinking-water, only allowing them about half the usual quantity for two or three days; then discontinue water altogether. If it is hot weather soak the corn in water. Use soft meal in the morning with roup powder in it, and in ten or fourteen days the chickens will be in a healthy state again. When the throat becomes sore, chickens usually open their mouth very much, and people think it is gapes. When there is a sign of gapes discontinue the water, and give sharp grit, soft food with roup powder mixed in, and boil the corn for a week or ten days. These simple remedies will work wonders, bringing health and vigour to the chickens very quickly. Under any circumstances do not overcrowd chickens, and give them ventilation, but not draught.

LIVER DISEASE.

There are many fowls suffer and die from this complaint, while their owners are quite unaware of the cause of death, and often put it down to consumption or cramp, unless they happen to open the bird and find an enlarged liver.

Fowls in confinement appear most liable to this complaint, and this is often for want of some necessaries, such as green food, and sharp grit, the latter being of great importance.

When birds show symptoms of liver disease they should be killed at once, as this disease is incurable. It is only waste of time and money to try to patch them up. Some writers on poultry call it "going light," which in reality it is, as the flesh wastes away from the body. Those birds that are all right should have Roup Powders given them for a week or ten days, as this will usually check any symptoms of disease, and bring the system into good working order.

The symptoms of this disease are rather difficult to describe. In many cases there is a lack of gloss on the plumage; the feathers look rough, and the fowls seem to have lost all energy. First thing in the morning they go to the water and drink a quantity. They eat but little soft food; many of them will not touch it, and usually eat a great deal of hard corn, especially maize—more than a healthy bird. If allowed to have it, they will eat this until the hour of their death. There is usually a yellow cast about the face, especially round the eyes. The face appears sunken, especially under the eyes. This can be distinguished better if the sufferer is placed beside a healthy bird. The eyes are rather dull. There is often a peculiarity in the bird's walk, appearing as though it was rather stiff, and afraid to shake its body. If a bird in this condition is made to run, it will usually go a little lame on one leg. It is the heavier varieties which are more subject to liver disease. Their food does not digest, and their crops are seldom empty. There are several causes for this complaint. In-breeding in the heavy breeds is conducive to liver disease. An insufficient supply of sharp grit is a most frequent cause of liver trouble. My experience during the past few years is that where the birds are kept short of sharp grit there have been most cases of liver disease. I have watched this carefully and as I have visited some thousands of farmers and cottagers in almost every county in England I have had a good opportunity of judging this. People are not so careful with their stock birds as they ought to be. Fowls cannot keep healthy long unless they are supplied with sharp grit. Cayenne pepper should be avoided. The liver is usually the first organ to suffer. Sometimes it brings on consumption and roup. When the liver is not acting properly the fowl is much more susceptible to other diseases, as when this is out of order the circulation of the blood is interfered with.

When liver disease is first coming on in hens, and they are already laying, a certain portion of the disease, at least, goes into the eggs. When a diseased cow is giving milk, the disease is liable to be transmitted to those who partake of the milk. It is the same when a hen which has liver disease lays eggs. While she is laying she keeps fairly well in herself, but the last few eggs she lays usually smell musty or strong, and if they were boiled an adult person would be able to detect them at once, because they would smell badly and taste worse. A boiled egg should be examined by smelling before being given to a child, because as a rule, whether good or bad, the latter will eat it. I have known hens, which have liver disease coming on, lay one shelled egg and one partly-shelled egg; these eggs I have opened carefully and the stench has been very bad.

During the past few years I have called upon many scores of poultry keepers in the Autumn, particularly farmers. Many of the latter have complained of losing their new laid egg customers on account of the eggs being bad, though in each case the farmers were sure they were new laid. In one instance a farmer had seven eggs cooked for breakfast and had not been able to eat two or three out of that number, yet they were not three days old. From that very farmer's yard I picked out fifty hens with liver disease: I killed a number of them to show the farmer the state of their livers. The lightest weighed four ounces, and several turned the scale at eight and nine ounces each. I took one liver from a fowl weighing fourteen ounces. If the bird is healthy the liver should not weight heavier than 1¾ or 2¼ ounces.

It is very important that those who can do so should keep a pen of fowls for themselves so as to have eggs from their own birds. Fresh eggs are good food for human beings, but those laid by liver-diseased hens are certainly not fit to eat. Our medical men tell us an egg which weighs two ounces contains as much nutriment as four ounces of mutton, without any bone. Then again, liver disease is contagious, particularly if the fowl house is not properly ventilated. If one bird has liver disease in a poultry house others are sure to follow, therefore it is better to clear them off when the first symptoms show themselves. My experience is, an insufficient supply of sharp grit and too much maize, or Indian corn, will bring on liver disease, and if the poultry house is badly ventilated, that will help to spread it among the healthy birds. I am often asked if the flesh of liver-diseased fowls, when the complaint is first coming on, is good to eat. I should not like to eat it myself, but it would not be so likely to injure a person as eating eggs laid by liver-diseased birds. The liver is not only rotten, but usually full of white spots, some of which are as large as peas, but in the early stages these small spots are no larger than the point of a pin. In most cases the liver is much paler than it should be when this disease sets in.

Another cause of liver disease is over-feeding on too much maize. This should be avoided; a little does not hurt them in cold weather, but on the contrary is beneficial, but feeding heavily on it is ruinous to the liver, especially when the fowls are confined in runs, and do not get sufficient exercise. Sudden changes in the weather or temperature of houses upset the liver very much; such as roosting in a warm house one night and in a tree the next, or anywhere causing a sudden change. This brings on congestion of the liver. The bird should be kept in one temperature as much as possible. When fowls have the disease badly, their excrements are greenish yellow. In bad cases, the fowls waste away, so that there is scarcely anything of them left, with the exception of skin and bone.

There are medicines advertised for fowls that are going light, but it is only a waste of money, trouble and time to buy and adminster these advertised remedies; it is always best to kill them at once and save them the pain and the owner the trouble and expense, and the risk of spreading the disease.

Liver-diseased birds can often be detected when they leave off laying at the end of the summer or beginning of autumn, as soon as they begin to shed their feathers, as the disease spreads rapidly when they leave off laying. Sometimes they linger on for months, at other times they die quickly. In very bad cases they do not get their new plumage in the following autumn, but when they shed their feathers early, say at the end of July, or during August, and early in September, they may get their new plumage, and live all the winter, but never lay an egg. Such birds can easily be detected on a cold, piercing day, because their combs will turn black, and they do not scratch round the stack yards and other places as the healthy birds do. When they are getting bad they will often go to roost in the middle of the afternoon.

Liver-disease may be prevented by introducing fresh blood regularly every year. The birds should have plenty of sharp grit, well ventilated poultry houses, no Indian corn in the Summer, except in cases where a hen is sitting, and a good supply of green food, particularly where birds are kept in confinement. In addition avoid over-crowding in the poultry houses at night and the latter must be kept very clean. Fowls are easily managed and many diseases may be avoided by strict attention to cleanliness.

LEG-WEAKNESS.

Sometimes young cockerels that have grown quicker than the others are taken with this affection, the symptoms of which are much the same as cramp, viz., tumbling over frequently, sitting down to eat their food, as though they had no strength. The best remedy is to feed on stimulating food, such as meat, bone meal, &c., and to give a tonic; roup powder is the best I know of. The birds should not be allowed to roost, but should be put on straw, hay, moss-peat, or chaff for a time. They are best killed for table and not kept for stock birds. When young cockerels show leg-weakness for a long time together they should never be bred from, as it is sometimes gout in the limbs that causes it.

GAPES.

This disease is mostly confined to young chickens and pheasants, and requires different treatment from any other, as it consists of small red worms in the windpipe, which cause the chickens to gape and run backwards, coughing at the same time, and if some remedy is not applied immediately they live but a very short time. There are many thousands perish annually of this disease, more especially among farmers, and I have known as many as 300 to 500 die on one farm in a year. How the worms get in the throat is a mystery, but some scientific writers tell us it is from eggs deposited by a kind of tick often found on chickens; this may be possible, but not probable. It is also very plain to me that chickens reared in the country appear more liable to this disease than those in towns, and one reason is that country chickens often drink dirty, stagnant water, particularly in the farmyards, while those in towns generally get clean fresh water. Some few years ago I tried the experiment of giving a few chickens water from a tub that had stood some time, and found that many of them had gapes, while those with fresh water were quite free. I may also mention that there are many wild birds in the country die from this disease.

These worms may be extracted from the chicken's throat by putting the feather out of a chicken's wing down the windpipe. When withdrawn, after being properly twisted round two or three times, there will sometimes be as many as half-a-dozen worms on the end of it. Occasionally when the feather is drawn out of the windpipe the operator will often think there is blood on the feather, when it is really the red worm smashed up by the feather.

If many are attacked at once, they should be put in a box with a little common lime, and when the box is shaken the chickens will flutter about and breathe the lime dust, which is an immediate cure, as they inhale the dust, cough and throw the worms up. This is the simplest method I know, and much easier than the other. They should be left in about five minutes, and after shaking the box the lid should be left open a little way to observe them, so that if any appear overcome they may be taken out and relieved, which may easily be done by blowing down the throat, when they will soon recover, but if they are allowed to go too far before any remedy is tried nothing will cure. If the eyes are closed they should be opened and gently wiped (not washed) with a silk handkerchief. It is always best to feed on meal only for a day or two after any operation.

A preventive is better than cure, and I find a little poultry powder in the soft food once a day when the chickens are from four days to a week old until they are two months old, is an excellent preventive for chickens having gapes.

If a brood of chickens has gapes the coop that has been used should be cleansed with lime or some other disinfectant, otherwise the next year's brood will be similarly affected; and if chickens have been reared on the same piece of ground several years in succession that is also liable to bring on the disease, particularly if any have had gapes there.

The use of camphor is most effectual in checking diseases. It is worth a guinea an ounce to poultry-keepers. There would not be half the disease amoung chickens, turkeys, and pheasants there now is, if it were used in the water. It should be put in the drinking vessels. A piece as large as a walnut will last twenty chickens from three weeks to a month. It dissolves very slowly, and should be removed every day after the water is emptied and replaced in the drinking vessel with the clean water. The camphor makes the water taste strong, and this checks the chickens and keeps them from drinking too much, which is an excellent thing in cases of disease.

CRAMP.

Early chickens are often subject to cramp in the cold weather, when from one to six weeks old. The result is that the toes are contracted, and the chickens fall down in trying to walk, and shuffle about on the joints of the legs. When this is the case the feet and legs should be rubbed with turpentine, after which a little vaseline should be well rubbed in, and a piece of stick should be obtained with three prongs, the same shape as the chicken's foot.

The toes should be bound round with cotton wadding, and each toe strapped with wool or worsted separately to a prong of the stick, the chicken being put in a box on wool or flannel, and kept warm for a few hours. If very bad they should be kept away from the hen for a few days, but should be put under at night, being removed first thing in the morning and replaced in the box, which should be set against the fire. When the wood cannot be obtained, get a piece of cardboard. Wrap the whole of the leg and each toe in cotton wool, place the latter on the cardboard, and sew them separately on to it with worsted, putting the stitches over the toe and through the cardboard, so that they cannot be moved. I have known them quite cured if taken in time in from 26 to 36 hours.

Some chickens never get over cramp, but are always shaky on their feet. These should be killed for table, and not kept for stock birds. Cramp in chickens is usually caused by their being kept on hard floors, either boards or flagstones. It comes on through imperfect circulation, which causes the blood to get chilled as it passes through the legs and feet, so that these points are attacked first.

The symptoms in laying hens are: they sit down on the ground; their feathers are rough just across the rump *i.e.*, at the top of the back. When the hen is disturbed she holds her wings out, flutters, and falls over. She appears to have no use of her legs and feet. She is still very red in comb, bright in the eye, eats well, and is often in full lay.

They are very subject to cramp in the winter and spring months, and these are usually the best layers. They use up carbon too fast, and the blood gets chilled, and does not circulate in their legs properly. Their legs are quite cold, and the hens lose all the use of them, and cannot stand upon their feet. This often happens to good layers; and causes them to lay soft eggs. If the hens are not noticed when they are in this state, and taken from the male bird, they often lose their life. They should be taken from the other fowls, and their legs held in hot or warm water, just so that the finger can stand it, with a little mustard in. It is well to rub the legs with a nail brush. When taken out of the water they should be rubbed quite dry; then a little turpentine rubbed in and a little vaseline applied after. This keeps the skin from drying and cracking. Then wrap the legs round with cotton wool or flannel, put on warm. Then place the bird in a basket quite out of all draughts, in a moderately warm place if possible. This usually cures them the first dressing, often they can walk well in six hours, if not, repeat the same.

They should be kept on moss-peat, or straw, and then a warmth arises to their legs, and the blood circulates freely again.

EGG-EATING.

Some hens are addicted to egg-eating, and as these clear away all traces of the eggs so neatly it is difficult to find them out, and if not found out and stopped at once the other hens soon learn the bad habit. If there is a suspicion of any eggs being eaten, an egg should be laid in the run and the fowls carefully watched. If some of them turn the egg over but do not eat it, it proves they are not egg-eaters, but if any of them commence breaking the shell, the egg should be at once taken away, and after removing the white a quantity of mustard and ammonia or some other hot substance should be mixed with the yolk, and the shell with its contents replaced in the run. This will generally help to catch the thief, but it is as well also to try putting an egg in the nest, as they often eat them there, and in this case would not be tempted by the egg laid down in the run, and so might leave that one alone. In most cases the taste of the mustard, &c., proves a cure at once, but it may be necessary to repeat the operation, with another egg treated in the same way. If this proves ineffectual the egg-eater should be killed at once; if not, she teaches the others. Egg-eating is generally caused by soft-shelled eggs being broken, or eggs dropped from the roost and broken. The birds all rush to them at once and clear them up. Peat-moss is a good preventive, as it is soft to catch the eggs should the hens drop them from the roost. Another cause is the want of materials for shell-making, and if the birds are to be cured they must, of course, be supplied with these necessaries, such as oyster-shells and bone-meal. I seldom have an egg eaten. If egg-shells are given they must be broken up very fine, or this will teach them egg-eating.

Egg-eating is a very serious matter. I have known people sell their hens because they said they did not lay, while almost every hen was laying at the same time, but the birds ate the eggs. I have had many gentlemen complain to me these last few years, saying their fowls did not lay. I asked them to watch the birds, and in every case they were in full lay, but ate all their eggs. At one place they ate about 15 a day, and yet the trace of an egg was never to be seen. If there is only one hen which eats the eggs it is best to kill her at once, unless she is very valuable. Most hens may be cured by cutting the horn of the beak at the tip, both bottom and top, so that the blood shows through the horn, and when they tap the egg it hurts them just the same as cutting one's nail down to the quick, but they can pick up their food just as easily and without hurting themselves. If a fowl is carefully seen to in this way it will usually cure it.

EGG-BOUND

This is not a disease, but rather a misfortune, to which pullets and young hens are more susceptible than old ones. The cause of these accidents is that the egg-passage is too small to admit of the egg passing through. Symptoms :— The fowl is often on the nest, and in walking the tail will touch the ground, while the head and breast are reared straight up. If they are not extra valuable and quite young, it is best to kill at once, as they are then in excellent condition for eating.

The best remedy is to dip a feather in salad oil and pass it up the egg-passage, and this generally causes the egg to be laid; care must be taken so as not to break the egg inside the fowl, as when this happens it is generally fatal. Sometimes the egg breaks of its own accord, and the skin remains in the fowl. This should be attended to at once with the finger; if not, it causes her to rupture herself by continually straining, and the oviduct, which is the egg-passage, comes right out. If the fowl is seen at once, and attended to, she may be saved. The passage should be rubbed with a little salad oil, and then gently put back again. The hen should be held head downwards, then the egg-passage will fall into its proper place, after which she should be placed in a cloth, or a roller-towel is best, suspended from the ceiling. The towel should be pinned so that the head of the fowl is four inches lower than the tail, the legs are partly upwards but the feet do not touch anything. If left in this way for 12 or 15 hours the oviduct will fall back into its place, and as a rule keep there.

The eggs hang round the ovary in a cluster, something like a bunch of grapes, and are attached to the backbone of the fowl.

Fowls, after being egg-bound, should not have soft food or several days, unless it is a little soaked bread and not much corn, this prevents the hen from laying, and the organs get quite strong again. If they are not attended to at once, inflammation takes place, and the hen suffers very much pain. When this is the case the birds should be killed at once.

Fowls frequently die when they have a soft-shelled egg in the oviduct, as it is so much harder for them to pass a soft-shelled egg than a hard one, especially when the former breaks and only the skin is left in. It is very seldom a fowl dies through not being able to pass a properly-shelled egg, but deaths from soft-shelled ones are frequent. The oviduct leads right up to the ovary, and there is a fine skin like a cobweb lying over the cluster of eggs already mentioned, which conducts the eggs into the oviduct before shelling. A sudden jerk of the hen's body, such as would be caused by flying from a high perch, or being suddenly frightened by a dog, or anything of that kind, ruptures the skin of the ovary and the contents of the egg escape and mix with the intestines, causing inflammation and death sooner or later. There is no cure in such a case as this.

CROP-BOUND.

This is a common complaint, generally caused by carelessness or over-feeding, and sometimes for want of sharp grit or throwing long grass into confined runs. It generally occurs when the birds are in full lay, but if treated at once, the stoppage is soon removed. The first symptoms noticed are that the fowl mopes about, often taking up the food and laying it down again, and drinking a great quantity of water. The crop feels hard, and the passage from it to the gizzard gets stopped. The best thing is to give the fowl two teaspoonfuls of salad oil and a little warm water, and some time after to gently rub the crop with the thumb and finger, so as to remove every particle of its contents. If the crop is not softer in three or four hours, the dose of warm water should be repeated, rubbing the crop as before; and if, in another four hours, the crop is still hard, the warm water, oil, and rubbing should again be repeated, and if ineffectual the only remedy left will be to open the crop and remove the hard contents.

The best way to do this is to lay the fowl on its back and get some one to hold her; and then to part the feathers down the centre of the crop, taking care not to pull any out if it can be helped, as they keep the cold out of the wound.

The incision should be made at the top of the crop, with some sharp instrument or small penknife or lance, taking care not to cut any of the large blood-vessels in the outer skin. The hole should be about an inch long, or just long enough to remove the contents of the crop with the handle of a teaspoon. A little salad oil should be put on the wound round the inside before sewing up. It should then be carefully sewn up with silk, a fine needle being used. Each skin should be sewn up separately; it should be wiped dry and then a little vaseline put on the stitches. About half a teaspoonful of salad oil should be given to the fowl at once, as this heals the wound inside while the other does so outside.

The fowl must not be exposed to the cold for several days and no water must be given for two or three days, or it will find its way through the stitches and wet the hen's feathers, causing her to take cold, (especially if in cold weather) and preventing the wound healing. The diet should consist of soft food, such as soaked bread given warm, and soaked corn; the birds will in many cases not even stop laying, the operation affects them so slightly. Care should be taken in removing the contents of the crop, as sometimes there are pieces of glass, bone, or cinder inside.

Very often, when fowls are crop-bound, they drink such an enormous quantity of water that the crop becomes full and remains so, hanging down like a bladder. When this occurs, the best remedy is to hold the fowl's head downwards, and press the crop so as to force the water out, if not the crop will fall. The inner skin gives way and lets the crop down, and when the hen walks it is in her way when stepping. This is what is termed a ruptured crop, and birds that are like this should be killed, as a large mass of sour food, &c., accumulates in the crop and causes the eggs to taste musty.

A stoppage is often caused through the fowls eating long grass, or swallowing long pieces of hay. This accumulates and gets bound into a ball in the crop and partly causes a stoppage in the passage leading to the gizzard, and at the same time causes a little inflammation inside. The fowl becomes thirsty, drinks too much water, and the crop falls from the body, as it is only kept up by the skin of the fowl. When it once falls it seldom gets back into its proper place. Sometimes when the crop is cut open it is necessary to get hold of the long pieces of grass or hay, a little at a time and twist them, the same as one would a hay band, then draw out a little at a time. When an incision is made the crop should be held with one hand or it will turn round. It is difficult to find a hole in the crop unless something is put in at the time, such as the handle of a teaspoon.

SOFT EGGS.

Poultry-keepers are often troubled with fowls laying soft eggs. There are several causes which lead to this. It may be for want of shell-making material, but not this in all cases. Sometimes when hens have been laying a large number of eggs, they make eggs faster than Nature can shell them. I have had fowls lay one perfect and one shell-less egg in twelve hours. I have frequently had them lay one shell-less egg in the night and a perfect one early next morning. This is not an exception, but often occurs where good layers are kept. I thought it impossible for a fowl to lay two perfect eggs in 24 hours, or rather to shell them in that time; but I have proved it is not, having had pullets under eight months old do it. Fowls are not always out of order when they lay shell-less eggs, as many think they are; that is, if they are supplied with everything necessary to form the shell and keep the egg organs in a healthy state. A fowl often lays double-yolked eggs. This weakens the egg-organs, and sometimes causes soft eggs to be laid. When fowls are over fed and become very fat internally, they often lay soft eggs; also when they have been laying a long time without a rest their egg organs naturally get weak, especially if they are large eggs. The oviduct, or egg-passage, is wonderfully constructed. It is attached to the ovary (this is where the eggs first form). They hang much the same as a bunch of grapes, and can be seen through a microscope when not larger than the point of a pin. They are so constructed that the largest are at the bottom of the ovary, or rather they are encased in a skin, and as they grow they lower themselves into the top of the oviduct. After the egg is severed from the ovary it has to pass through the oviduct or egg-passage, which is from 12 to 19 inches long. I have found it seven inches longer in some fowls than in others. In some it has been known to measure 23 inches. It is while the egg is passing through this pipe, or passage, it becomes shelled.

The egg-passage does not lie in one straight line, but is constructed much the same as the entrails of a fowl are, rather more of the **S** or pothook shape. If an egg is examined in a fowl before it leaves the ovary there will be found some small blood veins upon it. These leave the egg before it passes into the oviduct. Should a hen be startled or very much frightened, or over-reach herself, the little blood-vessels become ruptured. This is one of the causes of small, dark spots being found in a new laid egg; they are usually found at the large end of the egg, not in the yolk, but at the top of it, just between the yolk and white. Sometimes it is caused by the male birds being too heavy. When these spots are found in a boiled egg people think they are not new laid, and that they have been sat on. In some cases they are as large as a pea. After a hen has been very frightened, sometimes a shell-less egg breaks in the egg-passage. When this is the case the fowl may be seen standing very erect, with tail down and head up. The feathers are usually wet behind, while the other part of her plumage looks very rough. If not attended to fowls often die when this occurs. They are usually found dead on the nest, and the cause of death is frequently put down as egg-bound, when it is really the skin of the soft egg left in the egg-passage. This irritates the fowl and causes her to strain, as she cannot pass it. This causes a rupture in the egg organs, and often of the body too, and is sometimes the cause of the laying hen being so large and down behind.

When any of these symptoms appear, the hen should be caught and examined. The skin of the egg can usually be found just inside the egg-passage, occasionally it is already protruding; if so, it can easily be withdrawn by gently pulling it when the hen endeavours to pass it. It must be done very steadily, if not, it will break inside. When it is broken inside it can be withdrawn with tweezers; a small piece of linen rag should be tied on the end of the tweezers and a little oil put on the rag. When this is done, it is not so likely to break the skin or hurt the fowl.

If this precaution is not taken, inflammation follows. This is partly caused by the hen straining herself. The vent should be bathed in warm water, wiped dry, and then a large feather dipped in sweet oil should be put up into the vent about three inches and twisted round two or three times, so as to leave the oil inside. She should have a little hard corn, so that she does not lay any more eggs until the oviduct is strong again. If so, it causes irritation and the bird becomes very ill.

Ground oyster shells are excellent things for laying hens, as they answer two purposes, viz., supplying material for making the shell, and helping them to digest their food. Old mortar and cinder-ashes are useful for them to pick up. When all these remedies fail, bone meal should be given, as this strengthens the egg organs, and helps the body generally.

Flint dust mixed with soft food is also a fine thing for the laying hens, as this will prevent them laying shell-less eggs when everything else fails, and especially in the breeding season, as it makes the shell of the egg more brittle, and the chickens are able to liberate themselves much better. In the spring and summer I use flint dust with a little ground oyster shell mixed in the soft food every day; in the autumn and winter three or four times a week. One single handful is sufficient for 25 to 30 fowls. A very small quantity will keep the organs in good order. If only given them three times a week it helps them very much.

COMB DISEASE.

This disease is rather a peculiar one, or perhaps I ought to say it comes in various forms and from various causes, and is very troublesome when it attacks the fowls. I cannot say what it arises from in the first place, whether it is chill or overheating the blood. I think both. When a fowl is killed, and the disease is well developed, the blood is almost black, but at the same time the cause cannot always be traced, as in some cases when the fowls have diphtheric roup very badly comb disease comes on. Of course this is when the fowls are to all appearance in perfect health. I have known them lay when they have been almost blind with comb disease. In many cases it does not affect the fowl's appetite if taken in time. If the fowls have a touch of liver disease as well, death is almost certain, but if free from this they can be cured and the disease stamped out. The symptoms do not always show themselves in the same form, but in most cases it appears in little spots similar to small warts or scales growing on the face of the comb, sometimes on the eye and wattles, and in a few cases on the neck, but the latter is very rare. It should be attended to at once, as it is very contagious.

The affected birds should be removed quite away from the others. These spots develop, after 36 or 48 hours, and as they get worse they come like a fungus and spread rapidly if not checked. When they appear round the eyes they entirely close them in about three days. I have tried many things for this disease. As an outward application I have found nothing better than Jeyes' Disinfectant. It is a liquid, and I have found it a certain cure if the fowl has no other disease. In bad cases I have used caustic.

A feather should be stripped within half an inch of the end, so that it does not hold too much, and just touch each place, so that the liquid does not run down too far, as it is very strong. Should it run on the fowl's face or comb, where there are no spots, it should be wiped off with a piece of linen rag immediately. Each spot should be touched with oil or vaseline. Every bird should have not less than half a teaspoonful of Roup Powder in one day; in bad cases three parts of a teaspoonful is not too much, especially if the affected bird is a cock. It is well to mix the powder with a little flour and oatmeal, not less than a teaspoonful of each. If the bird is very ill, and cannot eat, a double quantity of meal may be used, as food they must have.

Give each fowl one teaspoonful of salad oil for the first two or three days. When the fowls are taken ill it is advisable to dress them twice a day, and also give the pills before mentioned. After they reach the turn once a day is sufficient. If the remedies I have mentioned are given, the spots will come off like scales, quite clear, so that the comb and face get well again, and nothing can be traced. If neglected it is almost certain death, and will become a fearful epidemic, as it is so contagious.

If persons have no Jeyes' Disinfectant at hand, paraffin will answer the same purpose, only it is not quite so powerful. In all cases when symptoms of this disease are noticed give the affected birds a quarter of a teaspoonful of Epsom salts, and the unaffected birds a quarter of a teaspoonful to every eight birds, and the following day one teaspoonful to twelve birds. If fowls have anything the matter with their liver, followed by this complaint, they fall victims to it. In bad cases of comb disease, diphtheric roup often sets in at the same time, so that a good deal of cheesy matter will be found in the mouth. Where there are many fowls kept it is best and safest to kill the birds which are affected with it at once in case of its breaking out in the other pens; or take the birds quite away. It is well to purify each bird in the house in which the disease broke out. The best way of doing this is to add one teaspoonful of Jeyes' Disinfectant to one pint of water, and sprinkle it in the feathers; or a better way is to rub part in with the hand, sprinkle the other about the fowl-house, and give the unaffected fowls some roup powder. Proportion: one teaspoonful to six hens. When treated in this way it seldom spreads any further, if taken in time, and a preventive is better than a cure. It is well for all poultry-keepers to acquaint themselves with the symptoms of diseases, and then if any appear among their poultry they know how to treat them. If they keep clear so much the better. I have known £50 worth of fowls die in a fortnight of this disease for the simple reason that their owners did not know how to treat it. In all cases it is well to put a ball of camphor in the drinking water.

During the last few years quite a fresh disease has cropped up among poultry in both town and country. It comes in the shape of small white patches on the comb, altogether different to comb disease, though it is often taken for the latter. It has the appearance of flour or mildew, and spreads all over comb and face. When these white patches appear they should be saturated with paraffin so that it does not run on the feathers; wipe dry, and apply ointment (that which is usually called scaly leg ointment). As a rule the second dressing entirely cures. In many cases it does not affect the bird's health in the slightest unless it is very delicate. The complaint is called eczema, and in a few instances it has been known to spread over the whole body, but it very rarely does this. Sometimes a great many of the feathers drop off round the upper part of the neck and body, but that is usually where people make a mistake and use too much paraffin, so that it runs on the feathers. Care should be taken in dressing with the paraffin and ointment.

FEATHER EATING.

This habit is very common with fowls, especially those that are confined in small runs, and in a few cases where birds have a large range they will carry it on, and if not checked early it becomes very serious. I have seen fowls quite naked about the neck, breast, and back, and in the summer they will peck each other till the blood runs. I cannot always account for feather-eating, but neglected fowls are most subject to it. A good supply of green food and oyster-shell and a little corn scattered in runs with soil sprinkled over it, are excellent modes of giving the fowls exercise and keeping them employed. Of course this is a good thing, but it does not always stop them from feather plucking. It is a good plan to bury some corn in the soil as this gives them exercise.

The best way of finding them out is to stand some distance away, out of their sight, when the sun is shining, and the fowls are cleaning themselves; then the feather-pluckers do their work. They generally commence in the spring on the feathers about the head, or among fine fluffy feathers round the tail, this is caused by their pecking at the nits from vermin, which are generally found round the head and upper part of the neck, and also at the point mentioned. The fowls persist in pecking at the nits until the feathers come out, when they at once swallow them and repeat the operation. In a few days the quills begin to grow, and the feather pluckers observing the quills with the moisture in them, which consists principally of glutinous matter, peck them out also, and therefore keep the fowls quite bare if left with them. The first thing to be done towards effecting a cure is to remove the feather-pluckers at once, and place them in a coop by themselves for a fortnight, and as a rule, this will cure them.

If, however, they persist in feather-plucking after they come out, they should be put in with a bird that has Jeyes' Disinfectant diluted with water put upon its feathers at about the spot they have previously pecked in others. Steps should of course be taken to rid the other hens of the nits on their feathers, as described in the paragraph on vermin. If this fails their beaks should be cut. A small piece should be cut off the end of the top beak and the sharp edges at the side of the same and the edges of the bottom beak also. They cannot pluck the feathers, as when they go to pick them they slip through their beak. This is a certain cure. It does not prevent them from eating their corn. Care should be taken not to cut too deep, and then it does not hurt the bird in any way. But if not valuable birds it is far better to kill them, as one bird teaches the other.

CONSUMPTION.

There may often be noticed two or three chickens moping about with long beaks and pale faces, while their wings appear too long for their bodies, often drooping to the ground, and the chickens are sometimes too weak to stand. Dorkings and Hamburghs when in-bred too much are very liable to this disease, and when other birds are affected it is often for want of fresh blood in the poultry yard. If taken in time, the chickens may recover, but as they are seldom of much good, and take up the room of healthy birds, it is the wisest plan to kill them at once, as it saves much time and trouble. Cod-liver oil is the best thing to use for those desiring to try and effect a cure. The quarter of a teaspoonful to a chicken six weeks old is about the quantity. Occasionally a hen may go into consumption, and I have known cocks to do so. The symptoms in the old birds are much the same as those in liver disease, only they do not eat very much food; when they have liver disease they eat twice as much as an ordinary fowl, so to one that is observant they are easily detected.

DIARRHŒA AND DYSENTERY.

The cause of diarrhœa cannot always be traced, as arises from various causes. Sometimes it is debility; at others it is a thunderstorm Very stale meat will bring it on, or corn or meal that have been lying by for a long time, and the mites have taken their share out of it.

Corn that is full of small holes should not be given to poultry; if it is, other good corn should be mixed with it as what are commonly called mites have made these holes, and taken most of the nutriment out of the corn. If fowls are short of sharp grit, the liver does not act properly, and this brings on diarrhœa, and very often fowls will swallow pieces of glass, stone, or coal, and the inlet to the gizzard being about three times the size of the outlet frequently these hard materials get through the inlet, but stop at the outlet, and cause a stoppage, and the husks of the corn get matted together into a hard mass, which is most difficult and well-nigh impossible to disperse. This causes violent diarrhœa, which frequently proves fatal.

It is always safe to give fowls salad oil in such cases. A teaspoonful and a half for a hen, or two teaspoonfuls for a cock would not hurt them, and often is the means of saving their lives. Their excrements are of a yellowish colour when this is the case. If fowls are fed irregularly (*i.e.*, half starved one day, and the next a quanity of food allowed to lie by them), and also kept short of water, they become very thirsty, and when they have the opportunity they drink a large quantity of water. This not only brings on diarrhœa, but also ruptures their crops. Bread soaked in hot water and given to young chickens will bring it on. Bread should always be soaked in cold water for young chickens. Dry rice and a little raw meat chopped fine is a capital thing to stop diarrhœa in young chickens. If this complaint is not stopped or rather something given to the birds to relieve it, they become very thirsty, and lose their appetite, their plumage looks rough, and they move about as though hurt in some way. Broody hens are very subject to this complaint, as they usually drink too much water, and do not have sufficient grit to digest their food. The hen leaves her nest, and in many cases dies. There is not only the loss of the hen, but also the eggs, and disappointment of losing the prospect of chickens for the want of knowing how to treat her. She should be fed on dry rice and maize. Very hot weather will bring diarrhœa on in chickens. When this is the case, they ought not to have water, but the food must be soft, and the greater part of the corn soaked in water or boiled.

When a hen has diarrhœa she ought to have a teaspoonful of castor oil given her. A cock should have one tea spoonful and a half (chickens in proportion to their size). Also give one heaped-up teaspoonful of powdered chalk, and half ditto of ground ginger. In addition to this, I give a quarter of a teaspoonful of Roup Powder a few hours after to each adult bird. I have not known this remedy fail yet. It is very seldom it has to be repeated, unless the fowls are very much out of order. If a fowl will eat, the ginger, &c., can be mixed in the soft food; if not, it must be made into pills with a little baked flour; not oatmeal. Sometimes if a fowl is neglected, dysentery sets in. In this case, use about five drops of chlorodyne for a hen and seven for a cock. It is best given on a piece of loaf sugar; sometimes it requires two pieces. A teaspoonful of water should be given after; not quite cold, just tepid. When fowls have diarrhœa, it usually leaves them in rather a weak state. They should not only have a tonic, but also a stimulant. The Roup Powder will be found one of the best things to get the fowls' strength up again. It brings them along quickly, and they are usually in full lay in a week or two. For a day or two the bird should not have much corn, but chiefly soft food. A little corn should be given, as that does not pass through them so quickly, and it helps to stay the other food. I have not found the chalk and ginger fail for young chickens. A brood of ten from a fortnight to three weeks old can have about the same quantity as prescribed for a hen. It can be given according to age. If they have a little overdose it will not hurt them.

DROPSY IN THE ABDOMEN.

This disease is not often found in the poultry yard, not one out of every hundred that are kept. The symptoms are: the fowl stands about very much by herself, and does not care about eating soft food; is very inactive, and large behind. In bad cases they are very large, and sometimes a little lame. The comb does not usually lose its redness; they look very much like a fowl which is ruptured. The abdomen is very soft when examined, and the bird is very heavy. When they are in this state they should be tapped. This can be done by making an incision about three inches from the passage, that is just under the thigh, rather low down on to the abdomen. A small incision should be made with a lance or small penknife. The first skin should be cut through carefully, and the second skin looks very much like a bladder, that is, with the water pressing against it. After this skin is cut through the water will spurt. I have tapped hens and taken from $3/4$ to $1\frac{1}{4}$ pints of water from them. The hen should be held for a few minutes for the water to drain out; then let her stand upon her legs, and hold her up by the wings, and in the struggle to liberate herself she forces the water from her inside. The feathers should be wiped as dry as possible, and a little vaseline put on the incision. Then it should be sewn up with a fine needle and silk.

There may be a few drops of water drain out after it is sewn up, but it will soon cease. Two or three teaspoonfuls of cold water should be poured down the hen's throat, and a Roup Pill should be given. This acts as a stimulant to the bird. Put it in a basket or coop for two or three days, longer if in cold weather. If free from liver disease, the bird will be quite well in a few days. A fowl that suffers with liver disease is very subject to dropsy. If a bird is only a common one it is not worth the trouble.

INFLAMMATION OF THE LUNGS.

This is usually brought on through sudden chills. I have tried many remedies for it, and have found warm stewed linseed one of the finest. Give a few spoonfuls as warm as the fowl can take it, and keep the affected bird in a warm room. I have been trying an outward application for this, and also when there is a little cold on the lungs, and have found it answer very well. The region of the lungs should be painted with Iodine; the proper place will be found under the wings where the body looks naked. Before painting, the operator should watch till he sees the movement of the lungs, and then paint over the exact place. It is well to put a little vaseline on after the Iodine, if not the skin may crack. The operation should be repeated several times if required, but, as a rule, it relieves the bird at once. The symptoms are—the breathing is very bad, and at the same time the mouth is partly open, and the birds appear to be in great pain, and usually drink a quantity of water if not very bad. If not relieved they frequently close their eyes. It is not always inflammation, but a cold, and the bronchial tubes are a little stuffed with fluid. I have found them full of coal-dust or soot when I have made a post-mortem examination, especially fowls that have been bred in a town. I have mentioned the remedies which may be used, whether it is inflammation or a cold. Fowls after having recovered from this complaint should be taken care of and not allowed to run out into the cold air.

Fowls which are handled, frequently open their mouth and breathe hard. This is through fright. They should always be handled as gently as possible, both the old and the young ones. When they are being treated as I have described, they should be fed on soft food.

VERMIN.

When fowls are troubled with vermin they never do so well, particularly chickens, and I have referred to this subject many times in my writings in various papers, as it is most important that poultry should be kept quite free from them. When the chickens do not thrive, without any apparent cause, the best way is to examine them for signs of vermin about the head and neck, as it is on these parts that the nits or eggs mostly appear. If any should be found, the specially prepared nit ointment should be applied round the head and neck. This destroys the nits. Insect powder is a safe remedy for destroying the live vermin upon the fowls' bodies. It can be used on chickens of all ages, and is a certain cure. It does not injure the fowls as many other things do, such as lime, snuff, &c. These are apt to blind the birds.

The fowl should also be laid on its back, and the whole of the body, and especially the under part of the wings, should be thoroughly dusted with the powder, all the feathers and skin being entirely covered. The fowl should then be placed where it can have plenty of clean ashes to thoroughly clean itself.

When fowls have a plentiful supply of ashes or dust to clean themselves in, they are rarely troubled with vermin.

It is when hens are sitting they usually breed these. Dust them well with powder.

Old stock cocks should be thoroughly examined two or three times a year, as they do not clean themselves like the hens do; the vermin in these cases usually lie round the abdomen. In the hot weather they will be found all over the body. Occasionally when chickens get from one day to three weeks old they have a tick on the back of the head, which is almost sure to kill them. It is, therefore, wise, if there are any symptoms of chickens dying without any apparent cause, to examine them, and if a tick can be found a little nit ointment should be rubbed in at once. There is another kind of vermin which trouble the fowls very much. That is small red bugs, which get in the cracks of the perches and in the bark. The latter are found more particularly in the old fashioned fowl-houses, but they can be found in some of the new ones also (I mean under the bark on the perches). If the perches are not kept clean, the little vermin hide themselves in the wood, and suck the blood from the fowls at night, which irritates them very much. New perches fitted to the house should be saturated with paraffin.

BUMBLE FEET IN FOWLS.

Poultry often go lame, and in many cases the owner or attendant has not the slightest idea what is wrong. Adult fowls are more subject to this ailment than young ones. When chickens go lame it is usually through rheumatism or gout, but with adult birds the feet will begin to swell underneath. This is usually caused through a bruise in the first place. Sometimes the feet will swell between the toes a quarter of an inch higher than the toe itself, and in some cases the feet get cut underneath and the place gets filled up with dirt, which keeps accumulating until with the heat of the foot it becomes quite a hard substance, with a skin round it, just the same as a piece of scrofulous matter As soon as a fowl's foot commences to swell it is best to catch the bird and examine it, and should there be any dirt between the skin it should be pressed out. In many cases the bottom of the foot will become bruised from the bird flying off a high perch on to the ground. If this is taken in time and the bottom of the foot is dressed and poulticed with soaked bread or bran, either will do, it will usually draw the inflammation out and the foot gets well again. It should be poulticed about twice a day for a couple of days, then the bottom of the foot should have Spirits of Arnica rubbed upon it, after which a little vaseline is a good thing to soften the skin, and, lastly, a piece of linen should be tied carefully round the bottom of the foot. If a little care is taken in the first instance, bumble feet can easily be cured, but when neglected the sinews extend very much, and a cheesy matter forms between the bones and sinews, which in time gets quite hard. When a cock bird is afflicted with bumble feet, unless he has a very soft grass run he is very little use for stock purposes, as the eggs are very rarely fertile till the middle or end of April. Fowls which have bumble feet feel the cold and a change in the weather very much.

ENTERITIS.

This disease was little known in England until a few years ago. I had a serious outbreak among my birds and went to Dr. Klein, of London, who conducted a series of experiments which shewed that it was possible to modify the severity of the disease by means of inoculation, and to prevent its spread by a vigorous system of isolation, so that none of the excrement of affected birds came into contact with healthy ones, as by this means the germs of the disease are most frequently communicated. Where a case exists it should be dealt with promptly. An affected bird stands and sleeps, and is very thirsty. The excrements are thin and look like chalk tinged with green. It is better to kill an affected bird and bury or burn it at once, as recovery is very rare. The liver is much enlarged and congested ; the lungs turn grey, and the intestines are full of inflammation. When the disease is discovered a teaspoonful of Epsom Salts should be divided among every four birds. A ball of camphor should be placed in the drinking water, and the following day half a teaspoonful of Roup Powder mixed with meal should be given to each bird in the form of pills, and the next day a heaped-up teaspoonful of Roup Powder to six birds. The young three weeks old chickens should have the same quantity to every ten or twelve, while those six weeks old should have a like quantity to every seven, continuing these doses for seven or eight days. This is the treatment I have recommended for some years.

THE TREATMENT OF BROODY HENS.

Broody hens in the way—Some modes of curing—The only humane and effective plan for bringing the birds on to lay quickly The broody coop.

MANY breeds of birds come broody and give the owners a great deal of trouble when the warm Spring weather sets in, as, when eggs only are required, sitting hens are in the way, the owner having no use for them.

There are various systems recommended for curing them. One is to dip the hen in water; another is to put her under a basket or tub, and keep her in the dark, without food or water for three days. The former is of little use, and the latter a great deal worse, as where a fowl is kept witbout food for three or four days it takes seven to ten days to get her back into the same condition as when she became broody, thus losing from six to ten eggs each time she is treated in this way. Some people think when a fowl wants to sit she has done laying. This is wrong. It is because it is her nature to do so, and if she can be put off from sitting, and fed well, eggs begin to grow at once, and in many cases I have known they have not stopped laying for more than two or three days, and in other instances not at all. If a hen is treated properly and fed well it is seldom she goes longer than from seven to ten days before she is in full lay again, unless it is very cold weather.

The following treatment has been found by many thousands of poultry-keepers during the last fourteen years to be an easy and effectual cure, and at the same time inexpensive. Many people have a coop made specially, but the ordinary box coop answers the purpose, and is the least expensive of any I know of, which is made as follows:

Procure a box about three feet wide and 20 inches deep, in which three to six fowls may be kept at one time, and place bars across the front about two inches apart, so that the sitting hens cannot get out. The box must have no bottom, but bars from two to three inches apart should be nailed across length-ways, and when the box is stood, say upon four bricks, it will therefore be quite impossible for the hens to sit down in it except on the bars—which should be round; round bars keep cleaner because the excrements drop between them and they have not so much surface for dirt or excrement to collect upon—and this practically causes them to be on the perch day and night. An ordinary coop with bars across the bottom will answer the purpose.

The box or coop should be put in as light a place as possible in the run with the other fowls, and the water for the whole yard should be placed in front, so that the others must come in sight of the sitting hens to drink. They should also be fed all round the box, taking care that the sitting hens get as much as they can eat, as when fed with other fowls they generally eat more ravenously. By this means a broody hen can soon be cured, remain in a healthy condition, and quickly come on to lay again.

PREPARING BIRDS FOR THE SHOW PEN.

Novices, careless and disappointed—Untrained birds: their beauties not perceptible, and consequently overlooked by judges—Washing the birds—The care of cockerels after returning from showing.

THERE are many amateurs who show birds at exhibitions and are very much suprised that they do not win prizes, especially when the birds are bought, and those who are fortunate enough to buy them win all through the country with the same birds.

The cause of this is explained in a very few words. Poultry are often shown, and in many places are better than those which win, yet they do not get even a card when shown by a novice. This refers to some breeds more than others. The finishing touch, or the preparation for the show pen, is a very important point and goes a long way towards the success of the birds, and if they are to win they must be in prime condition.

For instance, Plymouth Rocks are often picked up out of the run by a novice, and sent direct to the exhibition before the legs have even been washed, whilst others in the same class will not only have their legs washed, but every particle of dirt is taken carefully from under the scales, and their legs are nicely polished.

Some breeds, of course, want preparing quite differently to others, but all varieties ought to be put in a large coop for a few days before they are sent away for the first time, if not, they are so wild when the judge goes round to award the prizes, that it is impossible to see the proper shape, as they will crouch up in a corner, and very often the male birds will put their wings over the saddle feathers.

After they have been standing in the show pen a day or so they get tamed down, and in many cases stand right before the winner in merit, though perhaps they have not got a card, then the exhibitor cries 'shame' on the judging, but in reality it is not the judge's fault at all, but the exhibitor's.

Birds with yellow and white legs should have the latter washed very carefully, especially Plymouth Rocks, Leghorns, Wyandottes, Dorkings and Scotch Greys, and Buff and White Orpingtons. After they are scrubbed with a little soap and water and wiped dry, it is well to get what is termed by jewellers a watch cleaner, that is a small piece of boxwood, as the dirt can then easily be got from under the scales, just as it is from a person's finger nail.

After every particle of dirt is got out, the legs should have another scrub with soap and water, and be wiped perfectly dry, then have a small piece of vaseline rubbed on. After this they should be rubbed hard with a soft piece of cloth, an old silk handkerchief will do best, that leaves a nice bright gloss on the legs, no matter whether they are white, yellow, or black. The comb, face, and wattles should have a little vaseline and salad oil rubbed in, then carefully wiped off, as much as possible, with a soft cloth. This leaves a brilliant red, which lasts for two or three days, in fact the bird does not look the same. Large coops should be provided for birds intended for show, standing about three feet from the ground, to put them in a few days before they are sent to the exhibition, and the owner or attendant should put his hand or a stick in and stroke the bird down. This gets them accustomed to the pen, and causes them to become tame. It is well also to get them used to eating out of the hand, then when the judge goes round giving the awards the birds, instead of being frightened, are more inclined to walk up to him and show themselves off to the best advantage.

Game fowls should always be fed from the top of a wire pen or coop, so as to make them stretch themselves out, as they ought always to stand in a very reachy position.

Breeds such as Leghorns, Minorcas, Hamburghs, Spanish, Andalusians, Black and White Rose-Combed Bantams, and all those which have white ear-lobes should always have a piece of canvas put over the front of the coop so as to make it dark, as the earlobes become very much whiter and improved by being excluded from the light, and their combs grow much larger if they are fed on a little meat and hemp seed. The white ear-lobes should be just rubbed down carefully with the thumb, to prevent any wrinkles coming in them.

Birds with black legs should have them just wiped over, or if there is any dirt on them, they should be washed and wiped carefully, then a little vaseline rubbed on, just in the same way as it is on the birds with white or yellow legs. The latter should then be wiped and polished. These little things are not what is called "faking the birds up," but merely getting them into good exhibition form. Unless they are prepared in this way they stand but little chance of winning, as when horses are shewn they are always got up to the best advantage.

Care should always be taken not to put a bird in the dark, or so that it is shaded too much from the light when it is a breed with a small comb, such as Orpingtons, Langshans, Plymouth Rocks, &c., if so, it is apt to make them grow too large, which may be a disqualification in the show pen.

Houdans should be washed throughout, although many have neglected this. A little soda and soap may be put in the water. If they are rather dirty, a nail-brush should be used. Hold the feathers on the left hand, and then they can be brushed. It is well to dip them into a tub or pail containing blue water just like that in which linen is bleached; then use a sponge to get the water out as much as possible; and afterwards a wash leather, and rub them. Always take care the feathers are rubbed the same way as they lie; finish them with a dry towel. The white, buff, or light fowls of any breed which really require washing to the skin, must be done as follows:—A tub or bath should be filled with warm water, five to seven inches deep, then add a little soap (Spratt's specially prepared is the best) and soda. The fowl should be placed in the water in a standing position, and the feathers well soaked. After they have been scrubbed, the soap should be well rinsed out of them, and they should then be dipped in blue-water, which should have the chill off, this should be almost as blue as that in which linen is steeped to make it white. After this is finished they should be dried as described. Give them two roup pills; this usually prevents them from catching cold. The room should be warm, and the birds should be put in a covered basket and set by the fire. They should always be washed two days before being sent to the show; if not, they may not be quite dry. When dry, it is well to brush the feathers carefully with a clothes brush, each feather the way it lies, and then with a fine hat-brush; this brings each feather into its natural state. The fluff feathers should be held in the left hand, then they can be spread out and brushed properly. After the comb, face, and wattles are washed, they should have a little vaseline and salad oil rubbed on them, if not they are liable to crack or look very pale. I have known them to chap. When the birds are in the pen, they should have a good supply of grit, green food, and water. When sent to a show, it is well to give a Roup Pill, as this often prevents them from taking cold, and gives them a good appetite when they arrive at the other end. When cockerels which have been accustomed to run with the others return from the show pen they should not be put with them, as they are apt to fight and injure themselves.

POULTRY FARMING AND KEEPING.

Questions often asked with regard to Poultry Farming—Ignorance—Failure — Distrust — Popular suspicions concerning Poultry Farming—The commencement: How to begin and how not to begin—Theory one thing and practice another in Poultry Farming.

THE question is often asked, "Does poultry farming pay?"

I have had some hundreds of letters during the last twelve years asking me this question. I will try and answer it in this chapter for the benefit of the public, or rather, those who read it. The first question that is usually asked is, "How many fowls must be kept to bring in an income of a certain sum?"—it usually runs from £100 to £500 a year. And, "How much capital will it require to start and carry it on?" And, "How and where could the produce be sold?" And, "How should the chickens be hatched—under hens or in incubators; and, if the latter, which is the best and where can it be purchased?" These are not easy questions to answer at all times. In reply to most of my correspondents on this matter, the first question I put to them is, Are they well acquainted with the management of poultry? And, How long have they kept any, and about the number? And, Do they understand diseases and the different little ailments which poultry are subject to? In many cases my correspondents have never kept a fowl: in some they have kept a small pen and have not had any disease in their fowls, and seldom know there is such a thing as disease in poultry; and because half-a-dozen fowls pay well, they think that if they have a few hundreds or thousands a fortune will soon accumulate in this direction, and with so much pleasure combined. There are many who have started, and unfortunately have lost their little capital. Some years ago nearly every poultry farm that was started came to grief, but I am pleased to say things have altered since then, as those who have started during the last few years generally have known a little about what they were doing before commencing, and some I know of are doing very well indeed. I have known as much as £4,000 to have been lost in one large undertaking in five years, and in small concerns from £200 to £1,000. So it was once a popular belief that poultry-farming would not pay. It will pay if started and managed properly by those who understand their business. Who would think of putting a sea-captain to manage a linen-draper's shop, or would a farmer engage a confectioner from a town to manage his farm? The contrast is as great in respect to people starting poultry-farming without any knowledge of the business. It is more often tradesmen who have had a business in large towns who start. They think poultry-farming is so simple that anyone can manage it. It is simple to those who previously understood it; but it still remains a mystery to thousands who have not had experience in it. Reading poultry books is not practical experience, though this may help very much in many respects. I know nothing that requires practical experience more than poultry-farming, especially if in a large way. It is a business that can soon be picked up if the owner is fond of poultry and starts in the right way. In most cases a poultry-farmer just begins to understand it when his money is gone. He tells his banker, or it may be his friends—he may have over-drawn his bank or borrowed a little from his friends—but they say "No more," so his business falls to the ground for the want of a little more capital to put him fairly on his legs.

He can see where the mistake was when too late. Most people have to pay dearly for their experience. In many cases where poultry farmers have started they have bought in several hundred stock birds, and, of course, they are purchased from different parts of the country, and often they arrive before proper house accommodation is provided. Some have been well housed, while others have been accustomed to sleep in open sheds, or, may be, in trees. When the new-comers arrive they are put into a house very thickly together. The owner soon discovers a few of them not eating, or, in many cases, the eyes of some of them are entirely closed, and from 500 newly-purchased hens he does not have 300 eggs in three months. This may seem a dark picture to draw; but nevertheless, it is a true one. My advice to all who intend to go into poultry-farming as a business is to commence with a few stock hens or pullets if it is in the autumn when starting; but, if in spring, purchase a few good eggs. It is well in starting not to have too many, so that they can be well managed. it is by far the safest plan to hatch and rear as many of the stock birds as possible for several reasons. Firstly, it is cheaper;

secondly, the owner gradually gets his experience and has more time to study his fowls, and becomes better acquainted with their habits, and soon discovers which breed suits his place best.

If little ailments or diseases break out, there is time to attend to them, and the owner gets a knowledge of how to treat the different diseases, or, better still, to watch his poultry so closely that he sees at once when anything is wrong with a bird, and takes it away and tries an experiment on it; and, if taken in time, they are usually well in a few days. Another great advantage is that, by starting in a small way at first, a better market can be found for a little produce than a large quantity, for as the poultry increases they become better known and fresh markets keep opening, while, if there is a large number kept the first year, the owner cannot always find a fair market. This business in every branch requires to be worked gradually. "Practice makes perfect."

If a person commences in a small way he is usually successful. It is well to work up a fair stock of poultry, where it can be done, before a large place is taken. If a few small pens of good layers or well-bred birds are collected together there is a good foundation to build upon. It is not a matter so much of how much capital is required, but how it is managed. It is well to have another source of income, if possible, unless there is a good account at the bank. If the owner can use a hammer and saw, much can be saved in building the houses, coops and runs, as these are large items where they have to be bought. If the owner has not time or cannot build them, it is better to buy the timber and employ a carpenter to make them, and also the gates. It is very easy to put up the posts and wire. If a poultry-man is employed, he should be able to use the hammer and saw fairly well, as if he does not do the building there are always things that require repairing and keeping in repair.

A poultry-man should be industrious, or he will be but little good to his employer, as an extra pen is often required quickly, or a coop made for a sick fowl, or a perch may get broken, or the hinges off a door. All such little things as these get out of repair where a number of poultry are kept.

The question arises now, What branch of poultry-keeping pays best? This greatly depends upon which way one's fancy runs. Some have a better knowledge of one branch than another. If there is a good sale for eggs this branch pays, and in fact every branch, if a good market can be secured. One cannot be done well without the other. If fowls are bred for laying eggs for the market only, a number must be bred every year; for instance, if only 100 pullets are required, there must of necessity be about the same of cockerels, and if it is 300 or 40c, the young cockerels have to be sold at a very low rate, whereas if they are fattened they make half as much again.

If good poultry are bred there will be many cockerels, which are of no use for stock purposes; even if they were there would be no purchasers for them all. The fattening coop will come in very useful, as nothing need be sacrificed. If this is not used, the cross-bred cockerels and the wastrels out of the pure, or I might say those which will not do for stock purposes, must be sold when young to make room for the pullets and younger broods coming on.

If poultry-farming is to pay, these little things must be strictly attended to, as farthings make pence, and pence shillings. It becomes one to count the cost before the investment is made. There is no money to waste, especially in these days, when trade is so bad, and everything should be turned to good account.

This is put down to the importation of different articles into our country. The importation of grain has considerably lowered the income of farmers. They say it does not pay to grow grain and sell it in the London market. This indeed is too true, and as most of the foreign corn makes about the same as the home-grown there is not much inducement to farmers to grow at home. In poultry and eggs it is different, as one dozen of home-fattened fowls will fetch from 12s. to 18s. more than the same number of foreign. Ducks will fetch from 18s. to £1 10s. per dozen more; Turkeys from £2 to £4 a dozen more; and Geese from £1 10s. to £2 10s. a dozen more than the imported.

This, of course, is when they are well fattened. English eggs fetch from 1s. 6d. to 3s. 6d., and often more when sold in the market, and from 5s. to 7s. per hundred retail more than the imported eggs. I have under-estimated rather than over. As I am frequently in the markets, I have good opportunities of seeing how things sell. Is not this an inducement for English farmers to keep fowls to consume their grain, or a good part of it? Corn is usually fairly cheap, and poultry and eggs make a fair price all the year round, and generally it may be called a ready money trade. I know farmers who make from £40 to £200 a year out of their poultry in various parts of the country; but little attention is being paid by many farmers to the enormous sum paid out annually by this country for eggs and poultry alone—over £5,000,000. These figures are rather startling, or ought to be, to the home producers.

I do not say the country should be all poultry farms, but most of the people should be poultry-keepers. The words "poultry farming" are usually taken to represent a place where eggs and poultry alone are produced. Whatever it means it should not be so, as where there are a number of poultry kept there should of necessity be other stock, if everything is to be turned to good account. For instance, the poultry cannot eat all the grass in the summer months.

It cannot well be made into hay if a large number of poultry are running over it, as, if so, the cattle will not eat it. Then some other stock must be kept. Sheep and horses are the best to keep if they are required to run where there is wire-netting, as cows are apt to upset the wire with their horns. Jersey cows, however, are not so tiresome in this respect, as they do not knock the wire down. I have had two in my poultry pens many years, and have never known them to injure the wire. Then if sheep are kept, a few mangold wurtzel or turnips should be grown to help them through the winter months. The same for the fowls, as they should have roots of some kind in frosty weather if cabbages cannot be provided.

Where there is a large number of poultry, there ought to be cows kept, as the skim milk is so good for fattening purposes, rearing young chickens, and for laying hens. If a farm is taken with the intention of making it a poultry farm, fruit trees should be planted of the best kind. When worked in this way, there is what may be called three crops growing at once, and yet one does not interfere with the other, but the contrary. The trees shelter the poultry from the hot sun, and the fowls manure the ground, thus improving it. Sheep or young calves may be kept in the orchard where the young fruit trees are planted.

When worked thus it is not at all likely to fail, whereas where only poultry are kept the grass runs to seed and then dies. Then all through the autumn and winter this long grass is trodden down by the fowls. It is not only waste, but it is not so good for the fowls, as, while they are searching after insects on a wet and dewy morning, their plumage gets very wet, whereas if the grass were eaten down by cattle, the poultry would eat a large quantity of it—as then it is young, tender, and continually growing—and be able to find the insects better.

Poultry will pay if managed properly, either in a small or arge way, but the former the best. A large farm will pay if managed in a practical way, even if poultry only are kept. I know many who get a good living by breeding ducks only, and yet have not two acres of ground. They pay best when not too many are kept, as they get better attention. If one hundred laying hens are kept, and from three to four hundred chickens are reared, they will clear from £50 to £100 in a year, but this does not imply that if double the number are kept, the profit will be doubled. It is usually *vice versa*.

Poultry should be kept much more by those who own land and not too many in one place. Where poultry farmers have made the mistake is by commencing with little or no experience. Several pamphlets and books issued years ago were very misleading to the public. One stated that eggs could be produced for 1d. a dozen, and fowls 3d. a lb.; another that the total on each hen is 16s. 6d. clear profit. It is all worked out in figures nicely. I need not say how misleading these glowing accounts are. I do not say that half-a-dozen, or even ten might not give a profit of 16s. 6d. each, or even £1, if the eggs can be disposed of at a good price, and the greater number of them produced in the winter months. Poultry profits are not like those in most other businesses—the more business done, the greater profit.

It is usually the other way about; the less poultry the greater comparatively the returns. I have known thirty laying hens pay £29 clear profit in a year; while a neighbour of the same person had over 300, and lost about £30 a year. It is the management. I find nothing else in the way of live stock pay like poultry. Before I published the first edition of my book I made my poultry pay over 360 to 600 per cent, per annum, one year considerably over, but I put nothing down for labour and rent. I do not make them pay 300 per cent. now that I keep a large number, but they pay very well. They require the owner's personal supervision, with a good practical experience, and then they cannot well fail.

I have made arrangements in different parts of the country to have fowls bred and reared for me from my own stock, although I farm from two to three hundred acres. I introduce fresh blood in each breed every year.

Corn and land are both cheap, and farmers and cottagers ought to go in for poultry more than they do. Poultry and new-laid eggs should become a regular food and not merely luxuries.

FATTENING FOWLS.

Disappointment in young birds for table overcome by fattening—Fattening coops and food—Skim milk and fat for fattening fowls—Cramming by hand and by machine—Hints for helping fattening fowls—Killing.

FATTENING or cramming fowls is a business comparatively few understand, though they may be acquainted with other branches of poultry-keeping. Owners of young fowls are usually dissatisfied with their young cockerels when they are killed, as their own fowls do not eat so tender as some that have been bought from the poulterer. From 13 to 19 days is long enough to have them up, but as a rule very young chickens are not in the coop more than 16 days. Big fowls when being fattened for Christmas are usually kept shut up for three weeks. The best meal to use is ground oats, a little barley meal and a little Indian meal with it. When ground oats cannot be obtained it is well to buy some fine oatmeal and mix it with the barley meal. French buckwheat, ground, is a very fine meal for fattening. A little barley and pea meal may also be mixed with it. Oatmeal or ground oats mixed with skim milk makes the flesh whiter and more tender than anything else. The latter is rather difficult to obtain in some parts of the country. The fowls should be put in a coop on small round bars. They should be from 1 to 1¼ inches apart, and always put long-ways, so that the poultry can stand and eat out of the troughs. The bars in front of the coop should be about two inches apart.

One coop, three feet long and about 16 inches wide, is large enough for six fowls. It should be 18 inches high, otherwise the young cockerels will injure their comb when crowing, and cannot stretch themselves up. For the biggest fowls it is well to have the coop 21 inches high. Where small chickens are fattening a smaller coop will do. The fattening coops are best kept in a shed or outhouse where it is a little dark.

The trough they eat out of should be fastened outside their coops, about four inches higher than the bars they stand upon, otherwise they waste the food. The trough should be made like a pig trough, narrow at the bottom and wide at the top, and should be from five to six inches across the top. The food ought to be mixed up soft, so that it does not cling together when the fowls peck it up. In this way they cannot peck up much at once, so they peck away as fast as they can. In this way one induces the other to eat.

They do best where two or more pens are together, as they eat one against the other. Their food should not all be put in the trough at once, but a little at a time, then they clear it up and look for more. Nothing sets fowls against their food more than giving them too much at once, especially when put up to fatten, as they do not have any exercise to give them an appetite. They should not have a particle of food left in their troughs. It is well to let two or three fowls come into the house where the others are penned up to fatten, to peck up the few odd pieces that may have fallen down. This prevents any waste, and also induces the penned birds to clear up their food. If the food is mixed with hot water in the winter and spring they fatten much faster. Skim milk is the best where it can be obtained. The last eight or nine days they should have suet or rough fat mixed in their food. An ordinary fowl should have from ½ oz. to ¾ oz. in a day, but to large birds more must be given.

To make the flesh of old hens tender, they should be given a good deal of fat for three weeks before killing. If they are boiled gradually they cannot be distinguished from young fowls when fed in this way. If for market, it is best to cram them the last week, as a fat young fowl usually makes 6d. to 1/3 more than one the same weight not fat. If crammed by hand the meal should be made into pellets from 1½ to 2 inches long which should be dipped into milk or warm fat, then they slip down easier. They should be worked down with the thumb and finger; if not, they are apt to get lodged at the bottom of the neck.

When they have to be crammed by hand it is well to let them eat as much as they will first, and then give them a few pellets just so that their crop is well filled. They should have a little fine grit in their food about twice a week, but do not require any water to drink. After fowls have been shut up about four or five days they occasionally lose their appetite. When this is the case use a little fattening powder; it helps the fowls when put up to fatten. When fowls are required to be large, weighing from 8 to 10 lbs., they require three weeks fattening, with very generous treatment ; if not, they fall back the last few days. When first put up they should be allowed a little boiled corn three or four times a week, and a good supply of green food cut fine helps them very much, though the Surrey fatteners do not trouble about this. They also require cramming the last fortnight. When there are many fowls fattening it is best to use a machine. This saves time, as with the improved machines a man can do 18 to 20 dozen in an hour nicely. Cramming machines can be procured from Neaves, Sussex ; Hearson, London ; and from Every, Lewes.

Fowls should always be killed fasting ; if not, they usually turn a bad colour. There are different modes of killing. Some just break the neck and do not let the blood run ; but it remains draining from the body into the neck. Another way is to stun the fowl and then put the knife up into the brain. In this way it will bleed well, and no pain is given, as when stunned there is no feeling.

When there are only a few to kill at a time it is best to have a nail or nails knocked into a wall or beam to hang the fowls on. The legs should be tied and grasped in one hand, while the wings are held in the other ; the head should be struck hard against a post and the fowl hung on a nail at once ; a knife should then be run into the brain through the inside of the mouth, passing it through the roof as quickly as possible. Another way is to dislocate the neck. This is easily done by holding the fowl's head between the thumb and finger. The operator should press his thumb against the back of the head and with the fingers bring the neck right back, and it is put out in a second, this is the Surrey way of killing and the most popular. The fowl should be hung head downwards to allow the blood to run from the body; if not, the flesh will be dark.

There are many farmers, particularly in the Midland Counties, who never think of putting the birds in a coop to fatten, but shut them in a pig-sty or out-building, and give them a lot of food in a trough so that they can run to it when they like. This is wrong. When fowls are shut up in such places they ought to be fed carefully, so that they clear up every particle of food. A little fattening powder should also be mixed with it about three times a week, as very often when they are shut up for a few days they waste instead of putting on fat.

The place they are shut in should be well ventilated, and about 18 inches from the ground, with straw underneath to keep them clean. Too many should not be put in one place. What corn they have should be boiled, and boiled maize and barley should be given three times a week for the last meal. As a rule fowls do not care about barley when it is boiled, but if a little fat is put into the saucepan with a piece of salt they will eat the barley readily. They like boiled wheat better than anything, but it is not so fattening as the other grains.

"SANITAS"

Used exclusively at nearly all the prominent Dog, Horse, Cattle and Poultry Shows, and by Kennelmen generally.

"Sanitas" Crude Disinfecting Fluid—A concentrated and cheap form of "Sanitas," to be diluted with water, for disinfecting stables, kennels, poultry houses, drains, etc. Its use will keep hen houses free from insects. 1/- **Bottles and 5/- per Gallon.**

"Sanitas" Disinfecting Powder and "Sanitas" Disinfecting Sawdust—These preparations are rapid Air Purifiers. 1/- **Tins and in bulk at reduced prices.**

"Sanitas" Disinfecting Veterinary Ointment—Invaluable for wounds, sores, sprains, broken surfaces and skin diseases. Prevents and cures mange. 1/- **and 2/6 Tins.**

"Sanitas" Disinfecting Animal (Soft) Soap—For washing dogs, cats, sheep and horses; for the cure of mange and other skin diseases. It improves the hair and keeps the skin healthy. A certain cure for cracked heels. 1/- **Pots and in bulk at reduced prices.**

"Sanitas" Dog Soap—A splendid line. In 6d. **Boxes.**

"Sanitas" Distemper—For fowl-houses, cow-sheds, stable walls, cellars, etc., etc. 7-lb. **Tins 1/9 and upwards.**

"Sanitas Embrocation"—For human and veterinary use, the best and latest article.

A magnificent preparation for aches, pains, strains, sprains, bruises, stiffness, lumbago, rheumatism and veterinary use. In Bottles 8d., 1/- and 2/6.

"An exceedingly nice preparation"—A. J. SEWELL, M.R.C.V.S.

"HOW TO DISINFECT,"

A Guide to practical Disinfection, in everyday life, and during cases of infectious illness.

COPIES OF THIS BOOK WILL BE SENT FREE ON APPLICATION.

THE SANITAS COMPANY, LTD.,
Bethnal Green, London, & 636/642, W. 55th Street, N.Y.

SURREY AND SUSSEX FOWLS.

Surrey Fowls: their excellence and consequent leading position as market Fowls—The Author in Surrey and Sussex—The Surrey system of Feeding—Surrey Fowls, past and present—Sharp Grit for Surrey Fowls—How Surrey people keep their chickens dry.

THE Surrey fowl takes the lead in the London market because the Surrey people were more successful in fattening poultry years ago; no fowls could equal the Surrey fowls for fulness of breast, whiteness in colour, and at the same time an excellent flavour, so much so that the consumers of fat poultry usually ask for Surrey fowls, and when the salesman in the London markets is selling poultry, all the best fowls take the name of Surrey fowls, no matter where they come from. Surrey takes the lead.

I have driven many times through Surrey, Sussex and Kent, calling at farmhouses and cottages, and having a little chat with many of the inhabitants. I am very much interested in the branch of poultry-keeping the people manage so successfully. I think I may say I always return a wiser man, with some fresh hints and ideas. In some cases I was able to obtain a little information, and in others to impart a little, especially in the way of breeding, as there is plenty of scope for this. In many places their breeds want revising. In many cases I had introduced fresh blood, which they needed badly; where I had done this, many pressing invitations had been given me to call upon them, as they said they could then show me the difference in their birds. Where they had introduced fresh blood there certainly was a marked difference in the chickens. The laying qualities are what they most need in these localities, which I will refer to later on.

Though they are called Surrey fowls, the greater part of them are bred in Sussex and Kent, and I believe there are more than double the number of fowls fattened in Sussex than in Surrey. There is one country station in Sussex where 25 tons per week, on an average, of dead poultry, are sent to the London markets, and from the 1st of April to the middle of June they average 36 tons per week, and just the very busiest week 46 tons have been sent away in one week. When I heard of this I thought there must be some mistake, but I obtained from the station-master himself the figures that I now quote. The chickens are from eight to twelve weeks old when they are purchased, that is in the spring and early summer; in the autumn and winter they are older—from four to six months old. I have known them hatched in May, and weigh 10 lbs. by Christmas.

Of course, they are fattened by those who thoroughly understand their business, with a cramming machine. These large fatteners will kill from 300 to 500 in a day, according as the market runs. When the London season is principally over they send them to seaside places—Brighton, Eastbourne, Hastings, &c., so they really command a good price all the year round. They use oatmeal, or what they call Sussex ground oats, a little barley meal, skim milk, suet, and rough refuse fat from the butchers, which is boiled and passed through a sausage chopping machine, so that it will mix up nicely. The milk is bought up from farms. The rough fat is purchased in London at from 2d. to 3d. per lb.; this is chopped fine and mixed with the meal into quite a soft substance (about the thickness fat pigs are fed on), so much so that it does not hold together when the birds peck at it. It is so soft the feeders have to put it in the trough with a spoon, or pour it in out of the pail.

The fowls have neither corn nor water while put up to fatten. They are usually up from twelve to fourteen days, according to the condition of the fowls. They are fed morning and evening with as much as they can eat. Care is taken not to put too much in the troughs at once, then they soon clear it up and look for more. This is one of the secrets in fattening, not to put too much in the troughs at once; if so, they soon turn away from the food. If it is given them a little at a time, each one of them eats faster, which entices the others to eat, as each one tries to eat it from the other. The last seven or ten days of fattening they are crammed by machine; it took formerly two men to cram a fowl, but now with an improved treadle machine one man can perform the operation as successfully and quickly as the two could under the old system, viz.: about 20 dozen in an hour.

Some of the fattened chickens are in sheds, and some out in the open air, six or eight in one coop together. In large fattening establishments one large pen, size 10 feet long by

16 inches wide, is divided into three compartments, and six birds are kept in each. There is usually sand scattered underneath the pens every morning, for the excrement to drop on, which is all swept up every few days. There appears to be very little smell, as they are out in the open air or in open sheds. The pens are about two feet nine inches from the ground, and arranged so that there is just room to pass up between the rows of coops.

The principal place for fattening in Sussex is Heathfield, the country village I spoke of as sending off so much poultry from its station, which is about 16 miles from Hastings. There are hundreds who fatten poultry in a small way. Fattening in these districts is a distinct branch of the business. I know a few who fatten their own, but these are few and far between. Almost all cottagers in some districts in Sussex, Surrey, and Kent keep poultry and hatch chickens all the year round. They keep a few old stock birds to lay, and many of them never think of selling an egg; they set them all, unless a few are consumed in their own family. I am told the poor rates in those districts are very low, as poultry-keeping is the means of keeping many poor old people out of the workhouse. When old people get beyond work they can keep poultry, and if they have been accustomed to it it gives them great pleasure in their old age; more than that, it butters their bread, and enables them to put on a warm coat or a warm dress, whichever the case may be.

How different the whole country would be if this thrift and industry were carried out through England, Scotland, and Wales, or even throughout the world, wherever there is a race of people. I have not met a man yet, either white or coloured, who would say " No " to either new-laid eggs or a good roast fowl if he had the opportunity. I must say the cottagers of Surrey and Sussex are patterns to our English people for industry. Their gardens are full of flowers during the summer. I call them kings in their own castles. Many of the women are up at from five to six in the morning through the spring and summer.

Some may ask what breeds Surrey fowls are. They are no particular breed, being all mixed crosses. The breeds vary a little in the different districts. Many of the owners have not the slightest idea what breeds or crosses they are. The breeds are left in the hands of the higglers (who go round to buy up the birds from the poultry-keepers and sell them to the fatteners) in most cases. They change the cock birds, and their choice is usually a good one, as far as the table qualities go. They pick good plump fowls with white legs and full in the breast, and in most cases they produce good table birds; but there are not many good layers amongst them, in the winter more especially. They lay fairly well in the autumn, as they have several rests during the spring and summer with bringing up young chickens. There are some hens bring up as many as six broods in a year. Many of them rear three or four broods; but the great difficulty is they cannot get sufficient eggs in the winter; there are many of the breeders who have to buy. There are some farmers who keep hens for laying only, and do not rear any chickens for market. They sell the eggs to the higglers, who distribute them among the breeders. Each higgler they are successful in rearing fowls. Many of them place their young chickens under sheds in coops. There are but few use a bottom to the coops, not more than one out of ten. They use old sacks or bags at the bottom of the coops in wet or cold weather in the middle of the winter and dry them by their large wood fires, so that the chickens are kept as dry as possible.

TO PRESERVE EGGS.

The quicklime system—Buttered eggs—Eggs preserved in sawdust.

PUT into a tub or vessel one bushel of quicklime, two pounds of salt, half-a-pound of cream of tartar, and mix them together with as much water as will reduce the composition or mixture to that consistence that will cause an egg put into it to swim with its top just above the liquid; then place the eggs therein. Half the quantity will do three or four hundred eggs. The eggs preserved in this way will keep twelve months if required.

Another way is to butter the eggs as soon as they are laid, and lay them in tissue paper and set them on the small end. If buttered when warm they will keep four or six months quite fresh.

A very simple plan for keeping eggs is to have shelves made so that the eggs can stand in an upright position. Small holes, of course, have to be made in the shelves for the eggs to stand upright in. In this way they can be kept from two to six months, and they will be perfectly fresh. In all cases where eggs are intended for putting by for the winter, they should be collected from the nest twice a day, if not those which are laid first thing in the morning, and are kept warm all day by the hens, have germinated, and they will not keep. The germ becomes putrid. This is one reason for so many eggs going bad.

Another, and the best, plan is to make a cupboard or box, which may have fitted into it drawing shelves or trays with holes in, so that eggs can stand in with large end upwards. Kept thus eggs will be eatable or fit for cooking purposes from three to six months after laying, and if required will keep twelve months. The cupboard should be put in a cellar or other dark position where the temperature is even, and they will keep better than if they were put in lime or pickle.

ADVERTISEMENTS.

POCOCK'S PATENT EGG BOXES

Felt Interiors.   Iron-bound Corners.

Made in all sizes to carry from 1 Dozen to 80 Dozen Eggs

WRITE FOR SIZES AND PRICES.

THE "HAMMOCK"
Parcel Post Egg Box

Strongest and most Durable Manufactured.

Egg Boxes with Card Divisions for Wholesale Trade.

		s.	d.			s.	d.
To carry 20 Dozen Eggs		12	0	To carry 50 Dozen Eggs		21	0
,, 30	,,	15	6	,, 60	,,	25	0
,, 40	,,	17	6	,, 80	,,	30	0

DAIRY OUTFIT Co., Ltd.,
KING'S CROSS, LONDON.

Catalogue of all Dairy Appliances Post Free.

ADVERTISEMENTS.

WILLIAM COOK & SON'S
PRICE LIST OF EGGS FOR SITTING.

OUR fowls are carefully mated, and are on large grass runs, and Poultry-keepers placing their orders with us can depend upon having eggs from reliable birds. Each season we mate a number of our Special Cup and Prize Winners, and supply eggs as follows. Full particulars of our winners will be forwarded, and we cordially invite inspection of our stock of 8,000 breeding birds.

Buff and Black Orpingtons—From Cup Winners 21/-; from winners at a number of shows 10/6; and from pure birds with excellent laying qualities 6/6 per dozen. Rose Comb eggs at same prices.

Diamond Jubilee Orpingtons.—From finest birds 10/6; and from good birds 6/6.

White Orpingtons.—From finest birds 10/6; and from good birds 6/6.

Eggs of each of the following breeds from Prize Winners, with laying qualities combined, 10/6; and from pure birds and excellent layers 6/6 per dozen.

Golden Wyandottes	Light Brahmas	Buff Dorkings
Silver ditto	Dark ditto	Houdans
White ditto	Black Hamburghs	Anconas
Buff ditto	Brown Leghorns	Black Rose Comb
Plymouth Rocks	Buff ditto	Bantams
Buff ditto	White ditto	White ditto
White ditto	Black Breasted Red	Silver Sebright ditto
Black Minorcas	Game	Black Breasted Red
Buff Cochins	Old English Game	Game ditto
Partridge Cochins	Indian Game	White Silkies.
Andalusians	Dark Dorkings	
Langshans	Silver Grey ditto	

FIRST CROSSES FOR LAYING PURPOSES.

Houdan-Orpington	Langshan-Minorca
Houdan-Leghorn	Plymouth Rock-Brahma
Houdan-Minorca	Indian Game-Dorking
Houdan-Plymouth Rock	Indian Game-Buff Orpington

5/- per dozen.

TURKEY EGGS.

William Cook & Sons have some of the finest Turkeys in England.

	Each.	Per sitting of 12 eggs.
American Mammoth Bronze from magnificent prize and imported birds ...	2 6	1 7 6
American Mammoth Bronze (from grand birds) ...	2 0	1 0 0
Cambridge (from grand birds) ...	2 0	1 0 0

GEESE EGGS.

	Per egg.	Per doz.
Toulouse ...	1 6	16 6
Chinese ...	1 6	16 6

DUCK EGGS.

	s. d.
Prize Aylesbury ...	12 6
Aylesbury (from good birds) ...	6 6
Prize Rouen ...	12 6
Rouen (from good birds) ...	6 6
Blue Orpingtons (from selected birds) ...	15 0
Blue Orpingtons (from very good birds) ...	6 6
Indian Runners (from very large stock and excellent layers)	7 6
Indian Runners (grand layers) ...	6 6
Rouen-Aylesbury ...	5 6
Pekin-Aylesbury ...	5 6
Buff Orpingtons (from selected birds) ...	15 0
Buff Orpingtons (from good birds) ...	10 6
White Runners (selected birds) ...	7 6
White Runners ...	6 6

Twelve Eggs to a Sitting, all eggs guaranteed fertile, and unfertiles replaced. A reduction is made when a number are required for Incubation.

Please note that these Prices are Reduced after 1st of May.

William Cook & Son's Orpington House, St. Mary Cray, Kent.

ADVERTISEMENTS.

The New Patent Hot Water Incubator
"The BEDFORD."

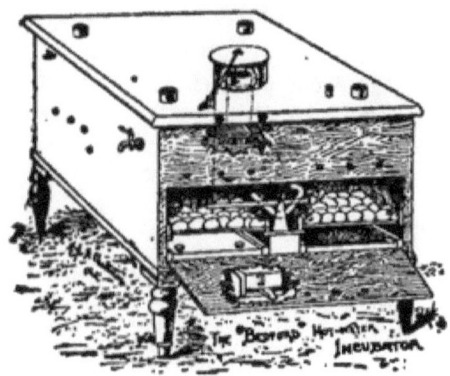

PRICES:

50 Eggs £5 0 0
100 ,,   £6 0 0
200 ,, ...   £8 0 0

Cases, 5/-, 7/6, and 10/- extra.

Carriage Paid in England & Wales

The New Patent Hot Air Incubator
The "CONQUEROR."

PRICES:
26 Eggs   £3 0 0
50   ,, ... £3 15 0
100 ,, ... £4 5 0

Carriage Paid in England and Wales.

The "CONQUEROR" REARER.

Price for 50 chicks, 37/6; for 100 chicks, 45/-; wheels, 4/- extra; with 6 ft. run, 7/6 extra.

Carriage Paid in England and Wales.

The "BELLEVUE" Ordinary Fowl House.

For 50 Fowls, 50/-

9 ft. x 6 ft. x 7 ft. 3 in.

Cheapest in the Trade. Carriage Paid in England and Wales.

The Cottager's Poultry House and Cold Rearer.

21/- each.

Wheels 4/- extra.

6 ft. x 2 ft. 8 in. x 2 ft. Carriage Paid in England and Wales.

W. W. GREENWOOD, Sidney Road, Bedford.
PLEASE NOTE NEW ADDRESS.

ADVERTISEMENTS.

Sold in 1/3 & 2/6 tins, postage paid

Write for Price List and Book of Testimonials.

CAMLIN (Registered)

THE CERTAIN CURE FOR

GAPES

IN GAME AND POULTRY

✦ ✦ ✦ ✦ ✦ ✦ ✦ ✦

Sole Proprietors and Manufacturers:

GILBERTSON & PAGE
(LIMITED),
HERTFORD, HERTS.

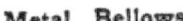

India-Rubber CAMLIN Distributors, 1s. each, postage paid.

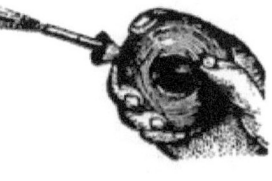

Metal Bellows for Distributing CAMLIN 2s. 6d. each, postage paid.

ADVERTISEMENTS.

THE PROBLEM SOLVED. CHICKENS ALL THE YEAR ROUND.

Hearson's Patent Champion Incubators
ARE ALL FITTED WITH COPPER TANKS.

They are the most complete and only ones which are Thermostatic. We supply the world with Incubators, and all who use our Machines acknowledge them to be without a rival.

BEWARE OF WORTHLESS IMITATIONS.

The CHAMPION has now superseded all others, as since its introduction no other Incubator maker in the world has been awarded a first prize at any show at which this apparatus has been entered for competition. It is the only Incubator in the world sold with a guarantee not to vary 5 deg. for 12 months together without readjustment, and in no other Incubator is the ventilation and damping so scientifically and practically carried out.

HEARSON'S PATENT CHAMPION FOSTER MOTHER

Made in one size only, for 50 Chickens, measuring about 6ft. 6in. by 2ft. 6in. and 26in. high.

A Masterpiece of Construction.
A Paradise for Chickens.

HEARSON'S PATENT CRAMMING MACHINE

For the Forced Feeding of Fowls, Turkeys, &c.

Try our "Eureka" Poultry Meal, 16/- cwt.

Illustrated Price List, One Stamp. Mention this book.

CHAS. HEARSON & CO., LTD.,
235, REGENT STREET, LONDON, W.

The average SALE of this Journal is greater by many thousands of copies per week than that of all similar publications combined.

Farm Field & Fireside

An Illustrated Agricultural, Rural and Domestic Journal.

PRICE - ONE PENNY - WEEKLY.

For the Country Gentleman, Farmer, Rural and Suburban Resident,

AND ALL INTERESTED IN

The Farm, the Dairy, Live Stock, the Stable, Poultry, Bees, Garden, or the Household.

(Poultry Section conducted by Mr. Wm. Cook.)

In all cases where possible, it is advisable to obtain the Paper through a Newsagent, Railway Bookstall, or Bookseller, or direct from the Publisher.

Subscription Rates - ONE YEAR, 6s. 6d. ; HALF-YEAR, 3s. 3d.

A Journal for Everybody.

QUERIES AND ANSWERS.

Especial attention is called to this feature of the Paper, as the columns of every department of "FARM, FIELD, AND FIRESIDE" are freely open to all, and offer a means of exchanging opinions and obtaining information such as can be met with in no other way.

PUBLISHED BY

WILLIAM A. MAY,

1, ESSEX STREET, STRAND, LONDON, W.C.

ADVERTISEMENTS.

German Moss Peat Litter

Moss Peat, instead of dust, ashes, or lime, in the house, is the greatest boon to poultry-keepers. It saves time, keeps the house clean, and is in every way a comfort to the fowls themselves. See remarks on this subject in the "Poultry Breeder and Feeder." If the houses are cleaned out three or four times a year, it is quite often enough, as the peat does away with all smells, an occasional stir up being all that is required. When once used, a poultry-keeper would not be without it for anything.

Sold in half-hundred weight bags ... 3/3	Bag and free delivery in Carter Paterson's London District included.
Three bags 9/-	

Bales weighing from 2 to 3 cwt. 9/-	Purchasers must pay carriage on these quantities.
By the ton 45/-	
,, half-ton 23/-	

William Cook & Sons, Orpington House, St. Mary Cray.

ADVERTISEMENTS.

Opinions of the Press of past Editions of this Book.

Practical Poultry Breeder and Feeder; or, How to Make Poultry Pay (by William Cook).—The idea of likening poultry unto machines for converting waste and worthless matter into very good and profitable delicacies, is a happy one, and the author explains it very thoroughly. With little labour and attention, fowls may be kept so as to yield a good return; but there are conditions which must be observed, and these are simply and plainly laid down by the author, who is the most careful instructor we have met with for a very long time.—*Daily Chronicle.*

Practical Poultry Breeder and Feeder; or, How to Make Poultry Pay (by William Cook).—We are perfectly sure none who follow the plain instructions given will fail to keep poultry at a profit.—*Glasgow News.*

Cook's Practical Poultry Breeder and Feeder.—Mr. Cook says that poultry may be likened to machines for converting waste and worthless things, into good and profitable delicacies. Much good poultry food is no doubt, thrown in the hog-tub, or otherwise wasted. How to turn many things to account may be found in Mr. Cook's valuable manual, which is full of practical knowledge of all kinds of fowls and their management. Poultry breeding and keeping not only *may be*, but *it is* profitable when carried out on the system recommended by Mr. Cook.—*Land and Water.*

How to Make Poultry Pay.—This is the title of a practical work on poultry breeding and feeding, by Mr. William Cook. It is especially adapted for cottagers, or those having limited accommodation for keeping poultry, and the author has been successful in his endeavour to impart plain and practical information, which will be of service to the amateur poultry breeder, and enable him to make it a profitable pursuit. —*The North British Agriculturist.*

ADVERTISEMENTS.

Mr. Cook in his useful little book, *How to Make Poultry Pay*, remarks that the number of eggs annually imported by this country is about 750 millions, worth (say) £2,400,000. As is generally known, the majority of these eggs come over from France, where they are produced by cottagers and farmers, nearly all of whom keep fowls, and make them pay well. Mr. Cook thinks that if our cottagers and farmers would only devote themselves to a little practical study of fowls and their rearing, at least one half this sum of money could be kept in this country. A friend who followed Mr. Cook's sensible advice was able to increase his store of eggs from 400 to nearly 800, without, at the same time, adding to the number of his fowls.—*Society.*

How to Make Poultry Pay (by William Cook).—Mr. Cook points out so many facts concerning the numerous errors universally made, either through ignorance or prejudice, about poultry, its rearing and breeding, that the little manual deserves to be widely dispersed. It has often been said that the English working-classes might be much better off than they are if they only knew how to take advantage of things, as do the French, who in reality are exceedingly poor, but at the same time very frugal, and admirable in their perfect knowledge of domestic economy, often knowing how to live comfortably on what their English fellow labourers throw away. Mr. Cook's book, however, has a wider scope than that of teaching *poor people* how to keep poultry. It addresses itself equally to the rich, and so practical are the hints it contains that one gentleman by following them managed to increase his store of eggs in one year from 1,800 to 2,300, and yet he did not add to the number of his fowls. He simply punctually obeyed Mr. Cook's rules for dieting his poultry, and the result was such as greatly to surprise and delight him.—*The Morning Post.*

Poultry Breeding and Feeding.—So much has been written of late years in connection with the subject of this little work, that one feels disposed to doubt whether there be anything that is to be told. Mr. Cook, however, takes up the subject in a somewhat different spirit to that of most writers.—*Journal of Horticulture.*

The Practical Poultry Breeder and Feeder. By W. Cook.—The book abounds with useful information requisite for the management of poultry with a view to profit as well as pleasure, the information being explained in a thoroughly practical and simple manner.—*Norwood Review.*

Practical Poultry Breeder and Feeder: or how to Make Poultry Pay. By William Cook. The fifth edition, re-written and revised to date.—This would enable anyone who had little or no idea of poultry " to keep fowls and make them pay well, thus combining pleasure and profit both in town and country." (Queen's Head Yard, 105, Borough, London.) —*Newcastle Daily Chronicle.*

ADVERTISEMENTS.

Practical Poultry Breeder and Feeder; or How to Make Poultry Pay. By William Cook. Fifth edition, re-written and revised to date.—A very complete and plainly-written manual for those who wish to keep poultry and to combine in so doing both pleasure and profit.—*Literary World.*

———

A fifth edition of *The Practical Poultry Breeder and Feeder*, a useful and well illustrated manual for those who wish to know the ways of fowls and profit by them, has come from Mr. E. W. Allen, London. The author of the work is Mr. William Cook, who has increased its value in this edition by a thorough revision and addition of some new matter.—*The Scotsman.*

———

Practical Poultry Breeder.—Many people would like to know "how to make poultry pay;" still more, perhaps, would like to know how to manage fowls for amusement or domestic purposes. Such persons may be glad to hear of a little book under the above title written by WILLIAM COOK, an expert in poultry raising.—*Gardeners' Chronicle.*

———

Poultry breeders should welcome the appearance of a new edition of Mr. William Cook's *Practical Poultry Breeder and Feeder* (E. W. Allen, Ave Maria Lane), as the many valuable directions on management, feeding, &c., contained in the work cannot fail to prove serviceable to all who keep fowls, whether for pleasure or profit.—*Graphic.*

———

Poultry Breeder and Feeder. Published by the author, William Cook, at the Queen's Head Yard, 105, Borough, London, S.E.—Those who had the pleasure of perusing Mr. Cook's valuable work when it made its appearance a few years ago, will not be surprised to learn that it has run into the fifth edition. But though the present issue is styled a fifth edition, it is to all intents and purposes a new book. It has been re-written and brought fully up to date. Everything of special value that appeared in former editions has been retained, and a variety of new matter, rendered necessary by the altered state of things under which we live, has been added. The book in its new form, should therefore be of exceptional interest to breeders and rearers on poultry, whether for fancy or for the market. The growing importance of the latter point has not been overlooked by Mr. Cook. For the guidance of those who would give attention to this matter, the author imparts a deal of useful practical information which should assist the poultry-raiser in making it

ADVERTISEMENTS.

a profitable pursuit. The most suitable class of houses, the best system of breeding, feeding, and rearing, are all dealt with in detail; while several valuable hints are given as to the selection of the best pure breeds for crossing. The best poultry for egg-producing and table purposes are indicated, and altogether the work should commend itself to all who are interested in the question of poultry-raising, which is receiving increased attention every year. Mr. Cook's book comes up to its title in a much fuller degree than any other work on the same subject with which we are acquainted.—*North British Agriculturist.*

Cook's Poultry Breeder and Feeder; or, How to Make Fowls Pay.—Mr. Cook's success not only as a writer about the history of poultry and the points of the various breeds, but as an instructor and example how to manage breeds to make them pay, is generally acknowledged. As this is a fifth edition it is plain that the public only require to be told that the book is "in print" once more.—*Live Stock Journal.*

Practical Poultry Breeder and Feeder; or, How to Make Fowls Pay. By William Cook. Fifth edition revised to date. London: Published by the author.—The writer of this handbook makes hens and eggs his business, farming them himself at "Orpington House," St. Mary Cray, and going up and down the country to help others in doing the same by lectures and advice. So far as we can judge the book seems sensible and useful.—*Liverpool Mercury.*

Poultry Breeder and Feeder.—There is no work better known and appreciated than this work of Mr. Cook's, the fifth edition of which, re-written and revised to date, we now welcome.—*Bell's Weekly Messenger.*

The Practical Poultry Breeder and Feeder; or, How to Make Poultry Pay. By W. Cook.—Unlike many writers on Poultry and their management, Mr. Cook is a large breeder himself, and has spent many years in making experiments with most kinds of poultry. His writings should be more valuable on that account. The opening chapters of his work have the most interest for ordinary poultry-keepers, as they contain general directions for breeding and feeding.—*Farm and Home.*

William Cook and Sons, Orpington House, St. Mary Cray.

ADVERTISEMENTS.

LECTURES.

WILLIAM COOK gives Lectures on Practical Poultry Keeping and Management, throughout the Country. His object is, as fully expressed in his book, to draw the attention of the labouring classes to this easily-attained means of adding to their income. Write for terms. Special arrangements made with Secretaries of Technical Education Committees or Poultry Societies for Courses of Lectures.

ADVICE & CONSULTATION.

WILLIAM COOK & SONS give information free to all poultry keepers and duck rearers, on the management of poultry, also answer any question by stamped and addressed envelope. All communications concerning this should be addressed to "Orpington House," St. Mary Cray, Kent. They also travel to all parts of the United Kingdom for the purpose of planning-out poultry farms and runs, mating breeding birds, &c., for the nominal sum of £1 1s. and travelling expenses.

NOTICE TO VISITORS.

WILLIAM COOK & SONS are always pleased to show visitors over their poultry farm at St. Mary Cray, and give advice on all matters relating to poultry keeping. Intending purchasers will do well to visit these yards, as there are over 8,000 birds on view, at various prices.

The Poultry Farm is open for inspection every week day. W. COOK is at home on Wednesdays and Saturdays from 1.30 p.m., or his son can be seen any day, for the purpose of giving advice and all information concerning the birds. For the benefit of the working classes the place is open for inspection on Bank Holidays. Orpington House, St. Mary Cray, is 3 miles from Orpington Station on the South-Eastern Railway, a mile and a half from St. Mary Cray Station on the L. C. & D. Railway, and 2 miles from Swanley Junction on the same line. Cabs are to be had at Orpington and St. Mary Cray stations. Address all telegrams: "Cook, St. Mary Cray."

Inspection of poultry farm cordially invited.

IMPORTANT NOTICE.

We desire to make it quite clear that we have no connection whatever with any other person of the same name. We are anxious this should be thoroughly understood, because persons have been misled by advertisements that have appeared, and so have mistaken other totally different firms for our own.

William Cook & Sons, Orpington House, St. Mary Cray, Kent.

ADVERTISEMENTS.

WILLIAM COOK & SONS'
PRICE LIST OF STOCK BIRDS.

We are the largest breeders in England of high-class poultry, as we not only have a large stock of the world-famed Orpingtons (of which we are the originators) but also of every useful pure breed known. We are most successful in the show pen with birds of all varieties and can always supply high-class specimens, fit for the keenest competition, at reasonable prices. We have always made the laying qualities of fowls our careful study and have never sacrificed these to mere beauty of plumage, as so many breeders have done. Customers placing their orders with us can rely on having GOOD layers combined with well-bred birds.

We have won over 2000 Cups, Medals, and Prizes at all the leading Shows.

Our terms are cash with order, and all birds sent on approval.

ORPINGTONS—We hold the finest Stock of these in the country, and being the Originators of the breed buyers may rely on having genuine birds. We have for Sale, Black Hens, at 8/6, 10/6, 12/6, 15/6 and upwards. Pullets, 8/6, 10/6, 12/6, 15/6, and upwards. Cockerels, for crossing, at 7/6 and 8/6 each; and for pure breeding, 10/6, 12/6, 15/6, 21/-, and 30/- each; and for exhibition, at £2 2s. 0d., £3 3s. 0d., and £5 5s. 0d. A few fine Cocks, at 10/6, 12/6, 15/6, and 21/- for mating with pullets. Rose-Comb Black Hens and Pullets, 8/6, 10/6, and 12/6 each. Fine Cocks and Cockerels, 10/6, 12/6, 15/6, and 21/- each, and upwards; and a few birds for crossing at 8/6 each.

BUFF ORPINGTONS—*Rose and Single Comb*—Hens, 10/6, 12/6, 15/6, 21/-, 30/-, and £2 2s. 0d. each upwards. Cocks at 10/6, 12/6, 15/6, 21/- to £8 8s. 0d. each. Pullets, 8/6, 10/6, 12/6, 15/6, and 21/- each and upwards. Cockerels, for crossing, 7/6, 8/6, and 10/6; and for pure breeding, 10/6, 12/6, 15/6, 21/-, and 30/- and up to £10 10s. 0d. each. We have for sale a number of first-class birds of the Black and Buff Orpingtons, fit for the keenest competition. Prices will be sent on application.

JUBILEE ORPINGTONS—Pullets and Hens of this popular variety, at 10/6, 12/6, 15/6, and 21/- each; and unrelated Cocks and Cockerels, 12/6, 15/6, 21/-, 25/-, and 30/- each.

Orpington House. St. Mary Cray, Kent.

ADVERTISEMENTS.

We can offer Hens and Pullets of the following varieties, in pens or otherwise—Anconas, Dark and Silver Grey Dorkings, Houdans, Minorcas, Indian, Old English and Black Breasted Red Game, White, Buff and Brown Leghorns, Golden, Buff, White, and Silver Wyandottes, Langshans, Light and Dark Brahmas, Buff and Partridge Cochins, and Plymouth Rocks, Andalusians, Buff and White Rocks, White Minorcas and Hamburghs, at 8/6, 10/6, and 12/6 each. Cocks and Cockerels, at 8/6, 10/6, 12/6, and 15/6 each upwards.

We have several distinct strains of each breed, so that Customers may rely on having quite unrelated birds sent to them.

COCKERELS FOR CROSSING—We have always a few good birds of different breeds for Sale, at 7/6 and 8/6 each.

FIRST CROSS PULLETS—of the best laying first crosses of all varieties (including Houdan-Leghorns and Houdan-Orpingtons) at 5/6 and 6/- each. If twelve are taken, 5/- each.

TURKEYS—We have a splendid flock of American Bronze for sale, bred from imported cocks, weighing 38, 40, and 42 lbs. respectively, and very heavy, large framed hens ; fine cockerels from 17 to 30 lbs. each (not fed up) at 30/-, 35/-, £2 2s. 0d., £2 10s. 0d., £3 3s. 0d., and £4 4s. 0d. each ; unrelated pullets, 25/-, 30/-, £2 2s. 0d., £2 10s. 0d., and £3 3s. 0d. each ; all will make enormous birds and come from excellent layers.

DUCKS—We have always a large flock of Indian Runners and White Runners. These we can specially recommend as layers, and mated with an Aylesbury Drake they breed fine table birds. We can offer Ducks as low as 6/6 each ; and others at 7/6, 8/6, and 10/6 each ; and unrelated Drakes, 7/6, 8/6, 10/6, and 12/6 each ; also a number of Aylesbury, Pekin, and Rouen Ducks, 9/6, 10/6, and 12/6 each ; and unrelated Drakes, 10/6, 12/6, 15/6, and 21/-, and smaller ones 8/6 each.

BLUE ORPINGTON DUCKS—Fine Ducks of this handsome breed, at 10/6, 12/6, 15/6, and 21/- each ; and unrelated Drakes, 12/6, 15/6, 21/-, 25/-, and 30/- each and upwards.

BUFF ORPINGTON DUCKS—A few choice Ducks, at 12/6, 15/6, 21/-, 25/-, and 30/- ; and unrelated Drakes same prices.

GEESE—We have a fine flock of Chinese, Embden, and Toulouse Geese, and can always supply good Geese and unrelated Ganders at moderate prices.

Queen's Head Yard, 105, Borough, London, S.E.

ADVERTISEMENTS.

"THE HORSE:
ITS KEEP AND MANAGEMENT."

Horses in the Stable—Colds—Diseases—Shoeing—Breeding—Rearing Colts—Breaking in—Driving—The Stable Floor—Fever in the Feet—Weak Joints, &c.—Illustrated.

Contains Chapters on Feeding—Watering—Tying up and Bedding down in the Stable—Cleaning—Clipping and Singeing—Horses' Feet—Bandaging and Managing

If you want to make your Poultry pay, read the

POULTRY JOURNAL:
EDITED BY WILLIAM COOK.

Published by E. W. Allen, 4, Ave Maria Lane, E.C., and to be obtained of all Booksellers. It is a Monthly Publication, entirely devoted to practical information on Poultry Keeping in all its branches, and is the only Monthly Journal in England which is devoted entirely to Poultry. In each number there is a chapter of Hints for the current month, according to the season of the year, showing how to manage both the old and young stock, &c. Also short chapters on Ducks, Turkeys, and Geese, and their management, &c., when kept in small runs. Questions are answered through the columns of this paper, and also free by post by enclosing a stamped and addressed envelope. Post-mortem Examinations are made on all kinds of Poultry, for the nominal sum of 1s. each. All specimens for examination to be sent, carriage paid, to 105, Borough, London, S.E. The Reports appear in the Monthly Journal, and in cases of urgency, if a stamped and addressed envelope is enclosed, they are answered by post. In cases of contagious disease, a letter of instruction is sent free of any other charge.

'WILLIAM COOK & SONS'
OINTMENT FOR SCALY LEGS

Sold in 6d. and 1s. boxes.   Post free $8\frac{1}{2}$d. and 1s. 3d.

Orpington House, St. Mary Cray, Kent.

SPECIAL OFFER.

In the Autumn we have the majority of our breeding pens for Sale at reduced prices. This affords an exceptional opportunity to those requiring first-class birds at low prices.

We have always for Sale a number of odd birds at very low prices to clear. Full particulars of these; and special quotations for pens of birds at reduced rates, will be quoted per return of post.

FOREIGN ORDERS EXECUTED.

We having exported over 1000 Birds to all parts of the World during the past three years.

Baskets to be returned and all letters addressed:—

WILLIAM COOK & SONS,
ORPINGTON HOUSE, ST. MARY CRAY, KENT.

RELIABLE POULTRY MEAL
FOR ALL PURPOSES.

WILLIAM COOK & SONS beg to call the attention of all poultry keepers to their poultry meals, which have been before the public for thirteen years. Having made the rearing of all classes of poultry their special study for many years, they have gone into the question of the most suitable meals with the greatest care, and they can confidently recommend the following as some of the best meals it is possible to produce. Many hundreds of visitors to their Poultry Farm, Orpington House, St. Mary Cray, have remarked upon the size and grand appearance of their birds, which is entirely owing to careful selection, and feeding them on their specially prepared meals, with Poultry and Roup Powders occasionally, and an ample supply of Sharp Flint Grit.

Orpington House, St. Mary Cray, Kent.

FLINT GRIT FOR FOWLS.

Sharp grit is most essential to all birds, and they cannot thrive properly without it, as it is their only means of digesting their food. Hand-broken Flint is the best material that can be used.

Grit to be of service to fowls must be both hard and sharp. Much that is sold for grit does more harm than good, as it only blocks up the birds' gizzards.

WILLIAM COOK & SONS supply FLINT GRIT broken in proper sizes for Fowls, Turkeys, Ducks, Pigeons, Chickens, and Cage Birds, and it is all broken by hand, as Grit broken by a machine loses the sharp edges it is so necessary to retain, and 28 lbs. of hand-broken flint will last Fowls longer than 112 lbs. of flint broken by machinery. FLINT DUST is also invaluable for laying Fowls and Ducks, it being strengthening to the egg organs.

WILLIAM COOK & SONS recommend both the FLINT GRIT and the DUST to be mixed in the Fowls' soft food, waste thus being prevented. Fowls require about half a teaspoonful each weekly of the Grit, and when in full lay three teaspoonfuls of the Dust daily to about 10 hens will be sufficient.

WILLIAM COOK & SONS have supplied for many years flint grit for Fowls, Turkeys, Pigeons, Chickens and Cage Birds. State which it is required for when ordering. This grit is hand-broken, and consequently the hardest and sharpest to be had : and a small quantity lasts a long time.

Prices :—9/- per cwt.; 5/- per half-cwt.; 3/- per quarter-cwt. Carriage is paid on 1 cwt. and half-cwt. bags to any Railway Station in England.

WILLIAM COOK & SONS'
FATTENING POWDERS.

These powders are very useful in assisting poultry to put on fat and to keep them in health at the same time; they give them a keen appetite, and assist digestion.

For 12 Fowls, one dessert-spoonful three times a week.
,, 10 Ducks, ,, ,,
,, 6 Turkeys ,, ,,

Sold in tins, post free, 1s. 3d., 5s. and 10s.

Special Quotations for Larger Orders.

Orpington House, St. Mary Cray, Kent.

"FOWLS FOR THE TIMES."

By William Cook.

THE HISTORY AND DEVELOPMENT OF THE ORPINGTON FOWL.

This book surveys the whole poultry keeping position up to date; contains many scientific facts in connection with poultry keeping that have never come before the public before, tracing many of the details of the new poultry management back to their origin in the laws of Nature, and giving many interesting particulars concerning the development of the industry. To farmers and fruit growers especially this work will be valuable, and being fully illustrated throughout, with new portrait of the Author, will form an interesting record of many details of interest to all advanced poultry keepers.

Price, 2s. 6d. Nett.   Post Free, 2s. 9d.

PHEASANTS, TURKEYS & GEESE:

Illustrated.

Their Management for Pleasure & Profit.

PRICE, 2s. 6d. NETT.   POST FREE, 2s. 9d.

This Book treats on the Management of Pheasants, Turkeys and Geese. It describes how these birds can be kept profitably, and points out many mistakes which have been made in the past. It deals with all branches of Pheasant Keeping and Rearing. The instruction given will be very useful to all Game-keepers and those who are interested in sport, as well as those who are lovers of these beautiful birds.

WILLIAM COOK & SONS,
ORPINGTON HOUSE, ST. MARY CRAY.

ADVERTISEMENTS.

WILLIAM COOK & SONS'
POULTRY BISCUIT MEAL.

Is one of the best meals in the market. It is made of the finest materials and a small quantity added to a mixture of sharps and middlings, for laying fowls, prevents any stickiness. Given alone it is an invaluable food for Exhibition birds, as it gets them into fine form and gives them a very glossy plumage. The price is very low compared with the quality, and it will be found the cheapest Biscuit Meal before the public.

Price :—Per cwt., 17/-; per half cwt., 8/10; per quarter cwt., 4/8.

WILLIAM COOK & SONS'
Special Poultry Meal.

This is a mixture of meals carefully blended after many years' experiments. It is specially prepared for laying hens and young chickens, and contains everything necessary for the production of fine fowls and eggs in abundance. It is not fattening and should be used by itself. Customers who have used it for years say it is "*A Perfect Mixture.*"

Price :—Per cwt., 15/-; per half cwt., 7/9; per quarter cwt., 4/-.

WILLIAM COOK & SONS'
GENERAL MEAL.

This meal is of a fattening nature, and for laying hens should be mixed with sharps. It is a grand meal for young birds wanted for the table, and one of the finest mixtures ever made for Milch Cows, as, when fed on it, they give a larger quantity of milk and more butter than on any other food.

Price :—Per cwt., 12/6; per half cwt., 6/6; per quarter cwt., 3/6.

Queen's Head Yard, 105, Borough, London, S.E.

WILLIAM COOK & SONS' ROUP POWDERS.

These powders are used with excellent results for birds with roup. When badly affected they can be cured by the use of it, and it is also invaluable for those fowls which have the disease fully developed. Full particulars and directions are given on the tins. For preparing birds for the show pen, and for keeping fowls generally in good condition and plumage, there is nothing to equal these powders. If fowls are suffering from debility, or their liver is out of order, it soon puts them right and brings a bright lustre on their plumage, thus improving their health and appearance.

When fowls are out of sorts, more particularly when they cough and sneeze a little, the powders should be used at once, they have saved the lives of thousands of the young stock. They should be mixed in the soft food of a morning, about four times a week, and that will prevent the disease from spreading. When the birds have a thick mucus round the mouth the Roup Lotion should be used, 10½d. per bottle, post free.

Sold in 6d., 1/-, 2/-, and 5/- tins: Post free for 9d., 1/3, 2/4½, and 5/-. A 12/- tin is sent, Carriage Paid, for 10/-; or Customers can have part Roup and Poultry Powders to the value of 12/- sent, Carriage Paid, for 10/-.

WILLIAM COOK & SONS' INSECT POWDERS.

WILLIAM COOK & SONS' Improved Insect Powder will destroy all insects on poultry, pigeons, cage birds, dogs and cats; also destroys blackbeetles, and is used largely for household purposes; its use is indispensable in keeping the nest and sitting hen free from insects; is perfectly harmless. Should be freely used just before hatching, both on the hen and in the nest, as it is impossible for chickens to thrive when covered with vermin.

Sold in tins, post free, 8½d., 1s. 3d., and 2s. 4½d.; or 5s. tins, carriage paid.

Orpington House, St. Mary Cray, Kent.

WILLIAM COOK & SONS'
POULTRY POWDERS

These powders are an invaluable composition for poultry under all circumstances. They are prepared especially to act upon every organ of the body, being stimulating, strengthening, and warmth giving—in fact, they counteract many diseases poultry are subject to, improve their appearance by imparting a gloss and beauty to the plumage, and keep the fowls in good health.

They are especially useful to birds when moulting, when there is a great strain upon the system in the growth of the young feathers and they are down in condition and need something to help them. They are also useful in cases where fowls mope about and do not care for their food, being a little out of sorts. The powders will be found most beneficial by acting upon the liver and bringing the birds on to full lay. Those who use them are seldom without eggs all the winter months. They are used very largely and have proved a great boon to poultry keepers. They do not over stimulate the fowls and leave them weak, like most other tonics do; they strengthen every organ of the body and can be discontinued at any time without injury to the fowls. They should be used during the Autumn and Winter, about four or five times a week, and if the weather is severe every day. Many people have used them all through the Summer of the past few years with excellent results; they do not injure the birds in the least, or wear them out sooner, as customers testify. They are invaluable for birds during the breeding season as they help them to produce fertile eggs in abundance. The same powders are used for bringing up young chickens, turkeys, and pheasants, and also with great advantage with young ducks; they have a good effect on all young poultry, assisting them in their growth, getting their feathers, and giving them health and vigour.

Sold in 6d., 1/-, 2/-, and 5/- Tins. Post free for 9d., 1/3, 2/4½, and 5/-; 12/- Tin for 10/-, carriage paid.

PUPILS.

WILLIAM COOK & SONS have vacancies for pupils to teach them poultry keeping and farming. It is wise for those who have had no previous experience to avail themselves of the advantages for practical training, which their extensive poultry farm offers. The fee is ten guineas, and we have had a large number of pupils, both ladies and gentlemen, during the last few years, to learn poultry farming, many of whom are now doing well for themselves. Pupils can remain six months, or longer, if they wish, and gentlemen will find it pleasant and instructive to spend their holidays on the farm. For full particulars write to Orpington House, St. Mary Cray, Kent.

Queen's Head Yard, 105, Borough, London, S.E.

THE BOOK ON DUCKS.

ILLUSTRATED,

AND HOW TO MAKE THEM PAY.

ENLARGED EDITION.

PRICE, 2s. 6d. NETT.   POST FREE, 2s. 9d.

Duck rearing being an industry largely on the increase, WILLIAM COOK felt that those engaging in it would do better if they treated their birds more intelligently in many instances.

The book goes into detail concerning all the most important branches of duck breeding and rearing, shewing the characteristic features of the breeds, and giving directions for crossing, so as to produce birds suited to the varied requirements of the Markets and circumstances of small rearers.

PUBLISHED BY THE AUTHOR,

WILLIAM COOK & SONS,
Queen's Head Yard, 105, Borough, London;
AND
ORPINGTON HOUSE, ST. MARY CRAY KENT.

THE
POULTRY KEEPERS' ACCOUNT BOOK.
(WILLIAM COOK AND SONS').

The most complete method published. Price 1/-, post free 1/1½.

WILLIAM COOK & SONS,
Queen's Head Yard, 105, Boro', London, S.E.

WILLIAM COOK & SONS'
PRICE LIST OF MEAL AND CORN.

	1 cwt.	½ cwt.	¼ cwt.
Poultry Biscuit Meal	17 0	8 10	4 8
Special Poultry Meal	15 0	7 9	4 0
General Meal	12 6	6 6	3 6
Duck Meal	14 0	7 6	4 0
Fattening Meal for Ducks	14 0	7 6	4 0
Bone Meal	14 0	7 0	3 9
Granulated Meat	21 0	10 6	5 6
Ground Oyster Shells	8 0	4 6	2 6
Flint Grit for Fowls, Pigeons, Cage Birds, and Chickens	9 0	5 0	3 0
Flint Dust	8 0	4 6	2 6

Orders for ½ cwt. and 1 cwt. quantities of the above delivered free to any Railway Station in England and Wales. Half carriage paid on 1 cwt. bags to Customers in Ireland and Scotland.

	Sack.	½-Sack.	Bush
Wheat (Best)	18 0	9 0	5 0
Buckwheat (Best French)	18 0	9 0	4 6
Barley	18 0	9 0	4 6
Maize (Small Round)	18 0	9 0	4 6
Dari	18 0	9 0	4 6

Groats (Whole) extra quality, 19/6 per 112 lbs.; 10/- per 56 lbs.; 5/3 per 28 lbs.

The Corn is Carriage Paid only within the delivery of Carter Paterson. Orders for Corn cannot be executed unless a remittance for Sacks or Bags accompany the orders.

Sacks charged, 1/4; 1-Bushel Bags, 6d. each, but allowed for when returned to London Warehouse.

CASH TO ACCOMPANY ALL ORDERS.

All WILLIAM COOK & SONS' Meals and Grit can be had in 7 or 14 lb. bags by calling at Queen's Head Yard, 105, Boro', S.E. These small quantities cannot be sent carriage paid.

Customers should specify the Station to which their Goods should be addressed to avoid errors.

Customers favouring us with orders for Meals, Corn, and Moss Peat, should write direct to

Queen's Head Yard, 105, Borough, London, S.E.
ADDRESS OF POULTRY FARM—
ORPINGTON HOUSE, ST. MARY CRAY, KENT.

SAFETY EGG BOXES
(TULLY'S PATENT).
AWARDED THREE FIRST PRIZES AT THE LONDON DAIRY SHOW, 1896.

BY HER MAJESTY'S ROYAL LETTERS PATENT.

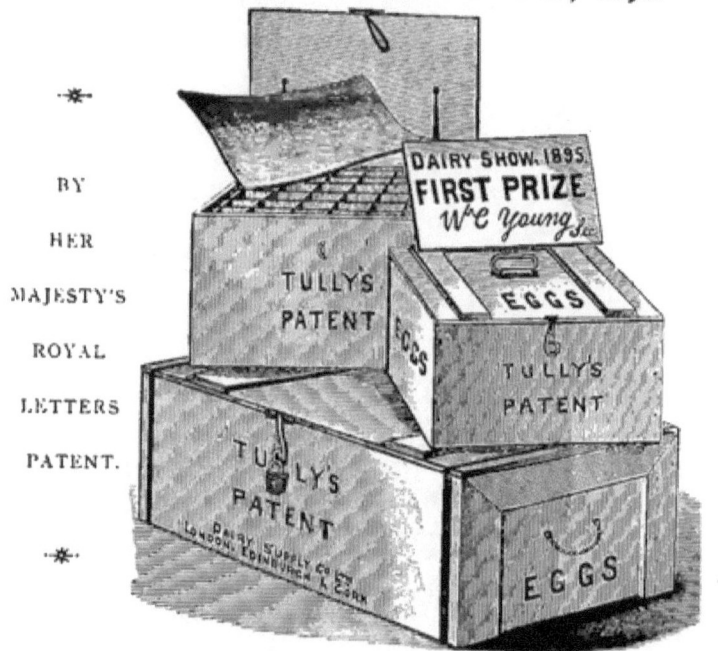

Unequalled for safely conveying Eggs by RAIL, ROAD, or POST. The Strongest and Cheapest Box in the Market. Fittings supplied separately.

PRICES.

			s.	d.				s.	d.
To carry 1 dozen Eggs	...	2	9	To carry 18 dozen Eggs	...	10	6
,, ,, 2 ,, ,,	...	3	9	,, ,, 20 ,, ,,	...	12	0
,, ,, 3 ,, ,,	...	4	6	,, ,, 24 ,, ,,	...	13	0
,, ,, 4 ,, ,,	...	5	0	,, ,, 30 ,, ,,	...	15	6
,, ,, 6 ,, ,,	...	6	0	,, ,, 40 ,, ,,	...	17	6
,, ,, 9 ,, ,,	...	7	0	,, ,, 48 ,, ,,	...	20	0
,, ,, 10 ,, ,,	...	7	6	,, ,, 50 ,, ,,	...	21	0
,, ,, 12 ,, ,,	...	8	6				

CAN ONLY BE OBTAINED FROM THE SOLE AGENTS—

DAIRY SUPPLY Co., Ltd.,
MUSEUM ST., LONDON, W.C.

SPRATT'S PATENT LIMITED
SPECIALITIES
FOR
CHICKENS AND POULTRY.

PATENT CHICKEN MEAL,

For Chicks during first few weeks after hatching, per cwt. **20/-**; per ½ cwt. **10/6**; per ¼ cwt. **5/6**; per 14 lbs. **2/9**; per 7 lbs. **1/6**; per 3½ lbs. **9d**. Also in 1 lb. and 2 lb. packets.

PATENT POULTRY MEAL,

Per cwt. **20/-**; per ½ cwt. **10/6**; per ¼ cwt. **5/6**; per 14 lbs. **2/9**; per 7 lbs. **1/6**; per 3½ lbs. **9d**. Also in 1 lb. and 2 lb. packets.

FATTENING MEAL,

For feeding Poultry for a few days before required for table or Show purposes. Per cwt. **20/-**; per ½ cwt. **10/6**; per ¼ cwt. **5/6**; per 14 lbs. **2/9**; per 7 lbs. **1/6**; per 3½ lbs. **9d**.

"CARDIAC,"

A Tonic Powder for Poultry and Game; per 7 lbs. **2/6**. Also in **1/-**, **6d.**, **3d.**, and **1d.** packets.

GRANULATED PRAIRIE MEAT.
TRADE "CRISSEL," MARK.

For Poultry and Game. A Preparation of Pure Meat, taking the place of Insect Life and Ants' Eggs; per cwt. **26/-**; per ½ cwt. **13/6**; per ¼ cwt. **7/-**; per 14 lbs. **3/9**; per 7 lbs. **1/11**; per 3½ lbs. **1/-**.

BONE MEAL,

For Chicks; per tin **1/-**, or post paid **1/6**.

BONE MEAL,

For Poultry; per cwt. **14/6**; per ½ cwt. **7/6**; per ¼ cwt. **4/-**; per 14 lbs. **2/-**; per 7 lbs. **1/-**.

SOLD BY ALL DEALERS.

SPRATT'S PATENT CHICKEN MEAL.

OF ALL DEALERS
In Sealed Bags or Sample Packets.

Samples Post Free of

Spratt's Patent Limited
LONDON, S.E.

Illustrated Catalogue of Chicken and Poultry Appliances Post Free on Application.

www.ingramcontent.com/pod-product-compliance
Lightning Source LLC
Chambersburg PA
CBHW050845300426
44111CB00010B/1134